The man who laughs has not yet
been told the terrible news

Bertolt Brecht

MUNGO:
THE MAN
WHO LAUGHS

by Mungo MacCallum

Duffy & Snellgrove
Sydney

Published by Duffy & Snellgrove in 2001
PO Box 177 Potts Point NSW 1335 Australia
info@duffyandsnellgrove.com.au

Reprinted in 2001

Distributed by Pan Macmillan

Cover design by Alex Snellgrove
Cover images of Mungo with permission of Fairfax Newspapers
Other cover images with permission of Newspix
Cartoons © Michael Leunig
Internal illustrations © Bruce Petty
Typeset by Cooper Graphics
Printed by Griffin Press

ISBN 1 876631 14 7

Contents

visit our website: www.duffyandsnellgrove.com.au

To the daughters in my life;
Diana, Gillian, Adrienne and especially
Gail, who talked me into it.

*Politics is the most important invention in
human history, because it is the only way of solving
disputes without killing people*

Robert A Heinlein

*a politician is an arse upon
which everything has sat except a man*

e.e.cummings

Whoever you vote for, a politician always gets in

graffito, anon

FOREWORD

This book does not pretend to be either history or autobiography. Instead, it makes the more modest claim to being a memoir of my learning about and involvement in Australian politics from the end of World War II in my childhood to the climactic dismissal of the Whitlam government just before I turned thirty-five. It is easy to say that the events of one's own youth were somehow special, that they had an intensity which has never happened before or since. But I think few observers would deny that the period in question covered some of the most dramatic events in the short life of Australian federal politics, or that it was a time of great contrasts and great questions for all those involved.

My own role was that of spectator or at best fringe dweller; I never joined a political party, largely because I could not cope with the discipline. But in my own way I was an activist and – unusually in these days – one who has remained committed to the ideals of the left, in spite of the frustrations and disappointments this has entailed. And of course there were some good bits too. I hope some of the excitement of the highs and lows comes across in what follows.

I have deliberately not attempted to do any serious

research; this is supposed to be a personal account and I have relied as much as possible on my impressions of what was going on at the time, even when my interpretations have turned out in retrospect to have been suspect, or at times downright wrong. I have, however attempted to check names, dates and places as far as possible. It goes without saying that any mistakes, like the views expressed hereafter, are entirely my own. However, it would be churlish not to mention at least some of the authors consulted: Bob Murray, Alan Reid, Laurie Oakes, David Solomon, Clem Lloyd, Andrew Clark and Paul Kelly have all made unwitting contributions and of course I have drawn on my own previous works.

I should also thank my editor Gail MacCallum (is nepotism involved here?) and my partner Jenny Garrett for their patience and encouragement during what turned out to be an unexpectedly difficult gestation. I hope they find that the infant has been worth the struggle.

Chapter One

My family used to run the place, but all I got was their worn-out genes

I come from a political family. This is less a boast than an admission. While a trace of convict or aboriginal ancestry, once a matter for shame and concealment, is now considered rather chic, politicians remain the pits. Moreover my mother's people, the Wentworths, were a bit fringe even by Australian political standards. D'Arcy, who arrived in the early days of the colony, was certainly a highwayman and probably a murderer. He had been tried at the Old Bailey and acquitted on four separate occasions before his aristocratic relatives decided the heat was too much to stand and shipped him out with an appointment as assistant surgeon on Norfolk Island; for practical purposes he was a remittance man. He came out with the second fleet on the convict ship *Neptune*, where he met and 'consorted with' (as record has it) Catherine Crowley, who was being transported for the theft of a bolt of cloth. Their first son

William Charles Wentworth, was born at sea.

Norfolk Island was perhaps the worst of all the prison hells of New South Wales; D'Arcy's duties consisted mainly of declaring convicts fit for flogging, a task he apparently performed with gusto. Having established his credentials, he was able to settle on the mainland, where he came under the patronage of Governor Lachlan Macquarie. As Macquarie's hatchet man, he quickly became a figure of wealth and influence.

Young William, after schooling in England where he met and admired his father's benefactor, Lord Fitzwilliam, returned to join the first expedition to cross the Blue Mountains and a blackbirding raid on Raratonga during which the ship's captain was killed and William took command and brought the ship home. He also attracted Macquarie's favour; at one stage the governor granted him the whole of Sydney's North Shore, which Wentworth promptly lost in a card game. Macquarie replaced it with deeds to the Illawarra region, which the family finally dissipated in the 1980s.

Wentworth was now a man of some fame; when he returned to Australia after another stint in England studying law and coming second in a poetry competition on the subject of Australasia, he was greeted as 'the native son', a title he immediately adopted to his emerging political career. He had previously circulated scurrilous verse about the military and civil elite who ran the colony. Now he opened a newspaper, *The Australian*, in which he attacked them with unbridled ferocity: 'little yellow snakes' was one of the milder descriptions. He made a particular enemy of Governor John Darling: when Darling was recalled Wentworth gave a party for 4000 people, which ended with many of them rowing out to the ship which was to take Darling back to England and farewelling him with a barrage of insults and several drunk choruses of 'Over the Hills and Far Away'.

Although he started out as a champion of the emancipists and native born, his increasing wealth led him inevitably towards conservatism. He bought Vaucluse House from an Irishman who had surrounded the estate with imported Irish soil because St Patrick would never allow snakes to cross it; the property was remodelled and filled with European antiques, with a modest family mausoleum attached – if such an attachment can ever be called modest. In 1840 he and his friends purported to acquire most of the South Island of New Zealand from some Maori chiefs for the privileged price of one farthing per thousand acres. Governor Gipps made them give it back on the grounds that the deal would have made Wentworth a bigger landowner than Queen Victoria. When he finally entered the Legislative Council he continued to campaign for self-government, but had now abandoned the idea of universal franchise for rights based on the ownership of property. He also proposed an Australian hereditary peerage – a notion ridiculed as 'a bunyip aristocracy.'

By now the fire had gone out in his belly. Once again he returned to England and was instrumental in piloting a constitution for the colony of New South Wales through Whitehall. He stayed to settle in Dorset. When he died in 1872 his body was repatriated for Australia's first ever state funeral.

William Charles Wentworth Mark I was clearly going to be a hard act to follow. During my childhood most of my family uttered his name with reverence, but with a conspicuous lack of detail; certainly his bastardry, both literal and figurative, was never mentioned. About all I knew of him was that he had crossed the Blue Mountains (in company, of course, with Blax-land and Lawson) and had consequently become a favourite of Macquarie's, as a result of which the family was supposedly stinking rich – although somehow none of this apparently untold wealth had trickled down to my mother. Then there was a gap in the family history which unfortunately will prob-ably never be filled because my grandmother burnt all the relevant papers in the backyard; a sturdy member of the Church of England, she believed in not speaking ill of the dead, and apparently there was a fair bit of ill to be spoken of the dead Wentworths. A glimmer of it can be seen in a 1912 news-paper article recording the death at the age of 91 of a man calling himself William Charles Wentworth and claiming to be the son of the original. An acknowledged son, Fitzwilliam, served in the Imperial Bushman's Contingent in the Boer War.

The next WCW, my grandfather, was qualified as a lawyer, but appeared to do nothing much apart from attending endless functions at the Union Club. A serious anti-Catholic, he is remembered for a visit to St Peter's in Rome during which he thumped his walking stick on the tiles to get the attention of the passing tourists, and roared: 'Jesus said: "Lay not up for yourselves treasures upon earth." Now just look around you.' He was removed by the Swiss Guard.

But with his son, William Charles Wentworth the Younger (as he chose to call himself), the political urge was revived in its full fury. My Uncle Bill was a brilliant scholar and studied economics at Oxford; he became a Keynesian long before it was fashionable. As advisor to the New South Wales premier Bertram Stevens during the Depression he pushed unsuccess-fully for expansionary measures; it was to be the first of many political defeats, none of which in the least dampened his enthusiasm. In fact Wentworth's ideas at this stage were far closer to those of the Labor Party and even to the maverick Jack Lang than to those of his fellow conservatives. He argued the need for subsidies to Australian industry and the creation of a general social welfare net. At the same time the young Robert Menzies was telling his supporters that paying British bondholders their dividend was really what mattered: 'If Australia was to surmount her troubles only by abandonment of traditional British standards of honesty, justice, fair play and honest endeavour, it would be better for Australia that every citizen within her boundaries were to die of starvation within the next six months.' But then Menzies and Wentworth were never to see eye to eye.

Nonetheless, Wentworth was a loyal lieutenant when Menzies remoulded the worn-out United Australia Party and its conservative allies into the modern Liberal Party and was elected to the safe seat of Mackellar in 1949. The good news is that he was to stay there for the next 28 years, and for 25 of them the coalition of which he was a part was in government. The bad news is that he spent all but about four and a half of them on the backbench. Even before entering parliament he had earned a reputation for eccentricity. As a wartime captain in the army reserve he led his men on a mock invasion from Cronulla beach, captured the vital military target of the local railway station, moved on to the battalion headquarters and arrested the colonel in his pyjamas.

In parliament he was no less belligerent. Even at a time when anti-communisn was more or less compulsory, Wentworth was seen as something of an extremist. Once when he was in full flight on the floor of the House Labor's Les Haylen entered the chamber in a borrowed white coat, watched judicially for a few moments and then, with a sad shake of the head, escorted the bewildered member out.

His ideas on social security were too far ahead of their time for the comfortable certainties of the Menzies years. But he had the occasional win; his campaigning for uniform railway gauges led to a single track between Sydney and Melbourne, although Wentworth himself was not invited to the official opening. His doughty wife Barbara turned up anyway, bearing a placard demanding 'Where's Wentworth?'

Ironically, it was the despised and neglected area of aboriginal affairs which led to his brief rise to power. Wentworth, an inveterate traveller around Australia in search of such phenomena as the Min Min light, had encountered many tribal groups, and developed some empathy and a great deal of sympathy. Unlike his colleagues, who dismissed the issue with the remark that there were no votes in aborigines (or boongs as they were commonly referred to at that time), he believed the government should do something. From the backbench he lobbied Menzies for a referendum to change section 51 of the Constitution to allow the Commonwealth to legislate on behalf of indigenous Australians. The vote had to wait until Menzies's retirement but the 1967 referendum which was passed overwhelmingly in all states was very much Wentworth's brainchild. When John Gorton, himself a bit of a knockabout who appreciated Wentworth's maverick tendencies, became prime minister, he made Wentworth Australia's first Minister for Aboriginal Affairs, and threw in Social Security as a bonus.

Happy as a pig in mud, Wentworth flung himself into the task of reforming the country, and attended as many cabinet meetings as he could wangle himself into with proposals for radical changes both inside and outside his portfolios. He was greeted at first with amused tolerance, later with mounting impatience. It couldn't last and it didn't. After three years his friend and political ally Gorton lost the prime ministership to Billy McMahon, an old Sydney enemy. That afternoon I went down to Uncle Bill's office to commiserate, and found him staring gloomily at the huge map of the world, with the gigantic communist bloc poised threateningly above little Australia, that adorned the wall behind his desk. Rather inanely, I suggested that things could be worse. 'Yes,' he snapped back, 'and they will be.' As it turned out McMahon allowed him to keep Social Security, though Aboriginal Affairs went to the smarmy and ineffectual Peter Howson, a McMahon sycophant.

Wentworth rather enjoyed his brief period in opposition during the tumultuous Labor years, during which he backed a series of extremely tenuous court actions against Gough Whitlam and several of his ministers. But when the coalition regained government Malcolm Fraser did not restore him to the ministry and he resigned from the party in disgust to stand, unsuccessfully, as an independent senator and later for the House of Representitives seat named after his famous grandfather under the slogan 'A Wentworth for Wentworth'. The blue ribbon Liberal stronghold was unshaken. In retirement he became a frequent correspondent on matters as diverse as the absurdity of economic rationalism and the necessity of a permanent colony on the moon. He was still trying to find a Diophantine solution to Fermat's last theorem when well into his nineties.

The Wentworths were, and are, a family of diverse interests. The man my mother called Wicked Uncle D'Arcy was bigamously married to a chambermaid by a bribed priest in a hot air balloon floating over Watson's Bay, while the family helplessly shook their fists from the beach below. Great Aunt

Dot spent much of her time talking to her garden, which bloomed spectacularly as a result, but chased relatives and strangers alike off her property on the grounds that they were spreading disease. Cousin Kate is an indefatigable litigant who went through a public and spectacularly messy series of law suits against her husband which featured rape, sodomy, obscene messages, a dildo, a shadowy individual who claimed to be a Polish count and an alsatian dog named Blitzen. Aunt Mary set something of a record by making seventeen separate decisions for Christ during a single Billy Graham tour. But it's fair to say that to think of the Wentworths is to think of politics – and of the wilder shores of politics at that.

Most of this was of course well ahead of me during my Went-worth-based childhood: Bill was just another presence, albeit a somewhat shrill one, at family gatherings. These usually took place at the imposing house (mansion is not too large a word) on top of the hill at Point Piper, where lived my maternal grandparents and in which my mother and father were some-what reluctant lodgers. Down the road in a smaller but even more exclusive residence overlooking Lady Martin's Beach, my father's mother Hilda held court, attended by her younger son Duncan. Her father-in-law, Sir Mungo MacCallum, had been chancellor of Sydney University, which coincidentally had been part-founded by the original William Charles Went-worth.

Anticipating the inevitable cracks, I used to volunteer that two great Australian families met in me, and both lost.

It need hardly be said that both houses were remorselessly conservative in their politics. Although Jack Lang had not been premier of New South Wales since 1932, and was now only a harmless if rather dotty backbencher in Canberra, he was still referred to in hushed and horrified tones as 'that man'. This was particularly hard on my father, a journalist who was broadened and radicalised by his years as a war correspondent and editor of the army magazine *Salt*, but was constrained by his position as a tenant of the still mighty Wentworth dynasty. I am fairly sure he voted Labor, which was close to high treason in those surroundings, but he certainly never admitted it.

Still, there were occasional hints. I remember a day in the early 1950s when parliamentary question time was on the wireless, and Menzies was asked if he recalled saying something earlier in the year which he was now contradicting. The great man was at his devastating best. It was, he said, an idiotic question which only illustrated the depths of desperation and despair in which the Labor Party now found itself under the communist-dominated union movement and its stooges, it would not be unfair to call them servants, who now ran this once great party, etc etc, and of course he didn't remember his exact words of six months ago, it was absurd to expect that of anyone who made as many speeches as he did, but if the honourable member would care to read them out he would undertake to inform the parliament that they made jolly good sense. 'Well,' I said to my father, 'that was pretty good stuff.'

'Yes,' he replied, 'but you'll notice he still couldn't answer the question.' I stared open-mouthed at such presumption; but then I thought, he's right, of course. It was my first critical look at Australian politics.

Chapter Two

IF THE WAR IS STILL OVER, WHY IS EVERYONE STILL FIGHTING?

I was born just before Christmas 1941; therefore I was con-
ceived some time before Pearl Harbor, when Japan entered
the war and Australia's part became rather more urgent than
the defence of a distant empire. Even so, the times were already
troubled ones, and my parents told me later that they were seen
as very brave, very irresponsible or just plain careless by their
respective families.

My father had resigned from what was regarded as a
promising career on the *Sydney Morning Herald*, where his own
father had been a leader writer, to run the armed forces magazine *Salt*. This involved a move to Melbourne, and in due
course my mother and I followed. This had the added advantage of getting us out of Sydney in the aftermath of the
Japanese midget-submarine attack, which had resulted in mild
panic by sections of the populace, especially those with harbour views.

My father was of course in army barracks and available only occasionally – he also spent some time overseas. My mother and I were ensconced in the home of a Wentworth family friend, Wilfrid (later Sir) Kent Hughes. Kent Hughes was a highly distinguished soldier, but politically well to the right of the soup spoon; like Uncle Bill he came into parliament in 1949, and like Uncle Bill was too extreme for Menzies, who left him on the backbench after a brief stint in Interior. He was still there when he died in 1970; I wrote a brief obituary for *The Australian*, in which I concentrated on the fact that he was a keen walker.

I remember almost nothing of the Melbourne years; the highlight was a solar eclipse during which I was taken down to the fowl house to look at the chooks asleep in the middle of the day. Even as a three-year-old I realised that Melbourne was hardly fun city. We were back in Sydney by the time the war ended, and on VJ day I, like many Australians, wept. Not, I fear, in relief; nor in sorrow over the huge death toll; nor in presentiment of the dangers of the atomic age ahead. It was because the ABC had substituted a program of thanksgiving for my regular favourite, 'Kindergarten of the Air'.

At Point Piper nothing much had changed, particularly rationing. In reality this made very little difference to the Wentworths; Uncle Neville owned a large sheep station in the west, and could be relied on for regular visits bearing fresh meat, butter, eggs and that unimaginable luxury, clotted country cream. In any case the Wentworths were in a comfortable position to top up their rations from the thriving black market. It would therefore be pleasing to report that they bore the minor inconveniences of post-war life with stoicism. They didn't. Grandmother in particular complained constantly, even when the local grocer, Mr Linke, treated her as a privileged customer and slipped a few little extras into her weekly shopping bag.

Mr Linke, incidentally, was at that stage my only link (no pun intended) with the non-Anglo-Celtic world. He was a perpetually harassed little man who had arrived from somewhere in Europe (I never found out where) just before the war and had tried to set up what would now be called a delicatessen. After discovering that the residents of Double Bay were deeply suspicious of any cheese that could not easily be substituted for soap and were appalled by the mere thought of salami, he reverted to the staples of the day – bread, milk, eggs and bacon. Soon after the war a magnificent continental cake shop appeared, and W.D. and H.O. Dullo opened a store selling the best chocolates in Australia. As with so many Australians, my first contact with multiculturalism was through the gullet.

But back in Canberra Prime Minister Ben Chifley and Immigration Minister Arthur Calwell had set what was to prove an irreversible process in motion. Until then the influx of migrants had been predominantly from northern Europe, and of these the overwhelming majority were Anglos. For Calwell at least the hope was that the balance would not change too much: his principal slogan was still 'Bring Out a Briton', and the program of assisted migration (the ten pound poms) was seen as the centrepiece. But the gates were opened wider and wider to southern Europeans as well, and what a difference it made.

The visionary Snowy River Scheme became the cradle of the New Australia, but private enterprise saw its own chance to recruit a cheap, hard-working and above all non-militant labour force. It was often said that the giant mining and metal-working conglomerate of BHP had more to do with setting the immigration program than any politician. The motives were not always idealistic, but the result was that Australia quickly became one of the most rapidly changing societies on earth. When the final barrier of the White Australia policy went down in the 1960s the great experiment was finally complete: Australia became the only nation in the world to have deliberately taken the road to multiculturalism and to have successfully finished the journey.

I still regard this as the best and noblest political and social achievement of any society during my lifetime; in some ways it ranks with the Greek invention of democratic government. However, in 1949 it just meant that eating was getting marginally more interesting. The politics of the time revolved around rationing and strikes, of which there were a great many.

Throughout the 1930s and 1940s the small but dedicated Communist Party of Australia had sought to extend its political influence, with mixed success. Its attempt to infiltrate the ALP had failed miserably and its various front organisations, usually based on an appeal to pacifism and/or internationalism, had not survived the gyrations of Moscow's foreign policy: the memory of the Hitler–Stalin pact was still too fresh. But in sections of the trade union movement the party, unconstrained by the need for strict observance of the democratic process, did much better. In particular the waterfront, effectively under the control of the charismatic Jim Healy, became a symbol of fear and loathing for those Australians who really cared about the preservation of capitalism at all costs.

The militancy fed off itself: anti-communist union leaders had to compete, to show their members that they too could face down the bosses. By 1949 Sydney's vehemently right wing

Daily Telegraph scarcely let an edition go past without a scream about strikebound Sydney, the country held to ransom, Bolshevik shop stewards and Moscow gold.

At Point Piper, where the *Telegraph* ruled, the atmosphere was uneasy, particularly as my father was writing a column for the *Sydney Sun* which became increasingly anti-establishment as he matured from being an unusually heavy social drinker into a fully-fledged alcoholic. Eventually he broke down completely and after a period in a sanatorium decided to go to England to recuperate, partly on the basis that it would be easier to be grog-free if he were also Wentworth-free. My Wentworth grandparents were torn between relief at being rid of him and annoyance at his abandonment of my mother and myself.

My mother said later that she believed he had ceased to love her from the time I was born; yet she clung to the marriage for another twenty years. After his return he too tried to make things work – or at least to maintain a civilised relationship. But it seldom lasted for long, even after we finally moved out of Point Piper and into our own house. Sometimes, as I took his feet while mother carried his shoulders when a taxi had deposited him home after a particularly severe drinking bout, I wondered why they stuck together, and hoped that it wasn't as a result of some mistaken belief that it was better for me.

For the Establishment the last straw was Chifley's proposal to nationalise the banks. The Establishment didn't actually like the banks very much; indeed, they were yet another object of constant complaint. But when all was said and done, the banks were still *their* banks, and no Labor upstart was going to get his grubby little hands on them. They mobilised in force and the banks themselves called out the troops. Labor's Fred Daly recalled a rowdy campaign meeting: 'I said to an interjector: "You're a bank officer and you're being paid time and a half to come here and interject." He replied: "That's a deliberate lie, I get double time." As it turned out the High Court ruled that bank nationalisation was unconstitutional anyway, but by then the damage had been done. Labor may have seen Australia through the war and set the wheels rolling for the great task of postwar reconstruction, but now Chifley and his team seemed tired and out of touch, especially when they insisted on continuing with petrol rationing. The silver-tongued Robert Menzies, on the other hand, had promised to abolish petrol rationing and also to do all sorts of nice, if vague, things like put value back in the pound.

Menzies had not wasted his time in opposition by simply opposing: after all, during the war years such a stance would hardly have been patriotic. Instead he concentrated on remoulding the conservative side of politics into something approaching a modern organisation. The old United Australia Party dissolved, as had its predecessor, the Nationalist Party. Menzies picked up the pieces and added in whatever allies he could find, including the Kooyong Ladies Auxiliary. He called his creation the Liberal Party in an attempt to bring back memories of the glorious past and Alfred Deakin; but of course it was and remains unabashedly conservative. The reborn Menzies had perpetrated his first deception on the electorate.

But the electorate didn't seem to mind, especially as Menzies had reinvented it as well; he addressed his appeal to 'the forgotten people'. This mysterious group was never really defined, but it was understood to include just about anyone who had ever had a whinge about the government. Chifley has frequently been described as Australia's best loved prime minister, but if this is true all it proves is that the Beatles got it wrong. Love is not all you need. Nor is the wistful but metaphysical goal of the light on the hill. Chifley of all people should have known. After all, he was the one who first identified the hip pocket nerve.

While Menzies failed to put much value back in the pound he did abolish petrol rationing and was able to ride the postwar recovery. Previously unobtainable goods began to reappear in the shops; I remember my mother triumphantly bringing home my first balloon, although in hindsight I am not entirely sure that some enterprising entrepreneur had not got hold of a case of army-issue condoms, inflated them and attached them to sticks. This was a high point; a low point was that my parents, no doubt from the best of motives, insisted that I should learn to write with my right hand. As a natural left-hander I found this impossible, and became a liar as a result. At the same time I was spoiled, selfish, wilful and moody – ideal material, one might have thought, for recruitment to the Liberal Party. It had certainly worked for Uncle Bill.

Uncle Bill was by now happily ensconced in Canberra, already making waves with his apocalyptic red baiting; the Labor Opposition claimed that he was at his best just before the full moon. At the time this suited Menzies, whose political luck had continued (it never really failed him) with the outbreak of the Korean War. Not only did this allow him to exploit the reds-under-the-bed paranoia which he increasingly used to smear the Labor Party; the jump in wool prices because of the demand for army uniforms turned a minor economic recession into a major boom. Graziers were quite literally getting a pound of money for a pound of fleece; many had no idea what to do with the windfall. The purchase of Rolls Royces, with extra wide running boards to make it easier to crutch sheep, was commonplace. One farmer was pictured seated on the steps of a country pub popping champagne corks at passers-by; well over a hundred empty bottles were beside him. Uncle Neville took a luxury round-the-world trip. Asked for the highlights on his return, he told my mother that the price of Scotch in Rome was outrageous. The hedonism made a nice contrast to the increasing dread that the Cold War would turn into a hot, indeed fusion-powered, conflict.

It was in this atmosphere that Menzies decided to introduce legislation to outlaw the Communist Party. Given his own long experience in politics, it is impossible to see this as other than an act of opportunism. He must have know that the CPA posed no threat to the political stability of Australia; it was certainly a nuisance in sections of the union movement, but the idea that Moscow had wriggled its godless tentacles through every aspect of Australian society was never more than a fantasy held by the seriously bewildered – and Menzies was not seriously bewildered. However, he had no objection to reducing the electorate to that unhappy state, especially if he could cause angst and division within the Labor Party in the process; and so it proved.

Although you would never have guessed it from listening to Menzies, the Labor Party was devoutly anti-communist. As a target of infiltration by the CPA, it had learned the hard way. However, it was also connected by an almost Siamese bond to the unions – indeed, a section of traditionalists within the movement believed that the ALP was, or at least should be, no more than the political arm of the industrial base. The party's structure reflected this belief: the majority of delegates to its national conference, and hence to its national executive, were nominated by the unions. They were not, of course, communist – party rules strictly forbade any crossover. But since some of the unions were communist dominated, it was easy for the uninformed to make a connection. Menzies and his allies constantly invited the uninformed to do so.

Thus Labor was at great pains to dispel any suggestion that it sympathised with the CPA. But many within the party saw that Menzies's proposals went far beyond mere anti-communism; they involved fundamental principles of human rights, including the right to remain silent, freedom of speech and association, even the right to believe what one chose. The Menzies bill allowed search and seizure without warrant, and it reversed the presumption of innocence: the onus would be on those declared by a ministerial committee to be communists to prove that they were not. Some thought these basics were far too important to ignore, whatever the political cost; others, more cynical, thought that in practice they would prove so unpopular that it made sense to let the government go ahead with them and take the consequences. After considerable agonising the executive decided that Labor should move amendments to get rid of the worst of the nasties, and if (when) the government refused to accept them, should allow the bill to pass.

But then, before it could be proclaimed, the communists announced that they would challenge it in the High Court, and Chifley's deputy, Dr Herbert Vere Evatt, announced that he would take their brief. Chifley had to put down a caucus revolt as a result, but he stuck with the Doc, who, as everyone now knows, won a famous victory both in the court and in the referendum that Menzies initiated to change the Constitution so that he could by-pass the court's ruling. Evatt, an outstanding lawyer, historian, internationalist and civil libertarian, had already received the signal honour of being voted in as the first president of the United Nations, but this was the high point of his political career; from then on it was to be all downhill.

In a funny way, it was also a turning point for me. Waiting on a corner in the city for my mother to come out of a shop I was surprised to see a woman climb to the top of a portable ladder and start haranguing the crowd; I was one of the few who paid attention. This fascist referendum must be defeated, she shouted. All our freedoms were at stake. She turned an eagle eye towards me. 'Do you want,' she screamed accusingly, 'the secret police to have the right to break down the doors of your home and carry you off to jail without trial?' A moment's thought convinced me that I did not. If nine-year-olds had been allowed to vote, I would certainly have voted no. My lifelong commitment to the left had begun.

Chapter Three

IF DOC EVATT HAD GONE TO CRANBROOK INSTEAD OF FORT STREET HE WOULD HAVE GONE MAD A LOT SOONER

The following year I started high school, and politics went on hold for the time being; a commitment to the left was definitely not something to be flaunted at Cranbrook. That this impeccably Establishment monument to the Anglican church should become my *alma mater*, as well as that of families like the Fairfaxes and the Packers, was purely a matter of geography. My kindergarten had been just down the road in Point Piper at Miss Peel's; transferring to Cranbrook was simply a matter of crossing New South Head Road at the bottom of the hill.

I first did so to enter what was somewhat grandly called the preparatory school in 1946, and was final released from the top end in 1958. These were decidedly not the happiest years of my life. As a gawky and asthmatic smart-arse I was a natural target for bullying, and despite all the *Boy's Own Annual*-style advice of my few friends, I could never summon up the courage to hit back; my adrenal glands always advocated flight rather than fight. Inevitably I became something of an outcast, with the derisive nickname of the Walking Encyclopaedia – which, in a spirit of mild revenge, I insisted should always be spelt with the diphthong. Actually it was seldom spelt at all, but I felt I should make the point.

The junior school was actually less trouble than the high school; the work came very easily to me and other expectations, especially on the sporting field, were mercifully undemanding. And, extraordinarily, there was even a smattering of politics. Mr Potter, widely hero-worshipped because he had fought in New Guinea, gave the assembled school a summary of last week's news every Monday. I remember almost nothing of this, except for one comment that the Russians had declared themselves peace-loving but had predicted war between Britain and America, and that was devilishly clever of them.

A more controversial moment came when Mr Lacaze, already suspect for his ability to speak French, organised an end-of-term debating competition; the final topic was, amazingly, an argument about whether communism was a good or a bad thing. Since all real Cranbrookians had been imprinted from birth with the certainty that communism was the ultimate evil, there was a certain amount of puzzlement among those chosen to defend the ideals of Marx and Engels; indeed, it quickly emerged that no one had a clue what they were. Mr Lacaze helpfully proposed the working definition that communism was a system under which the garbage man was paid the same as the bank manager, and the debate proceeded as planned. At its conclusion Mr Lacaze read out his own thoughts on the subject, of which no one understood a single syllable. However, some keen Cranbrookian must have dobbed him in, because next term Mr Lacaze was nowhere to be seen – a minor victim of antipodean McCarthyism.

I graduated, if such is the word, from junior school in 1952 and there was some discussion within the family as to whether I should stay at Cranbrook or not; my father would have preferred to move me to his own old school, the more prestigious (if scarcely less expensive) Sydney Grammar, a short tram ride away. By this time he had joined the ABC and risen rapidly through the ranks of radio features. The drinking, while still severe, was at least under control for sustainable periods and things at home were relatively stable, though far from idyllic. Inevitably I resisted change: I had been dux of the junior school, which gave me some kudos among my classmates, and I would rather stay with the few friends I had painfully gained. In the end I settled the matter by winning the annual Cranbrook scholarship which took care of all tuition fees as long as I could avoid expulsion. Swapping my cap for a silly hat (though not yet my shorts for long trousers) I set off down the hill once again.

For any pubescent boy (which I actually wasn't yet) of more sensitivity than a sledgehammer, there were two things wrong with Cranbrook, one permanent and one temporary. The permanent one was a reputation for effeminacy: a traditional chant from other schools went: 'Tiddlywinks old man, get a woman if you can; if you can't get a woman get a Cranbrook man.' It should be emphasised that the taunt was about sissies rather than homosexuals; in the latter regard

Cranbrook seemed neither better nor worse than any other boys-only school of the times. But, as I walked home alone, the jeers of other boys, and after we had moved to Paddington very much tougher boys, were hard to avoid.

The other problem, though temporary, was more serious: the headmaster, an English expatriate called Gwythen Hewan. It was my bad luck that my years at secondary school coincided almost exactly with Hewan's reign. Before him there had been Brian Hone, a muscular Christian who personified the cliché 'firm but fair'; a greatly respected figure who had left for the greener pastures of the GPS (Great Public Schools) system in Victoria. After came Mark Bishop, an enlightened and progressive educator who taught me chemistry and sex (the facts of life, as they were then coyly described) and with whom I had occasional congenial contact until his death. But in between came Hewan, a fossil and not an altogether convincing one at that: a sort of pedagogic version of Piltdown man.

Hewan was a fair maths teacher, a fitness fanatic and a good amateur conjurer. He was also an inveterate money snob and social climber, deficiencies which overshadowed whatever positive qualities he may have had. Wealth was his first criterion; after that came sport, meaning cricket and rugby union – attempts to start up a soccer team at Cranbrook were stamped out as being unmanly. And after sport came daylight, with intellectual and cultural pursuit so far back in the field that they might as well have been scratched altogether. His speeches at assembly, like his approaches to parents he considered worth cultivating, varied uplifting platitudes with meaningless banalities. A conversation with him was like spending half an hour head down in a tub of lukewarm bran mash.

But in spite of the Gusher, as Hewan was known, the

teaching staff was generally very good. Junior masters some-times had discipline problems, but seldom lasted long if they did so. The core group was dedicated, extremely hard working and usually literate and knowledgeable far beyond their spe-cialities. Most encouraged discussion and debate; there were very few taboos, although party politics appeared to be one of them. Nonetheless, we turned our young minds to issues like capital punishment, colour prejudice, pacifism – all the golden oldies – and solved most of them to our satisfaction if not that of our teachers.

Religion was more difficult: Cranbrook was, we were constantly informed, a Christian school, and attendance at chapel and scripture classes was compulsory – except for Jews. At one stage Hewan tried to make them compulsory for Jews as well, but a deputation of some of the richer Jewish par-ents forced a grovelling backdown. However, religious education was, to put it mildly, simplistic. In junior school we were ordered: 'Hands up all those who believe in God.' Only one brave hand (not mine) stayed down and when the order was changed to 'Hands up all those who would like to believe in God,' he too submitted. There were attempts to reconcile science and the Bible: I was solemnly assured that Genesis con-firmed the fossil record because it told us that grass was created before mammals and that scientists had constructed an artifi-cial amoeba that was perfect in every detail but they had been unable to give it life because that power was reserved for the Holy Spirit. But such gobbledygook was very much on the fringe; any attempt to take it to extremes – say, to suggest that creationism be taught as a serious subject – would have been laughed out of the staff room.

Without making any conscious effort, I quickly drifted

through agnosticism into atheism; the whole business of religion seemed patently absurd, not to mention logically unnecessary. The chaplain, an ex-army padre who later ran off with the school matron, pressed religious literature on me, but I treated the arguments in them as intellectual games, and concentrated on spotting fallacies and inconsistencies. Religion might be morally uplifting, although it frequently wasn't; ritual could be very beautiful, though it often descended into kitsch. But there was still no reason to believe in the Christian myth any more than in any other legend. Eventually the padre gave up on me; but I still had to attend chapel and scripture lessons.

The Jews, who didn't, spent their time in the library. Other than on these occasions, they were in no sense a group apart, and there was no ostensible anti-Semitism; I can honestly say that one of my best friends was a Jew. The same applied to the Asians, more often than not the sons of diplomats. Whatever Cranbrook's faults as social educator (and in the Hewan years they were many), it was mercifully free of any kind of racism. My disgust at the concept was thus a purely theoretical one, based mainly on media reporting of the uprisings in the American south. I was blissfully unaware of any local parallels. In the Point Piper and the Cranbrook of the 1950s, aborigines simply did not exist.

But by the time I left Cranbrook I was a confirmed leftie. If the school had taught me nothing else, it had shown me the power of money and the ways in which it can be used to enforce conformity. Like my father I had become an enemy of the Establishment, while happily drinking from its fountains.

Meanwhile, in the real world, the real left was in dire trouble. Menzies had capitalised on the arguments within the Labor Party to call a double dissolution in 1951; the ostensible reason was the rejection of an unimportant bill about bank employees, but the real purpose was to consolidate his power while he was still considered reasonably fresh. The campaign had an unexpected consequence: the strain of it killed Chifley, who died on the night of the celebration of fifty years of nationhood. Menzies seemed genuinely shaken, but he was enough of a realist to see that the loss of Labor's most popular leader in its history had to be a political bonus. This was spectacularly confirmed when the party elected Chifley's deputy, Bert Evatt, as his successor. Even in those days many in the party had doubts about Evatt; what was delicately referred to as his temperament was a bit of a worry. At times his enthusiasms got the better of him. Also his judgment could be more than somewhat awry. During Labor's years in power he had produced complex mathematical charts to prove that under a system of proportional voting Labor would control the Senate forever. Chifley, impressed, introduced such a system while Labor did in fact have the numbers in the Senate to pass it into law. Labor immediately lost control of the Senate and has never looked like regaining it since. But Evatt's huge talents, not to mention his recent successes against Menzies in the High Court and the referendum campaign made his accession inevitable. To have bypassed him for any of the other possibilities – Eddie Ward, Arthur Calwell, Alan Fraser – would have looked very dumb.

It will no doubt come as a surprise to most readers to hear that Evatt's election pushed the ALP not to the left, but to the right; for all his civil libertarianism (or perhaps because of it), Evatt was even more dedicated an anti-communist than Chifley. It was only when his own position was endangered by the events leading up to the split that he would turn, reluctantly, to a side he had always distrusted for salvation. His immediate aim – indeed, his obsession – was to win the next election, due in 1954. Wisely, he chose to fight it on the basis of domestic welfare; communism and foreign affairs in general were to be neutralised as issues. Thus Evatt, while privately conceding that communist control of mainland China would have to be recognised sooner or later, inveighed against it at the time; he even accused Menzies of secretly planning to allow a Chinese communist embassy to be built in Canberra in order to pre-empt any argument on the subject. (Meanwhile, in a small country far to our north, French troops were losing the battle for an isolated garrison called Dien Bien Phu and with it their last colony in Asia. In international circles there was desultory debate as to whether the West should intervene to stop Ho Chi Minh and his nationalist forces. Menzies said defensively that any suggestion that Australia would follow American policy in Indo-China was completely untrue. This was the foundation lie in the edifice of mendacity which became Australia's part in the Vietnam War.)

But at the time it appeared that Evatt would get his way; Australian politics would return to its traditional emphasis on living standards, the vital question being 'What's in it for me?' At least that was the position until Menzies rose in parliament to declare, with a solemnity unmatched since he had announced the death of King George a year earlier, that a minor Russian diplomat named Vladimir Petrov had defected to Australia and was ready to spill his guts about the various nests of traitors people like Uncle Bill had been carrying on about for years. Just in case the public did not understand the drama of the moment, we had interminable pictures of Petrov's tearful wife being dragged to a Moscow-bound plane by grim-faced Russian thugs, only to be rescued by heroic Aussie police when the plane landed at Darwin. There was to be no doubt about who were the goodies and who were the baddies in this case.

Menzies immediately set up a Royal Commission, which Evatt supported – he could hardly do otherwise. It held a preliminary hearing just twelve days before the election, promising a sensational spy trial with amazing scenes and shock-horror revelations. It was hardly the atmosphere Evatt would have chosen. During the campaign, Menzies took the moral high ground: the words 'Petrov' and 'communism' never passed his lips. The muck-raking was left to his eager deputy, Arthur Fadden, who used lines like: 'Can you afford to make Dr Evatt the nation's trustee after his association with communists and communism over the years?'

The decision, by a surprisingly narrow margin, was that they couldn't; but in the end Evatt's own desperation for a win may have been the deciding factor. Regardless of cost, he promised huge increases in pensions, child endowment and maternity allowances, abolition of sales tax on furniture, cheap loans, no means test, support for farmers – and all apparently with no increase in taxes or charges. It was everything you want for nothing. Asked where the money was coming from, he had no reply. Menzies poured scorn on his alleged innumeracy; given Evatt's cock-up with the Senate numbers, he may well have had a point.

Even so, Labor gained five seats; it was still three short of government, but it kept Evatt's hopes alive. Even after the Labor split next year and a disastrous loss in the snap election that followed, Evatt incredibly retained the leadership; by that time it was all about factional loyalty rather than winning government. After another loss in 1958 his record, combined with his erratic behaviour, finally meant it was time to go. With the acquiescence of the NSW Labor government, Evatt finally resigned in 1960 to become state Chief Justice, a job for which rationality was apparently not considered a necessary qualification. Two years later he was eased out of public life altogether, the end of a career which had become a tragedy for himself, his family, his party and the progressive side of politics as a whole. I only saw him once, when my parents took me to the exclusive Prunier's restaurant on Macquarie Street, I think in 1956. Evatt was alone in a corner. He had ordered the restaurant's signature dish, chicken in a basket, a roast spatchcock served in a basket cleverly constructed of potato straws. Speaking eloquently to an audience visible only to himself, the Doc was carefully dismantling the basket and sticking the straws in his hair – a phrase I had read, but never taken literally. Even then he was clearly a few straws short of a basket, not to mention a couple of drumsticks light of the full chook.

But for me, as for most Australians, the most vivid memory of 1954 was not the election, or even the Petrov affair, with all its Edgar Wallace overtones. It was, of course, the royal visit. I saw Our Queen twice on the first motorcade, once from the window of a dentist's surgery in Macquarie Street, and later from a prime spot on the roadside, where I felt that she was looking right through me. Later I, along with thousands of other hapless schoolchildren, was dragooned to the Showground where we waited for hours in the broiling sun for the royal party to appear. They were fashionably late. When the Landrover finally swept by the school captain called for three cheers for the Queen, but it was too late; I had already fainted. Unlike Menzies, I did not see her, passing out, and don't know what all the fuss was about.

Chapter Four

Onward Catholic Soldiers, sticking it to Labor Cheered along by Menzies, sitting on his caber

Royalty had two things in common with Anzac Day: both made me faint, and both were sacrosanct even to the furthest left. Presumably there were those who had some reservations about being ruled by a hereditary monarchy of dubious provenance and genetic unreliability – more than one royal tourist appeared to have lost his chin in an unfortunate breeding accident – but no one was game to remain seated during the ritual playing of 'God Save the Queen' which preceded even the most trivial movie from the fiercely republican United States.

But if there was in fact some invisible underground which wished to see Australia adopt its own head of state there was no, repeat no, opposition to the One Day of the

Year. When, some five years later, a bumptious young medical student named Graham Macdonald pseudonymously wrote a piece for the Sydney University paper *honi soit* querying some of the excesses that characterised the post-march activities of April 25 he was accused not just of bad taste but of treason and even sacrilege. The ranks may have been thinner but the faces were still proud, and not to be trifled with.

Cranbrook celebrated Anzac Day by assembling the entire school from the eight-year-olds up on the oval where, after various inept manoeuvres by the cadet corps, we were harangued at stupefying length by some military type dragged kicking and screaming from his local reunion. In the true army tradition, his success was measured by his body count; on a hot day there could be a couple of dozen victims sprawled unconscious on the grass before he wound up in a final burst of patriotism. I was invariably one of them, a habit which became more embarrassing after being forced into uniform.

The cadet corps was compulsory for fourth year and above. No one seemed to know why; even among most of the staff the general view was that it was an expensive waste of time that could be better spent on equally compulsory sporting activities. The company was under the command of the chief Latin master, who was also a captain in the Army Reserve; he was fond of quoting Horace's line '*Dulce et decorum est pro patria mori*', which, apart from being tricky to scan, means 'It is a sweet and glorious thing to die for one's country'. The other view was put by the head prefect, who besides being the company sergeant-major was also the son of a Methodist parson. (The alert reader may ask how such a seemingly humble scion could ever achieve top ranking in Hewan's

Cranbrook. The answer is simple: his mother was an heiress to the Grace Brothers empire.) This earnest young man spent much of his time inquiring of the junior ranks if they really believed it was appropriate to teach children how to kill.

However, his subversion was as ineffective as the Captain's exhortation. Cadets was neither glorious nor homicidal. It was unremitting boredom, the main ingredients of which were brasso, blanco and boot polish and the cleaning of ancient and mildly dangerous pieces of equipment. My pacifism, initially born more of cowardice than conviction, received a serious boost.

But the times were all wrong for pacifism. The Cold War was at its height and although it never reached the dizzying absurdities of the hysteria on the other side of the Pacific there was a feeling that an outbreak of the real thing was, if not inevitable, at least more likely than not. My fellow pupils read a lot of World War II books (Paul Brickhill was especially popular) and talked phlegmatically about 'getting the chop'. The Prime Minister would have heartily approved.

To that time Menzies's own military career had not been what even the kindest observer would have called successful. He had failed to enlist in World War I, an omission that led to his Country Party colleague Earle Page berating him as a coward and refusing to serve in coalition with him. Before World War II he had insisted on selling iron to Japan at a time when that country's aggressive intentions were clear to all but the purblind: this earned him the unflattering sobriquet of Pig Iron Bob. When the conflict broke out he attempted to wangle his way into Churchill's wartime cabinet and was unceremoniously rebuffed. On his return to Australia his conservative colleagues immediately ejected him from office and the populace overwhelmingly decided that he and his fellow conservatives could not be trusted with the conduct of the war. 'I have been done. I will lie down and bleed awhile,' Menzies announced, and retired to brood over his comeback. That having now been achieved in spectacular fashion, he was eager to crown his political achievements with a military triumph. For a heady few weeks it seemed as though the Suez crisis was going to provide it.

Seen from the post-colonial perspective of today the whole Suez operation looks like something dreamed up by Spike Milligan. Egypt's President Nasser nationalises the canal; the governments of Great Britain and France, in a fit of gung-ho jingoism, respond by bombing the place, presumably on the basis that these were the tactics that worked in Dresden (well, up to a point). The Americans, appalled, bang a few English and French heads together and tell them to settle things down or else; at which point the devilishly clever British PM, Sir Anthony Eden, murmurs to his French counterpart: 'You know, what we need here is someone to really balls up the negotiations so we don't end up as the ones with the egg on the face, and by George, I know just the man.' And so it was that Robert Gordon Menzies arrived in Cairo on what everyone except himself realised was Mission Impossible.

Actually things didn't get off to a bad start. Nasser gave a welcoming dinner for the Menzies party at the Manial Palace, and Menzies at first startled and then amused his hosts by doing his well-regarded (at least he told them it was well-regarded) impersonation of Winston Churchill. For encores he did Bernard Shaw and General Jan Smuts. Although the Egyptians had never actually met any of the three, they applauded vigorously. Nasser started referring to Menzies as the Bushman. Unfortunately this was as good as it got. Next day, as formal discussions got under way, Menzies offended just about everyone by brushing aside the orange juice proffered in deference to the Moslem majority and producing a bottle of Scotch from his briefcase. He proceeded to lecture Nasser on the need for an international body to administer the canal and, when Nasser rejected the proposal, warned that the refusal meant trouble would follow. Nasser chose to take his words as a threat and, although Menzies grovellingly apologised, broke off the talks. Menzies went home having fulfilled his designated role as scapegoat to the letter.

But if his excursion onto the international battlefield had been even more embarrassing than usual, he could be well satisfied with progress in the wars at home. Labor had now ripped itself apart so drastically as to appear beyond repair. Better still, it could not blame Menzies and his conservatives for the damage. Certainly the Libs had done their best to help; a gentle push here, a bit of niggling there. But the great split, a schism which made Labor's previous rifts look positively hairline, was almost entirely home grown.

So much has been written about the labyrinthine conspiracies, the violent clashes of personality and ideology, the backroom struggles and the public gouging that it is easy to forget that it really all began and ended as an old-fashioned power struggle between the left (which included some elements not unfriendly to the communists) and the right (many of whom were bound by the most unforgiving orthodoxy of the Catholic church). In the heady atmosphere of the Cold War the two would probably have tried for Armageddon sooner or later anyway, but the end of the party as we know it was brought forward by Evatt's desperation to hold on to the leadership long after it was clear he had passed his use-by date. In doing so he sought the protection first of the right, then of the left and finally of anyone who happened to be passing. The mutual fear and loathing that already existed was augmented by confusion.

But if Evatt filled the role of protagonist and clown, the Demon King, at least to those who saw themselves as the surviving True Believers, was undoubtedly Bartholomew Augustine Michael (but just call me Bob) Santamaria. In vain did Santamaria insist that he was just a normal, everyday supporter of the mighty Carlton footy club, a good bloke who was always up for a bit of fun. A small, prematurely balding man with piercing eyes and a sibilant voice, Santamaria looked sinister; he sounded sinister; and, by always working behind the scenes rather than in the open forums of the party, he acted sinister.

Such was the paranoia within the ALP that there was an unspoken rule against using his name in caucus meetings; the superstition was that if he remained unmentioned, you could pretend he didn't exist. And yet he was detected as the unseen presence behind every setback, every division.

There was just enough truth in this view to make it plausible. Santamaria was indeed the chief executive behind much of the Catholic right's offensive. His fine Italian hand was deeply involved in the industrial groups set up ostensibly to fight communists in the unions, in the work of Catholic Action and its so-called study groups and in the overall organisation known simply (and sinisterly) as the Movement. But what is often forgotten is that he was a passionate Labor man; never in his life, he claimed (and there is no reason to disbelieve him) did he vote for anything except the ALP or its splinter, the DLP. He also claimed to always have regarded capitalism as a greater threat to the body politic than communism; it was just that he was in a position to try and eradicate communism from the Labor Party before turning his formidable attention to the real enemy.

Well, maybe. But it always seemed to me that Santamaria saw threats and enemies everywhere; like another more recent politician he was born to conspire. His writings and broadcasts, which was how most Australians (including me, until many years later) mainly knew him were, to put it mildly, apocalyptic; they positively oozed fear and threat. And yet his idea of the ideal society was so naive as to appear positively loopy. For the wide brown land he envisioned a kind of feudal theocracy, in which happy smiling peasants would till their subsistence blocks under the benign guidance of mildly socialistic Catholic clergy, with a council of all-seeing bishops to administer the more serious issues of state. Or something like that; it was never entirely clear with Santamaria where social theory ended and personal fantasy began. Nonetheless, his shadow extended over the Labor Party far beyond those of many of its official leaders; even now there are those who would describe themselves as his followers. Santamaria spent his last days wrestling with the age-old theological problem of why a benevolent god should allow the existence of evil. There were many in the Labor Party still obsessed with the question of why any kind of god should have created Santamaria.

Although the damage to Labor was immense and lasted nearly twenty years, it should be stressed that the split, like Santamaria himself, was a peculiarly Victorian creature. The shockwaves spread from coast to coast, but the epicentre was firmly located in Melbourne – more precisely, in the triangle defined by Parliament House, Trades Hall and St Patrick's

Cathedral. It is part of Australian folklore that Victorians are more passionate about their sport and their politics than other Australians and the split would seem to confirm this theory. But there were also sound historical reasons why the debate reached its greatest intensity in the so-called Garden State.

The principal one was Archbishop Daniel Mannix, Santamaria's patron and mentor. Mannix was a crusty and ambitious prelate who emphatically did not believe in the separation of church and state; a turbulent priest who made more than one prime minister regret that he did not have the powers of Henry VIII. During World War I Mannix had led the anticonscription cause against Billy Hughes and had won. He was seen as the chief force behind Victoria's wowserish laws on drink, gambling and censorship, which were markedly more repressive than in New South Wales. Moreover Victoria was seen as a naturally Liberal state: the jewel in the crown, Menzies called it. Mannix had nothing much to lose in terms of temporal power by tearing the ALP apart.

In contrast, New South Wales was a naturally Labor state: even after the mini-split engineered by Premier Jack Lang and his followers, the ALP was in government more often than not. And importantly it was largely controlled by good middle-of-the-road Catholics with whom Cardinal Norman Gilroy had few serious differences. The bird in the hand was too valuable to risk. While Mannix was exhorting his flock to vote against the ALP as a matter of conscience, Gilroy was content to wish all the parties involved in the 1958 election good luck – except of course the communists. As wearer of the red hat Gilroy was technically superior to Mannix, but he was far too shrewd an operator to declare open war. Instead he tended his patch with an affected avuncular naivety: he was famous for

attending first nights at the Catholic-sponsored Genesian Theatre, after which he would invariably go back stage and
congratulate the cast: 'Very good, my children, very good
indeed, but I'm blessed if I know how you can remember all
those words.'

As a result of Gilroy's studied neutrality (which his enemies called appeasement) the split in New South Wales could
be characterised as a very small earthquake, not many killed. In
Queensland the rump of Vincent Gair's Labor government
joined the newly formed Democratic Labor Party after losing
a long-running dispute with the party machine; but this was a
matter of convenience rather than ideology. In the other states
the DLP never had more than irritant value. But its secure base
in Victoria, where it continued to enjoy the support of the
Catholic church (and also generous under-the-table subsidies
from the Liberal Party), enabled it to keep Labor from power
both in the state and federally for the equivalent of a political
generation.

In the staunchly Protestant milieu that surrounded me at
the time, the split was more peripheral than it was for the state
as a whole. The Wentworths' virulent anti-Catholicism was
exceeded only by that of the Presbyterian MacCallums. Cranbrook's most reviled enemies within the Associated Schools
group where it competed were St Aloysius (Jesuit) and Waver-
ley (Christian Brothers) – the former despised because we
usually beat them at rugby, and the latter loathed because they
usually beat us. The DLP itself was a bit of a problem: on the
one hand it was clearly a diabolical invention of the Vatican,
and therefore automatically a Bad Thing, but on the other it
was an effective bulwark against the socialist ALP, and thus
undoubtedly a Good Thing. But overall it didn't really matter.

For those who voted number one Liberal almost by reflex, all other parties were more or less irrelevant.

Besides, there were more exciting things to talk about. At long last, television was coming to Australia. It had been a long time waiting, mainly because Menzies didn't really want this new fangled, Yankee-created devil box. Partly it was because he was an instinctive Luddite: he was fond of proclaiming himself 'British to the bootheels', yet another anachronism in a country in which city dwellers had long since abandoned such footwear. And partly it was because he feared, quite rightly, that it would change the political process forever. Menzies was a man for the town hall meeting and the carefully prepared press statement; he avoided press conferences as far as possible. The idea of having a camera thrust under his impressive eyebrows by a long-haired git horrified him. Indeed, the media as a class were among his pet hates. In later years he was to tell Richard Nixon: 'In all my life I have treated the press with marked contempt and remarkable success.' (Nixon commented later: 'No one would ever forget Robert Menzies. I learned a lot from him.')

But the evil machine could not be kept at bay forever and the newspaper barons were clamouring to get their hands on what they saw as licences to print money. Menzies depended for electoral support particularly on the Melbourne-based *Herald and Weekly Times* group and the Sydney *Daily Telegraph* owned by Sir Frank Packer. His position with regard to the Fairfax group was also tricky, as he was having an affair with Sir Warwick Fairfax's wife Elizabeth. The Prime Minister bowed to the inevitable, but with one proviso: when the ABC channel was opened, it was to be modelled as far as possible on the British example, not that of the despised Americans. And so it was that my father once again took off for the Old Dart, this time to examine the entrails of the BBC.

He returned a full bottle in every sense and quickly immersed his eager young staff in a flood of new technology and old panel games. As his son I had a ringside seat; by far the most interesting part was the outside broadcasts, particularly of sporting events. There was a certain urgency about this, as Melbourne was about to host the Olympic Games and the ABC would be responsible for the coverage. As it turned out Packer won the race to be first to air, but it hardly mattered; the ABC opening, produced by my father and featuring a rather unhappy Menzies, moved quickly on to the Games, which were seen as a triumph for both host city and broadcaster. And the ABC scored a notable scoop: the acrimonious water polo final between the USSR and Hungary which took place as Soviet tanks were crushing the revolutionaries in Budapest. Not since the rescue of Mrs Petrov had the Australian electorate had such graphic images on which to focus its well-tended dislike of the beasts of Moscow. Menzies was right: television had indeed distorted the political process, but not at all in the way he had feared.

Chapter Five

No wonder no one cares about the Abos; they never even invented the space shuttle

For most Australians 1956 was a pretty good year, what with television and the Olympics. For the broad left it was just another bummer of the kind the left was getting used to; in spite of the high hopes raised by the immediate postwar years it was now clear that Labor was no longer the natural government of Australia, if indeed it ever had been. But for the hard left — the communists and their allies — 1956 was an unmitigated diaster.

Stalin had died in 1953, an event celebrated by Sir Frank Packer's *Daily Telegraph* with the poster: 'STALIN DEAD HOORAY!' This predictably infuriated the leftists among the paper's editorial and production staff. Nonetheless there was a feeling that it was probably time for a change; even those who were prepared to defend Stalin's ruthless abuses of human rights had to admit that his public relations left a bit to be desired. Khruschev and Bulganin were not exactly a dream team, but they made an interesting double act: the earthy peasant and the stern marshal. Khruschev in particular was seen as a potential thawer of the Cold War; he may have been rough as guts, but at least he was demonstrably human, unlike the robotic apparatchiks who had preceded him. Political insiders even started referring to him as 'Khruschy'.

Hopes rose even higher as 1956 dawned. This was the year of the twentieth party congress; it was, of course, closed to all but the initiated, but rumours, whether orchestrated or not, started to seep back through the Iron Curtain. Soon it was common knowledge that Khruschev had made a speech denouncing Stalin's atrocities. Just how strong the denunciation had been was a matter of debate, but one story in particular gave grounds for optimism. It was said that while Khruschev was in full flight about the awfulness of the previous regime a voice shouted from the floor: 'And what were you doing while all this was going on?' Khruschev thundered back: 'Who said that?' There was dead silence. Khruschev allowed the moment to sink in before continuing mildly: 'Yes, comrade. That's just what I was doing.'

But then the invasion of Hungary brought it all undone. The Cold War warriors growled that they had told us so, and muttered homilies about leopards and their spots. Many communists left the party altogether and those that remained bickered uncomfortably among themselves. The DLP received a boost and the ALP was once again forced into a state of denial. The works of George Orwell made a comeback and became the property of the right, which was never the author's intention. While *Animal Farm*, published in 1945, was a straight satire about the development of Russian communism, *1984*, which appeared four years later, was a warning about totalitarianism of all kinds, from the left, the right, or even the centre. But in the climate of the times, Big Brother became interchangeable with Uncle Joe Stalin. A film version appeared in which Orwell's bleak conclusion that a truly ruthless modern dictatorship would prove indestructible was dishonestly altered to a Hollywood-style message that true love will survive whatever the state can throw at it. And to our north, barely noticed, South Vietnam, now under the hopelessly corrupt control of the Diem family, refused to take part in the scheduled elections to reunify the country, and the Americans enthusiastically backed the decision with more military advisers.

Menzies had never looked smugger. He was to call his autobiography *Afternoon Light*, and it could fairly be said that 1956 was where the long afternoon began. For the next decade Australia, politically at least, was indeed to resemble Tennyson's land of the lotus-eaters – the land where it was always afternoon. There was just one sudden squall during the election of 1961, but in the end that turned out to be little more than a sun shower. These were the years of steady growth, the years in which Australia achieved its position as one of the world's great primary exporters while locking its rusting secondary industry away behind walls of tariff protection. These were the times when it made its economic peace with Japan, becoming first a trading partner and then a trading dependant of the wartime enemy. And similarly a theoretically denazified West Germany became a key member of the western alliance. In this context skirmishes in Asia, notoriously unstable and unreliable, were the merest of distractions. And over it all towered the firm but benevolent, the invincible figure of Ming. As the students of the day sang:

> There'll always be a Menzies
> While there's a BHP
> For they have drawn their dividends
> Since 1863.

> There'll always be a Menzies
> For Menzies never fails
> As long as nothing happens to
> The Bank of New South Wales.

> If we should lose our Menzies
> Whatever should we do
> If Menzies means as much to me
> As Menzies means to you.

Or something like that. There were those who wished it would never end. And there were times when it seemed that it wouldn't.

For once my home life seemed to fit in with the national mood. My father was now in a senior position at the ABC, working more and apparently enjoying it more; he even found time to write a novel which was well received by the local critics. Mother was also writing: she did several radio features, including some on interesting (rather than famous) women which were well ahead of the time; in the late 1950s feminism was barely a twitch in Germaine Greer's hormones. But to my mind her best work was for children; she wrote a number of series for the ABC children's program which were classics of their kind. Although I had long since handed in my Argonauts club badge (Socrates 22) I remember them with great fondness.

We were now living in Paddington in the days before it became trendy. It was, however, pretty multicultural, not that the word had yet been coined. The family next door was Greek, with a tough young daughter named Aphrodite. Her mother, defiantly Aussie, pronounced the name to rhyme with bite or more usually shortened it to Afro. From time to time the street rang with cries of 'Afrodight! Afro! Get yerself in 'ere!' There seemed little connection with the foam-born love goddess of legend. Greek myths were in fact one of my great loves. I can't remember who introduced me to them – probably my mother – but I know that by the age of ten I had read all the standard childrens editions and was getting stuck into Robert Graves's *Golden Fleece*, which I still regard as my quintessential desert island book. My friends talked longingly of going to England (home) or America (Hollywood) when they left school. Greece was always my target.

And although the isles to which Byron took such a liking still seemed impossibly far away, the customs associated with them were finding their way into Australian households. My father, in what was seen by most of his contemporaries as a rush of blood to the head, took to drinking espresso coffee in vast quantities and even embraced the idea of garlic. This, he proclaimed, was the mythical herb moly, given by the goddess Athena to Odysseus after the enchantress Circe had turned his seamen into swine. Garlic was symbolic of civilised dining; without it, men were little better than pigs. Nonetheless, he was fairly cautious when using it himself. His preferred method was to rub a clove around the edge of a salad bowl before filling it with iceberg lettuce. As he invariably ate the lettuce rather than the bowl this always seemed an act of symbolism rather than epicureanism. The real adventure came with dining out: the height of continental sophistication came with steak Diane, a dish in which a cheap cut of beef was first beaten to a pulp, then cremated and finally buried in a concoction of equal parts of worcester sauce and cream.

In other ways too the world was coming closer. Foreign entertainers from both England and America were actually appearing live and in person at Australian venues, more often than not at the Rushcutters Bay Stadium, otherwise known as the House of Stoush. I attended a concert with Spike Jones and his City Slickers, a favourite comedy band of the era. It was something of a disappointment. So, sadly, was an appearance by the incomparable Louis Armstrong, who decided that the acoustics lent themselves more to vocals than to trumpet.

Armstrong's visit was still an important event, as much for the politics as for the performance. At the time the White Australia policy was still alive and very well indeed; Armstrong and most of his band were welcome to visit, but they would not have been allowed to live here. The same applied to touring sporting teams such as the New Zealand All Blacks and later the West Indians: a couple of years later Wesley Hall commented on the anomaly to no less a cricket buff than Menzies himself (who reportedly nodded judiciously and suggested another drink). The racial tensions, later to become riots, in the southern states of the USA were making headlines in the local press and the apartheid regime in South Africa was coming under scrutiny. The left was working itself up into a mood of righteous outrage. And yet, indigenous Australians remained politically invisible.

Indeed, for most Australians, including me, they were physically invisible as well. I honestly cannot explain this collective blindness, let alone my personal ignorance. Of course I knew aborigines existed: one of my favourite childhood books was *The Way of the Whirlwind*, by Mary and Elizabeth Durack. By the time I was sixteen I knew my way around Sydney and had explored suburbs a long way from the leafy communities of the east. On holidays I had visited the Blue Mountains, and, more significantly, had spent many weeks at Uncle Neville's property at Leadville near Coolah, home of the fabled Black Stump. On these stays I had travelled around the Mid-West to Coonabarabran, Mudgee, and Warren, not to mention numerous smaller settlements. Yet I have no conscious memory of ever seeing a black Australian, let alone actually meeting one. I was vaguely aware that they existed somewhere out there in the bush in squalid and primitive conditions and that they were to be pitied as a Stone Age race clearly unable to adapt to Australian civilisation. Yet I remained completely uninterested. I was able to take up the distant cause of American Negroes and South African Bantu (as they were known then) with genuine passion and indignation. But I didn't give a stuff about the Australians whose lands had been stolen, whose children had been stolen, whose culture had been stolen, whose very existence had been stolen by my ancestors and was still being stolen by my contemporaries. Okay, so none of this was taught at school and not much of it was known even to historians at the time. But sheer commonsense and logic should have made it obvious to all but the cretinous that something terrible had happened. And yet it didn't. I can only assume that we were all in a state of denial, that we simply were not ready to face the shame and the guilt of our history. Of course, some of us still aren't; but they no longer have the excuse of claiming that they weren't told. I like to think that if my teachers had been aware of the awful reality, they would have made an effort to let us know. As I said earlier, Cranbrook had many faults, but racism was not among them.

School was at its best in my last year. I had done the Leaving Certificate exams in 1957 at the age of fifteen, and although my pass (second class honours in French and five A passes in other subjects) was good enough to get me into university with a Commonwealth scholarship to cover all compulsory fees, my parents quite rightly decided I was too young and too emotionally immature to face the outside world. I thus was sent back to repeat the final year. At first I thought this was a waste of time and a pain in the arse, but it turned out to be rather fun. In those days Cranbrook put far less stress on learning than on rugby, but there were some parents who liked the idea of good academic standards. Since I was obviously going to do pretty well second time around I suddenly found myself a pupil of respect. The great truth dawned on me: the school needed me more than I needed it.

This was a hugely liberating experience. Now that I no longer had to, I started to enjoy sport and actually developed a minor talent as a left arm spin bowler; my best figures of five wickets for nine runs for the third XI don't quite stack up with Bradman's test batting average of 99.94, but they were a triumph at the time. I had always enjoyed debating; now I made the school team, which went on to win the state eisteddfod. I also won an individual speaking prize for refuting the notion that it was 'Sputnik or perish'. I played fourth board in the A grade chess team and was a star in the school play. My asthma disappeared forever and I took up smoking. I even started to lose my shyness (but not, alas, my virginity; that came much later) when in the company of girls.

But best of all, I could work at my own pace. It was accepted that if I wanted to shut myself in the library rather than attend regular classes, that was the privilege of those from whom great things were expected. Actually I used many of those hours reading well outside the set courses, including numerous forays into politics; my reputation as a leftie increased, although it was leftiness of the most naive kind. Actually anti-Americanism, on the basis that apart from having invented jazz (which was really African anyway) Americans were uncultured buffoons, was quite fashionable among what passed for the intelligentsia at Cranbrook. Indeed cultural snobbery, while not nearly as rife as money snobbery, enjoyed a brief vogue. I joined in with a few lines of doggerel:

No nightingale should raise its voice
(What would the neighbours think?)
No Milton may with God rejoice
(Is he the worse for drink?)

And yet these joys can still be found
(For culture we adore)
Beneath a pile of Carter Brown
(Which must be read before)

Fortunately my general scholarship was a bit better than that. At the end of the year I triumphantly delivered three first class honours and two A passes, coming second in the state in Maths I and English and fourth overall. I was interviewed by the

Sydney Morning Herald, to whose bored cadet reporter I pompously declared an intention to follow in the footsteps of my paternal great-grandfather, Sir Mungo, professor of English and chancellor of Sydney University. Actually I hadn't a clue what I wanted to do. I suppose I assumed that, as had happened in the past, events would take place and I would be dragged along with them. In the meantime I was off to the cricket. This was, after all, Menzies's Australia.

And yet even Menzies's Australia could change. Sputnik was the clearest possible evidence of that. The Cold War had a new component: the space race, limitless in both threat and promise. Although I had taken the straight pacifist line during my competitive speechifying (it made for a simpler argument, and one more likely to appeal to the judges) I was hooked on space from a fairly early age. The night after Sputnik was launched my parents and I went up the hill to a darkish park and, together with many equally awe-struck observers, saw the satellite (or more accurately its rocket casing) slowly crossing the sky. 'Wouldn't you feel like God if you'd put it there?' my mother murmured. I silently agreed, and I knew that I'd love to try. From being a vague thought in the back of my mind astrophysics (or at least its theoretical cousin astronomy – I had always been better with the calculation than the building) became a serious thought. Even the sacrifice of the dog Laika in a second sputnik, vigorously deplored in what had always been a dog-loving family, did not deter me.

And there was a chance I could have followed through; with a high distinction in maths in my first year at university I certainly qualified to take the second year astronomy course taught by the renowned astronomer Bart Bok. But understandably Professor Bok required a minimum of two students before he would agree to teach a class. I waited, at first hope-fully and then desperately, but no one else, either from Sydney University or from the University of Technology (later the University of New South Wales) was interested. Theory was all very well, but star gazing was just a bit too vague to pursue as a career. Reluctantly, I went back to the drawing board, still without any real idea of what I wanted to do. But something was bound to turn up. It was still Menzies's Australia.

Chapter Six

THE ONLY PROBLEM WITH LIVING IN A CITADEL IS THAT YOU HAVE TO LEAVE IT TO GO TO THE PUB

What turned up was Sydney University. Nowadays, looking back into what was seen as that golden era evokes visions of endless sex and drugs and rock'n'roll, even if the song was yet to be written; but in practice these undoubtedly desirable commodities were neither as abundant nor varied as legend has it. Sex took me another couple of years to discover, and even then I was largely monogamous in my student days – more, I hasten to add, through incompetence than policy. The drugs were still the old stand-bys of nicotine and alcohol; the possibility of other more arcane substances was occasionally hinted at, but remained outside the mainstream curricula. But the rock'n'roll – well, if by that you mean the general culture and ambience, that was indeed something else.

The years between about 1957 and 1963 have gone down in folklore as a sort of golden age at Sydney University: an outpouring of creative talent unmatched since the Athens of Pericles or the Florence of the Medicis. Even I, as one who was there, am prepared to admit that this is probably something of an exaggeration. But at the time I was at one with Wordsworth: 'Bliss was it in that dawn to be alive,/But to be young was very heaven.' And with a naivety as touching as that of the poet, I didn't realise that it would not always be thus. The great privilege of my generation was that it was the last that could really afford to treat uni as the end of play rather than the beginning of work. We knew we didn't really have to pass; we could always come back next year. There were students around who were as much institutions as the stone lions outside the Fisher Library. And what was more, we knew that whether we passed or failed there would always be a congenial job of some kind or other waiting at the end of the tunnel. We were not only the elite, we were the invulnerable. *Gaudeamus igitur* indeed.

We were also in one of those hiatuses in which politics, at least in any formal sense, was completely unimportant. Sure, there were the political clubs, and those pathetic oxymorons, the student politicians, played their sad little games while jostling each other for the odd overseas trip, usually funded (as we now know) by the CIA. But they were at best second class citizens; the people unable to aspire to the higher, more creative projects offered by the literary and dramatic cliques who also put on by far the best parties. There were those brave (or insanely ambitious) souls who tried to straddle both worlds. But by and large the arty-crafties kept themselves as a race apart.

It didn't take me long to find my chosen milieu. During Orientation Week I had enthusiastically joined every society which would have me as a member, up to (or perhaps down to) the speleological group. But once I discovered the dramatic societies and the university newspaper, *honi soit*, my purpose in life became clear. As my passions increased, so my studies declined. In first year I managed high distinctions, in my second distinctions, in my third I was tossed out of the English honours class and barely held my place in the pure mathematics group, and in my honours year I scraped a pitiful third, purely on the strength of a barely comprehensible thesis which sort of extended Kurt Gödel's use of metalanguage to explain the nexus between life and art. I had long since abandoned such peripheral pursuits as lectures and tutorials.

Unlike most of the arty crowd, I was living on campus in St Andrew's College. My father had gone there and I had won some sort of son-of-old-boy scholarship. As one who had never attended boarding school I found it an unnerving experience. The initiations for first year students – freshers, as we were derisively known – were at best unpleasant and at worst mildly sadistic. While they no longer involved actual bodily harm as (we were assured by our seniors) they had in the good old days, they still seemed unnecessarily humiliating to those who now considered themselves young men rather than boys. Only after going through the ritual of being 'bashed' both physically and psychologically by one's seniors could one be considered that apex of evolution, a college man. This gave one a licence to bash the next intake of freshers.

College society was blokey at every level. Women were there for one reason only; any encounter was only tolerable if it was aimed at seduction. The ideal relationship involved the expenditure of two shillings and nine pence: threepence for a phone call to the Prince Alfred Nurses' Home, two coffees at the place on the corner at one and threepence each, and a speedy retirement to the long grass beside the oval. The more sordid and commercial such transactions could be made to sound the better. This at least was the public display; the reality may have been a shade less grim, but it is hard to believe that too many college men enjoyed genuinely caring, sharing, sensitive new age companionship. The Andrew's ethos simply wouldn't permit it.

Still, college life had its advantages. I tried out unsuccessfully for the cricket team, and with better luck for the debating and dramatic societies. The latter was run by Ken Horler, who then inducted me into Sydney University Players, one of two rival theatre groups. I found my own way to the *honi soit* office, and was accepted as an occasional contributor. I even acquired a steady girlfriend, although it was many moons before our passion was consummated. I started drinking. Life was good.

It was also far less cloistered than the above might suggest. Although the arty-crafty crowd were predominantly arts students there were overlaps; the then editor of *Honi* was doing medicine, as was one of the better writers and at least one of the outstanding actors in Players. The Law Faculty had a regular and active presence. The group included a couple of science students, one of whom was also an officer in the university's RAAF squadron. One enthusiast came from the Engineering School, despised home of Alfs and Ockers. And there were those who were not really part of the university at all; Leo Schofield, for instance, had left the previous year having failed Arts I. A slightly mysterious character called simply Chester was the backbone of the Revue writing team, but seemed never to have enrolled at all. His principal collaborator John Cummings had a job in the library. Between them they offered a wider perspective on life than that seen from the ivory tower and its numerous adjacent beer gardens.

Another outlet was the Push, which could be found in different pubs at different times; at this stage its natural habitat was the Royal George in Sussex Street. The Push was sort of anarchist, sort of libertarian, sort of sleazy; it included some talented musicians, sporadic poets and dubious philosophers. To an Eastern Suburbs lad like me it seemed attractively bohemian, not least because it included several women who actually said fuck and could therefore be presumed to do so. Alas, I never really tried to find out; as so often, I remained on the fringe, a somewhat frustrated observer. I did, however, attempt to join in the jazz, the versifying and the philosophy, in a manner which I like to think neatly balanced the pretentious and the satirical.

For the University Jazz Club I wrote the 'Ultimate Blues', a poignant number which began:

Well, I never ain't been so blue not yet before
I said I never ain't been so blue not yet before
Because that railroad train run right through my
   back door

and got worse from there on. I went through a prolonged Edith Sitwell phase, and wrote verse which at least sounded jolly:

Birds gather together in feathered profusion
In orderly ornithological rows
And fatherly pheasants in frequent collusion
Resent the intrusion of corpulent crows.

Flamingoes flamenco with bellicose pelicans
Allocate jelly beans, lamington buns
Till hunters in hundreds surround them with billy cans
Sleeping bags, slippers and camera guns.

Dispersing, the birds display deep disapproval
And fly from the flash bulbs and fleshpots and cheer
Resigned to an emu parade for removal
Of cigarette packets and bottles of beer.

I, of course, was just having fun. Others, including Clive James (who at that stage liked to describe himself simply as 'poet') were more serious about it. Geoff Lehmann was probably the most serious of all. But for my money Les Murray, another who stayed on the outskirts, was the one to watch. I always felt Clive, while boundlessly talented, was the better showman, but Les the better poet. My role was perhaps that of critic.

On the theatre side there was never any doubt that John Bell was easily the most dedicated actor around, or that John Gaden and Arthur Dignam were two of the more interesting. But there were many others, including a number of women, who seemed destined for a successful career. It was not to be; perhaps they were overtaken by the establishment of the National Institute of Dramatic Art and its subsequent stream of graduates. Then there were the other writers, the film-makers and editors: Ron Blair, Bob Ellis, Bruce Beresford, Geoff Barnes, Richard Walsh ... The list is now all too familiar to readers of magazine features. Not to mention, of course, the outsiders who spent some of their post-student life at Sydney Uni: Germaine Greer, Martin Sharp, Richard Neville. But lists like this are misleading; all they convey is an idea of the sort of people who made up the lucky generation. It was not the individuals but the total environment – the holistic experience, as one would say today – that made it special. Philosophising, carousing, dabbling in creativity and exchanging witticisms and partners, we were, briefly and delightfully, the chosen ones.

However, outside the citadel the barbarians were massing. In what now appears to have been a disastrous miscalculation even for a coalition treasurer, Harold Holt in 1961 had managed to put an otherwise booming economy in the grip of a credit squeeze, and that in the lead-up to an election. What made it worse, from Menzies's point of view at least, was that it was to be the first election contested by the ALP's new leader Arthur Calwell, an altogether more stable opponent than the Doc, and the first in which television, which Menzies loathed, was to play a significant role. What should have been a walkover suddenly looked like a damned close run thing.

The ABC did not help by running a series of programs in which the various candidates for each electorate were allowed to address the nation. On paper, the idea was admirably democratic. On the screen, it became an unparalleled opportunity for the candidates from minor parties to gain the kind of publicity of which they had only previously dreamed. The communists saw it as a heaven-sent chance to regroup. Instead of their normal practice of running only in seats where they had a chance of making a serious impression, or in seats in which some loony was prepared to pay all his own expenses including the electoral deposit which he invariably lost, the comms fielded candidates across the nation. They were invariably well dressed and softly spoken. They played down any talk of revolution, even of militancy; they were all about governing for the benefit of all and giving everyone a fair go – in fact they sounded rather like John Howard. And they invariably finished by thanking the ABC for giving them the chance – as indeed they might have.

There is no evidence at all that the ABC had planned it this way, but Menzies and the Libs were apoplectic as soon as the fiendish Red strategy became clear. For Labor candidates to have the same time to spruik as their own people was bad enough, but to have the comms on equal terms as well – this was approaching the end of civilisation as we knew it. And as if television wasn't bad enough, the Reds had devised a supplementary strategy: selecting candidates whose names began early in the alphabet, a practice which put them at or near the top of the ticket.

These days the order of candidates on the voting form is determined by a draw from a hat. Back then the Electoral Commission simply followed the alphabet. This had led to many interesting battles of tactics between the comms and their arch-rivals the DLP, who were also keen to get their people at the head of the ticket. The comms usually won, thanks to their recruitment of numerous members of the Aarons family: short of rechristening their own candidates something like Aardvark, there wasn't much the DLP could do about it. But normally the comms only stood in a handful of seats. This time they were all over the place, well publicised and well placed to capture a handsome percentage of the so-called donkey vote – the result of ignorant or confused voters simply numbering candidates straight down the page. The Libs saw it all as thoroughly sneaky, if not downright unfair.

But in the end it probably saved them from defeat. On voting day it looked desperately close; indeed it appeared to come down to the single seat of Moreton in Queensland, held for the Libs by the flamboyant lawyer Jim Killen. Killen was a deadset Tory, a supporter of the South African policy of apartheid, a fervent royalist and something of a pompous ass to boot. His seat would be decided on preferences, and there was a sizeable communist vote to be distributed. There seemed to be no way it could go to Killen. Calwell went to bed on election night confident that he would emerge from the poll as prime minister. He didn't. Those crucial ballots turned out to have been cast not by communists but by donkeys, and as Killen's name preceded that of the now forgotten Labor candidate in the alphabet, they flowed largely to the Libs. Having snatched an unlikely victory both for himself and his government, Killen waited for words of congratulation from his leader: they did not come. Hounded by the press, Killen claimed that Menzies had telegrammed: 'Killen, you are magnificent.' But it never happened. An unlikely and unwanted hero, he remained on the backbench until after Menzies's retirement.

This election marked Menzies's only real scare since 1954 and confirmed all his worst fears about television in general and the ABC in particular. Although the board and the general managers of the ABC were pretty much under governmental control and therefore part of the establishment right, the people who actually made the programs were far less trustworthy. Even the presence of secret police on the staff failed to deter them. My father recalled that shortly after joining the commission, he was told by colleagues to watch out for a particular officer, who was known to be the ASIO agent in the department. 'And he's on expenses,' they added, 'so be sure you don't spoil things.' My father took the hint. Soon afterwards the ASIO man asked him over the road for a drink, and after the first middy fixed him with a piercing glare and remarked: 'I think the communists have all the answers. What do you think?' Well, replied my father, he thought that was a very interesting viewpoint. Perhaps they should consider it over another drink. Unfortunately he had left his own wallet at the office ...

This kind of Cold War buffoonery may or may not have contributed to my father's early retirement; as it happened he was invalided out, as it was delicately phrased, at the end of 1960 – before the election which caused Menzies so much angst. But even during the credit squeeze Australia's security services were one of the few sectors to flourish. By the time of the 1963 election it was said that the Communist Party was so thoroughly infiltrated that ASIO held a comfortable majority at most branch meetings. But the communists, taking as Marx had commanded the long view of history, did not give up and one of the few places where they appeared to be making some progress was on the university campuses, even at staid old Sydney.

Chapter Seven

WHAT I DID ON MY HOLIDAYS AT THE UNIVERSITY; OR, THE GETTING OF IGNORANCE

Everyone knows that in Australia the 1960s didn't really happen until the 1970s. But it is often forgotten that even in America they didn't start until well into that decade either. J F Kennedy was inaugurated as president at the start of 1961, ushering in his short-lived and ultimately phoney Camelot period, but the overall mood remained bland and bourgeois. The rebels then were not the hippies but the beatniks, and while stream of consciousness mumblings of Kerouac and Ginsberg had their following, they did not have the mass attraction of Bob Dylan's nasal call to arms, or to peace, or whatever it actually was. Looking back, the Kennedy administration seems to have been a series of failures, from the abortive attempt to invade Cuba through the build-up in Vietnam and the confusion of the somewhat half-hearted desegregation program. Even the so-called triumph of the missile crisis was a

Pyrrhic one: America prevented the stationing of Russian missiles in Cuba, but, as we now know, had to scale down its own bases in Turkey as a *quid pro quo*. Yet there are many who still see those years a sort of mini-golden age for the USA. Perhaps this is because they were so much more peaceful than the upheavals that were to follow.

In Australia the feeling was much the same: there just wasn't much to get political about. In the late 1950s there had indeed been a mass student demonstration – to have a set of traffic lights installed where a student had been run over on Parramatta Road. But for some years that was the extent of the activity. In many ways the dramatic groups were far more political than the university at large; in the four years that I attended uni they premiered works by Jean-Paul Sartre, Albert Camus, Bertolt Brecht, Samuel Beckett, Harold Pinter, Max Frisch, John Arden, Brendan Behan and Alfred Jarry, to name but the most prominent. In the meantime political clubs held barbecues and sang rugby-type songs. The Labor Club had effectively been taken over by the communists; the ALP wanted nothing to do with it. The Liberal Club was pumping out unctuous lawyers who were good debaters but utterly unscrupulous in what they debated: some, like Peter Coleman and Michael Baume from the previous generation, went on to enter politics, and to gain reputations as effective muck-rakers and muck-spreaders, if not as statesmen. The attitude of the university as a whole was one of massive indifference.

The right had nothing to offer except more of the same, but the left lacked any real credibility. Since Hungary, Russia was pretty much on the nose. The old guard communists still looked to Moscow: for them the political imperative remained the preservation of the Soviet Union at all costs. The Eurocommunists were thin on the ground and totally irrelevant. The emerging Maoists suffered from the fact that China's closed door policy meant they had nothing much to say – and of course, when China did emerge from behind the bamboo curtain, it was to do something like invading Tibet. To put it mildly, such actions lacked mass appeal.

But by concentrating on a few gut issues the left was able to gain some recruits at the start of the 1960s. The race issue, which still meant America and South Africa rather than Australia, was becoming more urgent. The massacre of black South African schoolchildren at Sharpeville even got students back on to the streets and disrupted the traffic, prompting the police commissioner of the time to huff that those involved were nothing more that educated louts. At a larger follow-up demonstration next week Paddy McGuinness, then professing himself to be an anarchist, screamed at a policeman: 'Get your hands off me, you uneducated lout', thereby earning himself a few hours in the cells. I was entrusted with the task of getting him out on bail, which I duly did. All I can say is that it seemed like the right thing to do at the time.

The other concern which attracted support was that of disarmament, and particularly nuclear disarmament. For some years there had been protests against the testing of new weapons by both sides; in 1962 the Cuban missile crisis gave them new urgency. Even at Sydney University many people had spent the crucial hours listening to the radio for the latest news and some were convinced that neither side would pull out of the monstrous game of chicken that had developed. Bob Ellis was so certain that the end was nigh that he took off for the Blue Mountains with the daughter and automobile of the ageing but still vindictive David McNicoll, Sir Frank Packer's chief hatchet man and gossip columnist. Others were less despairing, but in the aftermath decided to form a branch of the Ban the Bomb movement. As a pacifist whose fashionable anti-Americanism had never involved barracking for the other side, I joined immediately.

So, in droves, did the communists. Being rather better organised and considerably more dedicated than the rest of us, they ended up more or less running the show. Occasionally, with considerable effort, we were able to get motions passed that deplored the actions of all involved in the arms race, but more often the line was straight anti-Uncle Sam. This applied equally to the wider Australian movement: I was invited to speak at a rally at the Rushcutters Bay stadium as 'the voice of youth' (a title I repudiated as too all-embracing) and made what I thought was a rousing attack on warmongers in general. I was later rebuked by a trade union heavy for not realising that the peace-loving leaders of the USSR were only arming themselves to defend the world against American imperialism, and would only go to war if it was absolutely necessary to keep the peace. I returned to my arty-crafty friends.

Other parts of Australia were rather more serious about their politics. When I visited Melbourne in 1961 for the intervarsity debating festival (I was captain of the Sydney University team) it was obvious that, as always, things in the South were both more radical and less tolerant. The left had coalesced into a formal structure called Student Action, which effectively issued the student body with its marching orders – quite literally. Notices of demonstrations were posted on an almost daily basis, and attendance, if not actually compulsory, was certainly expected. The right, though fighting back, was hopelessly outnumbered, a state of play which was to continue for some years. When I went back the following year to do some all too infrequent work on my thesis – Melbourne had some microfilm of Gödel's work that Sydney lacked – things had got even tougher. Dissent was treated as a reason for immediate expulsion from the ruling group. It was getting close to the ultimate position of authoritarianism: whatever was not forbidden was compulsory. Again I retreated. I quite enjoyed dabbling in politics, but not if it got too serious.

However, the debating festival brought its rewards. Together with two members of the winning Melbourne Uni team, I was selected to represent the Australian Universities on a tour of the Philippines organised by the Lions Clubs. I had been abroad once before: at the age of thirteen I had taken part in a student exchange trip to New Caledonia, ostensibly to improve my French but in fact as a hugely enjoyable holiday. Too young to worry about the politics of colonialism, I had nevertheless noticed that my (white) hosts consistently referred to 'les noirs' in tones of mixed fear and contempt. I found this puzzling, as the black people I met were unfailingly pleasant and cheerful, although invariably in menial jobs.

By this time I was more interested in such matters and I decided to make the most of the trip by including, at a slight extra cost, stopovers in New Guinea, Thailand, Vietnam and Cambodia. New Guinea in particular was starting to impinge on the Australian consciousness. Since World War I it had been our colony, on the understanding that we were nursing it towards independence. But to those few who took an interest in the area, it was clear that this was not a priority of the Menzies government. When ministers spoke of the place at all, independence was hardly a consideration. Control of the rich pickings from rubber, coffee and copra was a much higher priority. This involved protecting the white planters and their estates through the paramilitary kiap system – the kiaps being young Australians, usually of little education, in whom considerable authority was vested. Their power to inflict summary punishment on natives who bucked the system had led to what the media sometimes referred to as 'disturbing reports'. While a couple of days in Port Moresby would hardly allow for an in-depth investigation, the chance to get at least a feel of the place was too good to miss.

Of course I learned nothing, although my prejudices were confirmed by the dismissive attitudes of the whites I spoke to, who clearly regarded me as too young and ignorant to understand the special problems they faced – a cop-out used regularly by every oppressive regime in history. The Philippines was a similar story. A junior official of the Australian embassy was nominally in charge of us, but we were effectively taken over by Manila government, in all its vainglorious corruption. Princes of the church fed us on quails and San Miguel beer while rhapsodising about the wealth and security the present administration had brought to the country. At the state (as opposed to church) run University of the Far East some students attempted to talk to us about their grievances; they were quickly removed, never to reappear. We were flown to the American air base at Baguio in a plane in which one of the emergency doors blew off a hinge and flapped alarmingly during the hair-raising landing on a mountain terrace: the military might of the island's great and powerful protector was paraded before us. At Mindanao in the south, with its Moslems even then resentful of the Catholic hierarchy, we were not allowed out on the streets by ourselves. And of course the real rebel armies – the Huk Beluk – didn't get a mention.

At Bangkok I linked up with a local student who showed me the sights and spoke patriotically of the fact that Thailand was the only country of Indo-China never to have been directly colonised. His American accent and the proliferation of Coca-Cola signs made this difficult to accept. By now I was feeling ineffectual, lonely and somewhat homesick. I cut my tour short and flew home to Sydney via Hong Kong. The rest of Indo-China would have to wait for another thirty-five years. But in its own way the tour had been a success. We had won all but the first of our debates in the Philippines and done nothing to disgrace ourselves, our country or our sponsors, to whom I had to report on my return. The Lions turned on a lavish lunch and I gave them a very rosy account of the trip, with emphasis on the cross-cultural benefits their generosity had made possible. When I had finished they did not applaud; they roared in imitation of their namesake. Ever the coward, I tried to glide under the table before being pulled out and presented with a commemorative medallion.

As astute readers will have detected, I was by this time bludging on the taxpayer. While still drawing a Commonwealth scholarship to pay for my tuition, I was prepared to undertake very little of it. At least I could say I owed St Andrew's College nothing; after second year I abandoned it to go back to living at home, or wherever was available. While Andrew's had played a big part in socialising me and giving me the confidence I had largely lacked during my Cranbrook years, the culture was still too restrictive for my pseudo-bohemian existence. So, of course, were the meal hours. I did manage to graduate within the statutory four years, albeit in a manner which was faintly humiliating to my parents. By both the Wentworth and MacCallum standards, third class honours in anything, let alone mathematics, was a failure. Fortunately for me, their own problems had become too difficult for them to dwell on it, and given what they knew of my increasingly erratic lifestyle they probably anticipated it anyway.

Apart from somehow completing my thesis with the aid of quite a lot of Ritalin to keep me awake and brandy to put me back to sleep, my final year was something of a blur: I was now involved in so many extracurricular pursuits that lectures were not even an optional extra. Along with my ex-Methodist head prefect from Cranbrook, Mike Newman, I co-directed the 1962 University Revue; if there was no other reason to remember it, this included the first appearance on the Sydney stage of Germaine Greer, who had come up from Melbourne to complete a masters degree on the erotic poetry of Lord Byron. Germs, as she was affectionately known, was in her prime, and shook the Push and its affiliates to the bottoms of their schooner glasses. The leisurely and somewhat incoherent style of debate which had characterised the exchanges between the Libertarians and their few surviving opponents from the more ascetic school of Professor John Anderson was not for her. Teleological discussion was brought to an abrupt halt with the flat premise: 'God does not exist and if he did he'd be a fascist cunt.' I couldn't have put it better myself.

But the hard fact was that my university days were inevitably coming to an end. The head of the pure maths department, a mild mannered genius who had been a member of the British code-breaking team during World War II, sympathised with my inability to combine attendance at lectures with a full-blooded post-adolescence and suggested that I should stay on and do a masters degree. I thought about it, but decided that it was time to escape. Much as I had enjoyed (no, delighted in) my time at uni, enough was enough. My tentative forays into politics, as much as my half-hearted travels in Asia, gave promise of a much wider world out there. I still saw my future in the theatre: although I had long abandoned any ambition to act I had become a fair sort of stage director and was fascinated by the process that went on between playwright and production. I thought I could do something inside that gap, though I never really sat down to figure out what. I had shown myself to be a fast writer: no one was more reliable at filling a hole in *honi soit*. And if the worst came to the worst, I had a degree, a lowly one admittedly, in the field of pure maths, which wasn't a bad passport at the start of the computer age.

What was more I had a small nest egg. My maternal grandmother had left me a modest legacy – enough to do up the second-hand Morris Minor I was then driving and a bit of spending money left over. The exodus of my contemporaries to London had already begun: it was time to follow, but not just by ship to Southampton. With two friends I arranged to ship the Morris to Colombo and make our way west by road and ferry. Thus we could see the ancient civilisations of the world en route. The thought that the most ancient of all was in the very country we were deserting on the grounds that it had insufficient history never even occurred to us.

I left Australia a few days after my twenty-first birthday on a Greek ship called the *Bretagne*, which means Britain in French: there could have been no better symbolic reminder of my confused view of the world. London was to be the end of the pilgrimage, but the Holy Grail (for me, if not for my companions) was Greece. Asia, as Prime Minister Paul Keating was to say later, was just somewhere you flew over on your way to Europe. It would be exotic, it would be strange and somewhat primitive, and it would be a distant memory as soon as we crossed the Bosphorus. It would also involve a great many vitamin pills, an enormous supply of something called enterovioform and several miles of toilet paper. It might also be a bit hairy, but so what? However leftish and liberated we may have thought ourselves, we had been brought up on the theory that the white man enjoyed special privileges both as a matter of history and as a birthright.

When I left university I had boasted pompously that although the previous four years had opened my eyes to all sorts of things I might otherwise have never experienced, and given me the assurance, if not the grace, to deal with the world at large, they had really taught me nothing: I was now empty, ready to start learning. I was about to discover how true that bit of bragging was.

> When boys were men and girls were boys
> And every raindrop grew a flower
> Story books were only noise
> But travellers' tales were magic words
> And I'd discuss them with the birds
> From brillig to the witching hour.
>
> And half the things I nearly heard
> Were sometimes almost real.
> So now I'm off to see the world:
> Big deal.

Chapter Eight

IF GOD HAD MEANT US TO TRAVEL IN ASIA SHE WOULDN'T HAVE CREATED AMOEBIC DYSENTERY

For many of my contemporaries, leaving university was a terrible wrench; leaving home had been nothing in comparison. It was at uni that most had completed their rites of passage into adulthood and had discovered, however tentatively, their inner selves. The idea of having to go through the whole sordid process again in the outside world was almost too much to bear. For me, however, the prospect held no terrors, mainly because I wasn't planning to go anywhere near the real world for sometime yet. The dreadful notion of actually having to work for a living remained a distant threat. I was simply extending my carefree existence with a spot of travel. My student (to use the word loosely) days had undoubtedly been the happiest of my life, but it was time to move on. I felt I had embraced all that the university had to give me in terms of lifestyle, and saw myself as an open vessel, ready to receive whatever new and exciting experiences life had to offer. Rather than filling me with knowledge, my years of tertiary education, so called, had emptied me out. Unless I received immediate replenishment, nature would abhor me.

Unfortunately the good ship *Bretagne* was not the place to get it. Most of the passengers were disgruntled Poms complaining endlessly about the Australian weather and looking forward eagerly to a proper feed of fish and chips down the Old Kent Road, always one of the more worthless sites on a Monopoly board. A smaller group was made up of sinister and predatory Australian homosexuals offering small denomination American notes to the Greek cabin boys in return for unnameable favours. The balance was people like myself and my two companions whose main ambition was to get as far as possible from the whole scene. Entertainment was provided by a lachrymose Australian comic and his wife, who described herself optimistically as a chanteuse; one assumed they were on a freebie. Further diversion was provided by an obsessive body builder who insisted that as his obnoxious twelve-year-old had paid full fare, he had every right to hang around the adult swimming pool and push the unwary into it. I swore off sea travel forever.

A day in Singapore provided the chance to buy cheap shirts, which promptly fell to pieces, and a cheap typewriter which lasted remarkably well. I used the latter to write huge amounts of bad poetry for the girls I had left behind. When we reached Colombo I also sent some cheap jewellery which probably never left the post office; it certainly never arrived in Australia. Thus far the East was proving surprisingly unmystic; Ceylon (as it still was then) was about as exotic as Katoomba. It did, however, have some quaint and annoying customs.

Under the government of the Bandaranaike family, a kind of socialism held sway, one of whose benefits to the workers was the observance of religious holidays of all creeds – Christian, Buddhist, Hindu, Moslem and for all I know, Rastafarian. As a result no one ever did any work; it took us a fortnight to get the Morris off the wharf. In the meantime we sat around drinking immense quantities of iced tea and fending off a man who tried to sell us a piece of translucent rock he claimed was a diamond ('See, sahib, it scratches glass.')

Eventually we proceeded north through the various previous capitals; in the good old days each new king built his own. From the peaceful and beautiful Tamil country we took the ferry to India and then the train through marshes packed with flamingos. Then we started driving again and the strangeness really set in. I have now travelled to more than fifty countries, including such out of the way places as Botswana, Bolivia, Uzbekistan, Tibet and Easter Island. But India remains the most foreign. I have been back several times and have still never managed to come to terms with it; indeed, I have never even come close. It has been the setting of some of the most brilliant and sophisticated civilisations the world has ever seen, and is still a place of extraordinary and primitive savagery. It can be wonderfully fulfilling and incredibly cruel. It is kind, generous and inclusive, as we found when we arrived in Gwalior one evening at the start of Dewali, the great festival of lights; but underneath runs a seam of avarice, vice and secrecy. It is always life on the edge.

And just when you think you're finally getting it figured out something happens to make you realise that you really haven't got a clue. We arrived at the beginning of 1963 at the time of the border war with China. In the cities of the north at least this had led to a kind of jingoistic frenzy: the place was covered in posters exhorting: 'India needs your blood, gold and work.' Chinese restaurants had been forced to close and students from Hong Kong and Singapore beaten up and worse on the grounds of their appearance alone. It was all rather depressing, as I remarked to some fluent English-speaking students we met in Jaipur. Of course feelings were running high, but surely this was no reason to take totally irrational revenge on innocent individuals. They agreed enthusiastically. The war was bad enough without people behaving like barbarians. I asked if there were any Chinese students at the local uni; yes, they said there had been one. And what had happened to him? They looked at me as if I were a complete idiot. Oh, said one, we hung him of course. Back to the drawing board.

The days of the Raj were mercifully long gone, but whites in India still had certain privileges. We could sleep cheaply in what were called Dak bungalows, designed originally to accommodate travelling senior public servants. If none was available, we could doss down free in the first class waiting rooms of railway stations. And if any alcohol was available, which it seldom was, we could drink. It was assumed on the basis of a couple of centuries of observation and experience that all Europeans on the subcontinent were by definition alcoholics. In theory they were supposed to purchase a certificate stating this fact, which they could then on-sell at a vast profit to the first Indian they met; but in practice no one ever mentioned it. Whites drank, and that was that. We ate and drank the local stuff, and attempted to sterilise the drinking water as much as possible. We all got diarrhoea and I had a close shave with amoebic dysentery, losing some three stone in weight over a week; a passing medico got to me just in time.

But the car knocked and pinged its way on low octane petrol to the border with West Pakistan in exemplary fashion. We spent our last night in the golden temple at Amritsar.

Ajanta caves, the Taj Mahal
The templed vastness of Keral –
But did you like the Rann of Kutch?
Not much.

By now our travel plans had changed a bit. The original idea had been to go through Pakistan, over the Khyber Pass to Afghanistan, thence to Iran and Iraq, to Jordan to see the rose red city of Petra, then out through Syria and Turkey to Greece. However, advice received from others on the road was that Afghanistan was definitely a no-no; in the unlikely event that we got into the country, we would be most unlikely to get out of it. Also, while we were in Delhi news came through of a revolution in Iraq. I went to the Iraqi embassy to ask if it would still be okay to travel. Well, said the official, he couldn't see why not. He certainly hadn't heard anything to the contrary from Baghdad. In fact, he mused, he hadn't heard anything at all from Baghdad for some days now … We thus abandoned Afghanistan and Iraq, and consequently Jordan and Syria as well; for me, Petra would have to wait for another thirty-five years. The revised route took us straight through Pakistan to southern Iran and thence to western Turkey.

All went well until we got to the wild west town of Quetta where every second person offered to buy our guns and refused to be convinced that we didn't have any. There we learned that from the Pakistani border post at Nok Kundi to the Iranian post at Zahedan was ninety-odd miles of disputed territory, maintained by neither side. The trick was to find the tracks of a car that had come the other way and follow them diligently. Unfortunately, frequent sand storms made this a fairly chancy business. Insh'Allah, and were we really sure we didn't even have the odd revolver between us? As it turned out we got through it with only a few panicky pauses, and made out way through towns with names like Bam and Yazd to the fabled city of Isfahan, where I bought a very fine carpet. We pushed on to Teheran, which was by far the most sophisticated city I had ever seen, and celebrated by drinking large amounts of coffee and brandy.

As it turned out this was a wise precaution. On the road north to Turkey it started snowing heavily. We put chains on the tyres, but even so mud and ice kept jamming the wheels; we spent a lot of time chipping it out with a couple of inadequate screwdrivers. We eventually made it across the border to the town of Agri and drank a lot more brandy in the town's best and only hotel. When we woke next morning the Morris was entirely buried in snow. A couple of helpful Turks dug it out and lit a fire under it ; this, they assured us, was an infallible way of unfreezing the radiator. It wasn't. A few miles out of town the whole engine block seized up. I volunteered to walk back to Agri and seek help. After about half an hour I went snowblind and blundered off the road into a snow drift, from which I was retrieved by a providentially passing bus.

Back in Agri I found a man with a Landrover who offered to tow the Morris in. My half-frozen companions moved into the Landrover; I agreed to guide the Morris. The Landrover then took off as if in a drag race, making any control impossible and instantly masking the windscreen with mud. I tooted the horn madly and to no avail. I then stupidly tried to slow things down by applying my own brakes and succeeded only in burning them out. On arrival in Agri I ran heavily into the back of the Landrover. Miraculously no serious damage either to the radiator or the engine had resulted. I decided that if I could just get a bit of brake pressure back we might be able to get out of this accursed place. A beaming mechanic offered to help: he put the car up on a ramp and immediately let all the oil out of the shock absorbers.

So it was that we crossed the icebound mountains to what turned out to be the forbidden military town of Erzurum with neither brakes nor shock absorbers. As with intense pain, it was the kind of experience memory mercifully blots out. In Erzurum I found a Turk who spoke a little German and a German who spoke a little French. Calling my own schoolboy French into play, I was able to relay enough instructions to a Turkish mechanic to make the car vaguely roadworthy again. But I couldn't face any more mountains. By mutual consent we headed for the Black Sea and the town of Trabzun, formerly Trebizond of the towers.

Actually there weren't a lot of towers, if indeed there ever had been; perhaps Rose Macaulay was more zonked than she let on when she wrote her famous memoir. But Trabzun was a charming spot, a port town which faded away up a pretty gorge down which the Morris descended on its semi-repaired brakes. Although still technically in Asia, it had a very European feel about it; the transition to the West we had sensed in Teheran now seemed almost complete. So much so, in fact, that we decided we had driven enough in the East. There was a small cargo boat that did a milk run along the Black Sea ports to Istanbul. For a pittance we could load the Morris onto it and take temporary possession of a broom closet masquerading as a cabin. It seemed the sensible thing do.

In the meantime we explored Trabzun and did the properly romantic bit of going for a very fast drive along the Black Sea; well, as fast as the Morris could manage. Less romantic was my solo attempt to change a tyre on the outskirts of town. A group of small boys appeared and started stoning me. Eventually an aged Turk emerged from a nearby house and waved them away with stern reprimands. I thanked him extravagantly; he then approached with his hand out. When I smiled deprecatingly and made signs indicating poverty, he waved the boys back. I paid the protection money.

The trip to Istanbul reminded me instantly of how much I disliked sea travel. The deckspace was crammed with Turks, their baggage and livestock. The moment we untied from the wharf they were all violently sea sick and stayed that way for the entire trip, except when the boat was securely moored. The situation became so dire that we largely kept to our broom closet, even dining on highly dubious tinned sausages we had bought in India for emergencies. But arriving at the Golden Horn made up for it. Here, at last, was a city. Agra, with the Taj and its other monuments, had been wonderful, but it lacked the scale of Byzantium. Viewing the great church of Aya Sophia, the mosque of Suleiman, the Topkapi palace and the covered markets I experienced a severe attack of cultural cringe. Suddenly Australia seemed very young and very simple; also very straightforward. I had learned the Turkish for 'no' within seconds of crossing the border, but in the best part of a month I had never received a direct 'yes.' It was a relief to get back on the road and to cross into Greece. It was now early spring; we drove through Thrace towards Athens through meadows covered in wildflowers, especially the scarlet poppies the Greeks call Agamemnon's blood.

The trip had taken about four months. We had taken in six countries, including two military dictatorships and an absolute monarchy. Yet it was the biggest of the democracies that seemed the most alien. India, thanks partly to the war with China, was then as united as it has ever been. In Jawaharlal Nehru it had one of the great statesmen of the century. Yet it struck me as being not only extraordinary, but almost out of control. Where there was authority, it was usually corrupt and more often than not ignored by all but the most vulnerable. India was more like anarchy than democracy. Perhaps – just perhaps – Churchill was wrong after all, and democracy was not just the worst system of government yet devised except for all the others; perhaps there were circumstances where some of the others were better, even necessary. It was a treacherous thought with which to enter the country which had invented democracy. But then, even a raving Hellenophile such as myself had to admit that Greece in those days wasn't the most perfect example of the sacred principle in action either.

The hard right, then under the leadership of Constantine Karamanlis, had been in power for some time. It had no intention of allowing that to change. The last election had seen the splintered parties of the left attempt to organise a mass rally in Omonia Square, traditionally the site for such gatherings. Before it could begin, tanks appeared from the streets leading into the square and slowly and deliberately lowered their guns to cover the crowd. An officer with a loud hailer proclaimed that the meeting had been disbanded because it was a threat to public order, and that was that. It was to be assumed that Karamanlis had the support of the army – although, ironically, many years after he was to be the man who reinstated democracy after a period of military dictatorship.

I was told this story later, of course, along with the account of the rightist candidate who arrived on a remote island in his electorate and distributed photographs of his opponent. When puzzled observers queried this tactic, he informed them cheerfully that he was merely informing the voters that his opponent was wanted for the rape of a series of young children. As a result, the man was not even allowed to land on the island. Greek politics had always been devious and a trifle vicious, but in the modern era it seemed to lack the subtlety of previous ages.

However, politics was not at the front of my mind as we approached Athens, where the group was to split up. A more pressing concern was a series of phone calls I had made way back in Delhi. There I had been located by an enterprising officer from the Australian High Commission who told me to ring home urgently. After a wait of ten hours fearing the worst I finally got through to my father, who informed me gravely: 'Your friend Susan is in big trouble.' What he meant, it finally emerged, was that my long-time girlfriend was pregnant. After another agonising wait I was able to speak to Susan, who told me, as a fait accompli, that our respective parents had agreed she should have an abortion. I had no fervent moral position on abortion, although I found the idea thoroughly distasteful. But I was outraged that the decision should have been taken in what seemed, from that distance, so cavalier a fashion. In retrospect, there probably wasn't much choice; I could have been uncontactable for months. But as it was, I wanted a say. Having established that Susan did not actually want an abortion, I suggested she meet me in Athens and we would pick up from there; I can't remember whether marriage was actually mentioned, but the firm implication was that we would keep the baby. And so it was arranged. With, I suspect, considerable misgivings, the various parents combined to put Susan on the next boat. In the meantime I had about a month to ponder just what we would do when she arrived.

Chapter Nine

TO TRAVEL HOPEFULLY IS BETTER THAN TO ARRIVE; SOMETIMES EVEN TRAVELLING DESPONDENTLY CAN BE, TOO

Fortunately I had the perfect place to go. During my childhood George Johnston and Charmian Clift had been the most glamorous of my parents' friends. George had been one of the most dashing of Australia's war correspondents and had returned to become something of a golden boy in Sydney journalism. Charmian, a beautiful and free-spirited younger woman for whom he had left his wife, was undoubtedly the golden girl. Between them they had written an award-winning novel. Unexpectedly they decided to use the proceeds to escape what they found the stultifying mediocrity of Menzies's Australia and flee to the Greek isles, where they would do some real writing.

The decision was greeted with a mixture of apprehension

and envy by their friends, most of whom wished they had the courage to do the same thing but were certain that the enterprise was doomed; in those days Australians simply did not make a living by writing, and especially not on some god-forsaken island where they were the only speakers of English. Nonetheless George and Charmian were a much loved couple and they were sent off in grand style. My father contributed a lengthy document he called a vade mecum, to which I affixed a seal, liberated from my menagerie of miniature lead animals. Some twelve years later, I was ready to pick up the threads.

As predicted, life had not been easy for the golden pair. They had started out on the western island of Kalymnos, where Charmian had written her first solo effort about the local sponge divers. As children arrived, they decided to move closer to civilisation and ended up on Hydra, then a three-hour ferry ride from Athens. Since then both had written books which had enjoyed modest success but not the bestseller status that would have guaranteed them security. I learned later that only the generosity of the local grocers, a family named Katsika who were prepared to grant indefinite credit, had kept them from starvation.

However, news of their presence had spread among itinerant artists of all kinds, many of whom arrived to make Hydra something of a bohemian colony. When I got there the most prominent was the Canadian Leonard Cohen, then an introspective opium smoker who worried ceaselessly about the quality of his orgasms. He had just published his first novel titled *The Favourite Game*; an unkind English reviewer dismissed it with the line: 'Mr Cohen's favourite game is the same as everyone else's.' But at least he produced, which was more than most of us did – I include myself in the group, because I ended up staying for nearly a year.

George and Charmian made me welcome immediately, and I fell in love with them. In George in particular I found the wise and experienced elder brother I never had just when I needed someone in whom to confide doubts, hopes and fears. George was happy to oblige. His own relationship with Charmian was going through one of its frequent rocky patches and he was in the mood for a bit of serious drinking and philosophising. Moreover he was in a state of some expectation: the manuscript of *My Brother Jack* was with his publishers. Both he and Charmian were convinced that this could finally be the breakthrough; she even referred to it, with a minimum of irony, as the Great Australian Novel. On reading it, I enthusiastically agreed.

In this heady atmosphere it seemed only sensible to stay on the island as long as possible. Susan, when she arrived, agreed not too reluctantly; although she was English by birth and had relatives there she was in no hurry to return to the frozen north. We decided the baby should be born in Greece; we then decided to get married. The ceremony was performed by the Australian ambassador, a pompous diplomat who had been in the country for over a year and still did not speak a word of the language. I, a blow-in of a couple of months' standing, had to translate for him when he complained that the champagne at the Hotel Grande Bretagne was not cold enough. Not for the last time, I was astounded at the arrogance and ignorance of my country's overseas service.

The honeymoon, such as it was, gave us a chance to pump up the Morris and do a quick whizz around the more accessible bits of Greece; we went to Delphi and Mycenae, now demoticised to Mykini. We spent time on the Acropolis, and sat on the Pnyx where Socrates taught and the Areopagus where the citizens of Athens elected their leaders and threw them out. I had always been intensely attracted to the idea of Greece: to the myths of gods and heroes and to the all too brief glory of the fifth century. The Greeks, I would proclaim (and indeed I still do) invented almost everything worthwhile in western civilisation; the Romans were merely copycats. Even the much vaunted system of Roman law was pinched from the code of Lycurgus of Sparta. All the overlong and over boomed Roman empire ever gave the world was super highways, bureaucracy and genocide. Compare these with the Greek legacy of democracy, philosophy, science and art.

I am prepared to admit that I sometimes went a little over the top: the Athens of Pericles may indeed have been a glorious place to live if you were a native-born landowning male, but for anyone else it had its disadvantages. However, sitting in the theatre of the Acropolis watching the great Katina Paxinou in Euripides' masterpiece *The Bacchae*, or standing in the perfect temple of Poseidon at Cape Sounion which the ancients saw as the end of the civilised world and Lord Byron saw as a great spot for a bit of personalised graffiti, it was difficult not to be carried away by the emotion of it all. For me, for the moment, the reality fully lived up to my expectations.

Marriage and parenthood were more problematical. Neither of us was really ready for either. My mother came over for the wedding and stayed for the birth, which was well-meaning of her but a bit of a mixed blessing; she tried to hide it, but was clearly appalled at our casualness and ineptitude. The birth took place in a suburban but adequate hospital early in autumn. The waiting room was full of anxious Greek fathers-to-be, cigars at the ready. News of a boy was greeted with congratulation, of a girl with commiseration. I received the latter, but my mood was one of mixed relief and apprehension. Even then I feared that I was not going to be able to cope, which of course made it a self-fulfilling prophecy.

Back on the island things were settling down for the winter. The tourists were less frequent; the last gross German in pursuit of adolescent cadets from the naval college on the island next door was packing his bikini briefs (one particularly repulsive specimen had sported a pair with the word *'nein'* on the front and the word *'ja'* on the back). Decision time was approaching; even after further subsidies from my mother the money was running out, and I had faced the reality that the little writing I actually committed to paper was unsaleable. England beckoned, or rather loomed, but I still didn't have the faintest idea of what I could do when I got there. I took my insecurities out on George: his generation had causes, I railed: the fight against fascism, the Spanish Civil War – they could join the International Brigade.

Looking back I cannot believe my brash stupidity. Not only was the Australia I had left behind positively teeming with worthwhile causes domestically, but the Americans had now well and truly escalated their adventure in Vietnam into a hot war, with Australia's enthusiastic support. It was obvious to all but those who chose not to see that unless the conflict came to a quick conclusion one way or another – and given the constraints of the Cold War and the doctrine of Mutually Assured Destruction that was never likely – it would only be a matter of time before Washington demanded that we put our troops where our rhetoric was.

And, of course, back in Australia it was another election year; Menzies chose yet again to go early and consolidate his one-seat majority. Labor, having run it so close only two years ago was simply not ready for another full-scale campaign. And, of course, Menzies had a ready-made scare. Those two great stalwarts of Australian conservatives, the Red Menace and the Yellow Peril, had coalesced into a monster of limitless potential. Vietnam gave rise to the domino theory: if Saigon fell, then Chinese communism, propelled by the relentless force of gravity, would pour down through South-East Asia and leap the ocean to engulf our sparsely populated white land. A poster of the time, issued I think by the DLP, summed it up neatly: headed simply 'Is this your future?' it showed a picture of two gloating Chinese warlords in a rickshaw being pulled across the Sydney Harbour Bridge by a Bondi lifesaver.

But at the time I knew none of this. News of Australia, when it came at all, came only by mail and was almost exclusively personal. The last bit I had received was from my father, who announced that he and my mother had decided to split up; he was sure this would come as no great surprise. It didn't, even when it turned out that what he really meant was that he had decided to walk out. My mother was devastated, especially when he very publicly threw himself into the much younger, notoriously promiscuous, arty set. Just how devastated I was not to discover until I returned to Australia. But in the meantime my concerns were, understandably I think, mainly selfish. With a young wife and a baby daughter, broke and aimless, I set out for England.

London in those days was not quite as prohibitively expensive as it is now, but it was still a hell of a town to be broke in. England was meant to be swinging; perhaps for those in the know it was, but with the approach of a foreigner, the only thing that swung was the door, firmly in the direction of closed. Racism was rampant, and Australians were classed as honorary blacks. Having turned the already unbeautiful suburb of Earl's Court into Kangaroo Valley, they were now moving into more salubrious areas; it was seen as akin to an invasion by the hordes of Genghis Khan. The magazine *Private Eye* summed up the general attitude by printing what it called the Definitive Australian Joke:

> The Aussie bloke is feeling a bit randy, so he asks his girlfriend for a fight. But she says no, she doesn't feel like it, it's the wrong time of the month. He says, what do you mean, the wrong time of the month? And she says, you know, I'm bleeding down here. And she pulls up her dress to show him. He says: 'Christ, no wonder you're bleeding. Some bastard's cut your cock off.'

Such was the view from Soho.

My own arrival was inauspicious. Susan and young Diana had flown on in advance and were staying with relatives in Birmingham. I drove the Morris across, arriving by ferry at the distinctly grey cliffs of Dover. I pushed on to London behind a lorry full of youths who spat with remorseless accuracy at my windscreen. Arriving by chance at Victoria Station I stopped to ask for directions; a well-dressed man with bowler and briefcase came to inspect me. 'Excuse me,' I murmured in my best private school tones, 'could you please tell me the best way to get to South Kensington?' He looked me up and down for fully twenty seconds before replying freezingly: 'No, I don't think I could.' Screaming an obscenity at him I forced my way through the maze of one-way streets until I reached the house of my friends; they were out. Khaki-coloured snow began to fall. I took shelter in the Natural History Museum where I watched a gloomy Englishman sketching a stuffed warthog, to which he bore a certain resemblance. Finally my friends arrived. I had a restless night and woke early to wait for the sun to rise; it didn't. Resignedly I drove up the M1 and into a small but sturdy farmer's van, thereby writing off the Morris after bringing it halfway round the world. Welcome to Merrie England.

We returned to London to a one-room flat near Sloane Square owned by a villainous friend of George's named Vic; it was almost unimaginably squalid. As a concession to his Australian tenants Vic had installed a shower above the communal lavatory, which was a couple of floors down. To use either (or both) you had to take your own light bulb, as anything moveable was invariably knocked off. During our mercifully brief stay some enterprising thief also unscrewed the power socket; from then on you had to take your own candle, a difficult thing to manage while showering. Unable to endure the horror of it we moved to a lightless downstairs flat in Shepherd's Bush, which was made gloomier by the insistence of an arty friend that we repaint it in dark regency tones. But the neighbourhood was a cheerful one, with a majority of Africans, West Indians and Pakistanis. We spent most of our spare time with Australian friends; our group from Sydney Uni had now moved almost en masse to the mother country. Its native-born inhabitants remained aloof.

I had applied for a number of jobs for which I thought I was well qualified and missed out on all of them; although it was never stated as such, I felt that I was being discriminated against because of my nationality, an uncomfortable insight which was probably long overdue. Just when it appeared that there was nothing left except the ultimate fallback – sorting mail – my luck changed. I ran into a vague acquaintance who had a job at an advertising agency. The creative director was an Australian, and so were many of the copywriters. Would I like a knockdown? K'noath I would. (There was something about the Poms that made even the most cultured Australians defiantly ocker.) Next day a somewhat effete man with cufflinks like Chinese gongs cast an approving eye over samples of my writing and installed me in a cubicle with instructions to be creative.

Unfortunately there was little chance of it; the agency and its clients were studiously conservative. Most of the work consisted of revamping last year's campaign for this year, and as this took about two hours a week stringing it out, there was a lot of spare time for musing. My most interesting account was for Australian canned peaches and pears: Ardmona, the fruits of Australia's sunshine. Having failed to persuade the client to adopt the catchy anagram 'ARDMONA – NO DRAMA' as a slogan, I got more ambitious; I suggested we develop the sunny Australia theme by locating at a beach with waves (there were said to be a couple in Cornwall) where a kangaroo riding a surfboard would deliver a tin of the product. Unfortunately no actor could be found who could ride a surfboard while wearing a kangaroo suit. An attempt to provide stability by nailing the tail to the board only resulted in the kangaroo turning turtle, as it were. As can be seen, I found it hard to treat the job seriously; exhortations from the man with the big cufflinks to 'rev up the copy pluspointwise' didn't help either. An English copywriter started referring to me in hushed tones as 'that Bolshie', which I took as a compliment.

Through the Australian network in the BBC I also got

some casual work writing scripts for the science unit of the overseas service; they went over well, but I was never able to crack the full-time job for which I yearned. And I still dreamt vaguely of a career somehow connected with the theatre. This was one of the great years in London; we economised by eating a great deal of cabbage in one form or another, but we went to everything. We saw Olivier's *Othello* and Michael Redgrave's *Uncle Vanya*; we saw Peter Hall's production of *The Tempest*, and the *Wars of the Roses* series at Stratford – it was Shakespeare's quatercentenary. We saw Fellini's Italian version of *Hamlet*, a Max Frisch by the Schiller Theatre and a Feydeau by the Comedie Francaise. We saw Peter Brook's brilliant premiere of Weiss's *Marat-Sade* and his incomparable *King Lear* with Paul Schofield. To cap it off there was Joan Littlewood's wonderful satire, *Oh What a Lovely War*. Socially London remained a desert, but dramatically the desert bloomed.

And politically it was quite fun too. When we arrived the tabloids were still getting over the Profumo affair, one of those politico-sexual scandals which are as much part of England as cricket and cold showers. Briefly, it involved a junior defence minister who had shared a mistress with, among others, a Russian military attaché. Even worse, according to the more bourgeois editorialists, was the fact that the lady in question had also been involved with a black man. There were connections in high places. Oh, the shame of it, and what a ripping yarn it was. It was also a clear pointer to the election year which was now upon us. The Tories were, to put it mildly, in disarray. Lord Home, pronounced Hume, had descended from the House of Lords to replace the senile and batty Harold Macmillan as prime minister; he was now officially Sir Alec Douglas-Home, but with his stoat-like face and slightly

deformed carriage it was impossible to think of him as anything but plain old Lord. He was surrounded by a ministry of
staggering incompetence but wonderfully aristocratic names:
Selwyn Lloyd, Duncan Sandys, Quintin Hogg. They lurched
from folly to folly, to the great amusement of the populace.
Labour leader Harold Wilson seldom had much to say; he
didn't need to, and in any case his mouth was usually too full
of pipe. But he looked sound; one could not imagine him in
bed with anyone, let alone a prostitute. True, there were doubts
about some of his offsiders; deputy George Brown was a bit of
a worry. (Brown in fact went into the vocabulary. It was he
who, having fallen down the steps of Westminster leglessly
drunk, reassured passing journalists: 'Don't worry, I'm just a bit
tired and emotional.') But few people actually doubted that
there would be a change of government, and about time too.
Once again *Private Eye* summed it up best in a spoof interview:
'Now sir, can you tell me why you, as a member of the working class, are planning to vote conservative?' 'Well actually, it's
very simple. It's because I'm a stupid cunt.' There seemed no
other reason.

One of my friends was already doing some letterboxing
for Labour. I decided to offer my services as well and was
received by my local branch with very lukewarm interest until
they learned that I had a car. Actually that was something of
an exaggeration; it was in fact an ancient and unroadworthy
Ford Popular I had bought from a crook on the day John
Kennedy was shot, and was almost as big a disaster. The
exhaust bled into the back seats, it had no second gear and
the doors didn't lock, which made it a natural playground for
the neighbourhood kids. Often I would set out on a drive only
to discover a couple of small brown faces grinning at me over

the backrest. But for the Labour Party it was good enough to get reluctant voters to the polling booth, and that was all that mattered.

If that election taught me nothing else about politics, it made me a lifetime convert to compulsory voting. In Australia there is a lot of lofty talk about how it is terribly undemocratic to compel people to vote if they don't want to and how forcing the ignorant and uninformed to the polls can actually distort the result and how it is really better to be governed by the vote of an enthusiastic minority than a disgruntled majority. Proponents of voluntary voting insist that unlike, say, the payment of taxes, voting is a right and not a responsibility. To enforce a right is a denial of freedom. This makes for a jolly good debate, but it ignores the realities of the voluntary system. In the outer western suburbs of London in 1964, the first job of the candidates was not to get the populace to vote Labour, it was to get them to vote at all. It was conceded that a wet polling day might give the Tories anything up to an extra 10 per cent, simply because their richer voters were more likely to have access to cars and taxis to get them to the booths. The Labour Party devoted immense amounts of time, money and energy simply trying to overcome this disadvantage. Resources that should have been devoted to disseminating and arguing policy were instead locked up in organising a motor pool. Politics was debased in a way it never has been in Australia.

It is true that with a compulsory system voters may be attracted by superficialities and cast a ballot on the basis of appearance rather than deep analysis; but at least they get to cast a ballot and thus become involved in the mechanics of democracy. Under the voluntary system many – at times a majority – drop out. This leaves the way open for single-minded minorities to take control – consider how much greater the influence of the extreme minor parties ranging from the Greens to One Nation would have been in Australia if disillusioned moderates had been able to walk away from the process altogether. Compulsory voting has its problems but it makes it clear that participation, however brief, in the government of a free society is not just an option but a duty. It is with compulsory voting that we ensure democracy.

On that Saturday in London it didn't rain – well, at least not much. But the voters had their expectations. If their transport didn't arrive, they were going to stay home. When it did arrive, they often complained about the state of the car, or that I was a few minutes late. When they got to the booth, they wanted a cup of tea before accepting the how to vote card. It occurred to me that if the Tories had had the wit to offer them a hot scone as well, they would have switched sides on the spot. But they didn't. Labour won the constituency and the election. Back at headquarters the party offered me a warm beer and dismissed me for the next five years or the next election, whichever came first. I was not a comrade; I was just a colonial on wheels.

At about this time we were visited by both mothers, an occasion which was somewhat fraught. We were still pretty broke and pretty miserable. I had some social life, going out with the boys (Australian of course) to East End pubs and sometimes a sporting event; Susan had practically none apart from our visits to the theatre. I at least had a job of a sort, albeit one I despised; Susan was stuck at home with baby Diana except for occasional and unproductive forays as a door to door saleswoman flogging make-up. Her attempts to secure coaching work through advertising in shop windows had been an awful failure; in England 'coaching' remained a euphemism for prostitution, and nothing would convince her would-be clients otherwise. We were no match for two mothers determined to bring us home, especially when mine, appalled at the sight of the Ford, offered us a second-hand Morris and a brief holiday in Europe as part of the deal.

We quite literally could not afford to refuse. I sold the Ford to Clive James for a shilling; he later swapped it for a second-hand bicycle with one flat tyre. We fled from the flat, breaking a lease and leaving an unpaid Selfridge's account. We had a rather jolly four weeks travelling south through France and Italy, and boarded the *Galileo* at Naples. Halfway across the Indian Ocean the beer ran out, but it was the least of our worries. Returning humiliated to the country I at least had left with such high hopes was another matter.

Simple Simon wondered why
They always gave him humble pie.

When Simple Simon asked for more
They showed him firmly to the door.

They turned poor Simon out into the snow,
Told him to watch the flowers grow.

But Simon, who was ten feet tall,
Calmly decided to show them all.

So taking an ell without giving an inch
Simon went on a two year binge.
He visited Samarkand, Mars and Rome,
Bought a harem and a project home,
Beheaded a troublesome dragon or two
And cornered the market in Reckitt's blue,
Dived fifty feet to a bucket of water
And won the heart of the Kennedy's daughter …

Wondering why they never forgave
Simon went for a shower and shave

Humming a mournful tirra lirra
He looked at himself in the bathroom mirror

And saw the wreck of a thousand nights:
A skeleton hung with fairy lights.

So he took off his boots and he hung up his sword
And he hanged himself by his dressing gown cord.

Chapter Ten

IF YOU CAN'T FIND REAL WORK THERE'S ALWAYS JOURNALISM TO FALL BACK ON

Back in Australia at the end of 1964, nothing seemed to have changed. Menzies was still on his throne, still promising to put the value back in the pound, although he had been reluctantly persuaded of the need to adopt a decimal currency, which he wanted to call the Royal. Ho de hum. But in fact the oldest continent was finally showing signs of life, one of which was that Menzies was forced to abandon his preferred designation and settle for the common or garden dollar. It was increasingly obvious that he was at last on his way out, and that he would retire before the next election.

This did not make him a lame duck; far from it. Among other perquisites he effectively retained the power to name his own successor, since in those days the Liberal Party of Australia, unlike such upstart organisations as the College of Cardinals, saw elections for the leadership as the merest formality. Moreover such was his apparent omnipotence that it appeared that in retirement he would not so much disappear from the scene as be translated to another and higher realm, in much the same way that King Arthur is reputed to have entered Avalon. And he continued to collect imperial honours with the enthusiasm of a child wedded to matchbox toys. He had already been made a Knight of the Royal and Ancient Order of the Thistle, a weed held in greater esteem in Britain than in Australia; now he became Lord Warden of the Cinque Ports, a position which gave its bearer the right to salvage flotsam and jetsam from certain areas off the coast of southern England. This was too much even for the sycophantic press of the time, whose cartoonists started to lampoon the grand old man – something which would have been considered near sacrilege a couple of years earlier.

But journalism too was changing. The media, after decades of conforming to the most wowserish standards in the English-speaking world, were finally starting to have a cautious go. Part of the impetus for this switch had occurred when I was away: some university friends had started a satirical magazine called *Oz*, which poked somewhat undergraduate fun at the country's sacred cows. In one issue the artist and cartoonist Martin Sharp contributed a mildly salacious parody of a northern beaches party; the police swooped and a Jurassic judge sentenced the bewildered editors (who included Sharp) to jail. The trial was not quite as absurdist as the trial of London *Oz*, which took place a couple of years later, but it was quite silly enough to provoke a serious backlash even from the establishment media, who were sufficiently far-sighted to realise that the antediluvian laws might threaten their own interests if pursued to their logical conclusion. It was recalled that not long before Rudyard Kipling's 'Barrack Room Ballads' had been seized by a customs officer who explained aggrievedly: 'No, I didn't read it, but with a name like that it's got to be dirty.' The *Oz* editors were released on appeal, and the first tears appeared in the chenille curtain, although *Tropic of Cancer*, *Lolita* and *Lady Chatterley's Lover* remained unfit for Australian eyes.

At the same time the ABC was starting up its irreverent current affairs show 'This Day Tonight' and even commercial television dipped its toe in the water with social satire in 'The Mavis Bramston Show'. But the real breakthrough came in print. From the moment I got off the boat the talk was of Rupert Murdoch's new national paper, *The Australian*. Its style, its layout, its writers, its politics, its brilliant cartoonist Bruce Petty – even its back page comic strip, *The Wizard of Id* – all seemed to come from some brave new world unimaginable in the Australia I had left. To many, even most observers it was simply too good to be true. In those pre-electronic days the idea of a national daily in Australia's far-flung geography was an ongoing logistic nightmare. Copy had to be collated via teleprinter in Canberra and the offset matrices then flown to printeries in Sydney, Melbourne and Perth. With Canberra airport closed by fog for several days every winter, production often involved a headlong rush by motor transport to get the mats to Sydney and Melbourne, with the west missing out altogether. Even in later years when the editorial headquarters moved to Sydney the process remained incredibly hairy until technology finally caught up. It cost Murdoch many millions of dollars and untold sleepless nights before the paper settled down. Over the years there have been many critics of Murdoch's politics, taste and business ethics. But in those early days there were few who did not admire his courage, even when they privately believed it would all eventually fall in a heap.

Menzies was one of the recalcitrants who viewed the emerging media revolution with suspicion and distaste. He had never got over his distrust of television; now 'TDT' and 'Bramston', with long-haired whippersnappers thumbing their noses at tradition and authority, confirmed his worst fears. As for *The Australian* – well, he could now understand why Murdoch had briefly been known as Red Rupert at Oxford. Actually the newspaper's editorial standpoint was certainly to the left of the standard Fairfax and Packer lines, but then, so was about 99 per cent of human thought. *The Australian* was hardly radical. After an erratic start under Maxwell Newton, a somewhat wild-eyed purchase from *The Financial Review*, the editor's chair had passed to Walter Kommer, a solid and uninspiring business writer whose only known idiosyncrasy was a tendency to return from long lunches and jump on the subs' table singing 'I'm the queen of the May.' But actual political control was firmly in the hands of Douglas Brass, an old Murdoch trusty who had become something of a father-figure to his employer. Brass was an old-fashioned Liberal with small-l liberal views, a Whig rather than a Tory. Menzies was by this time the archest of arch-conservatives. *The Australian* was marked down immediately as a potential enemy.

There was no shortage of available battlegrounds. Censorship was one; aboriginal affairs, finally emerging as an issue through the nascent land rights movement and agitation at Sydney University which was to culminate in the freedom rides, was another. But the overriding political preoccupation of the times was unquestionably the escalating conflict in Vietnam. By now Australian advisers and support personnel were very much part of the American adventure. In the United States itself the protest movement was gathering strength. The administration of LBJ, stuck with an inheritance it really didn't want, desperately needed international support of a more practical kind than it was getting from its lukewarm European allies. With an acquiescent government in Canberra it was only a matter of time before the inevitable request for at least a token commitment of ground troops arrived from Washington. Brass, who had a journalistic background in Asia and an appreciation of the complexities of the struggle not shared by many of his compatriots – including those in Canberra – believed from the start that Australia's involvement was both morally wrong and ultimately against the national interest. In 1965 this was a lonely and unpopular view among all but the extreme left, which was not the company in which *The Australian* wanted to be found. However, Brass pressed the line and Murdoch went along with it, albeit with decreasing enthusiasm, until opposition to the war became acceptable and eventually the conventional wisdom. This alone made *The Australian* a standout in the media morass of the time.

As a returning pilgrim of the left, I regarded it with awe and gratitude. I also thought of it as the unattainable height of Australian journalism, reserved for the very best and the brightest. In fact, of course, many of the best and the brightest – especially those cosily established with the older organisations – wouldn't have dreamed of associating with anything they saw as such a risky proposition. In those days – and perhaps still – job security was the paramount objective for all but the truly fearless or genuinely reckless. Or, of course, the totally naive, in which category I found myself. I still had no real career plans, although it was becoming clearer that writing was my best bet. For a few months I sought to sustain myself by freelancing, before succumbing to the obvious truth that successful freelance writing requires either a solid reputation or a network of contacts or preferably both. Having neither, my early plans lapsed for want of a buyer. Facing up to reality I started doing the rounds of the radio and TV stations and of the newspapers, though not, at that stage, of *The Australian*, which I still regarded as out of reach. I was firmly knocked back. I had some hopes of the *Sydney Morning Herald*, where my godfather Guy Harriott was the impeccably conservative – even reactionary – editor, but failed there as well. My mother blamed it on my lack of dress sense; I had once delivered some freelance copy to the great, grey building on Broadway without a tie. Sartorially I was not good enough for Granny.

Eventually in something like despair I approached Murdoch's tabloid *Daily Mirror* with a written application and samples of my work. By some mysterious process they reached Douglas Brass. Brass called me in; he had read my efforts, he said, and was particularly impressed by my ability to use the semi-colon. With that in my mind he felt I would be more suited to *The Australian* than the *Mirror*. Could I start in the paper's Sydney Bureau as a D grade on Monday? Mumbling my gratitude I left. The following Monday I filed my first copy, which had to be sent to Canberra by teleprinter, the keyboard of which did not contain a semi-colon. I wondered if Brass knew.

It still wasn't quite a career; at the time I saw journalism as a useful stopgap, a way to earn a living while I decided what I really wanted to do. Like many before me I drifted into it. But it was a most satisfactory drift. In those days journalists were basically of two kinds: earnest grifters making their way out of the working classes and smart but basically lazy graduates who couldn't be bothered pursuing their real qualifications. I, of course, was emphatically of the second kind. I enjoyed the illusion of freedom journalism brings; for large parts of the day you can kid yourself that you are really your own boss. I was also smart-arsed enough to enjoy the challenge and quick enough to survive the pace, which in those days was frenetic. *The Australian*'s Sydney office was chronically understaffed, and we were expected to produce around five stories a day each. Moreover, we had to be highly adaptable. In the course of my first year I wrote on state politics, the civic rounds, industrial affairs, the equity court, the magistrates courts, the Supreme Court, company general meetings, crime, industrial affairs, science, drama and other arts, religion and sport — and that was just for the news pages. We were also expected to contribute features and quirky items for the back page gossip column, not to mention fill in for regular columnists who were on holiday, ill or just drunk. The working week included Sunday, but not Saturday; the standard joke was that perks of the job meant you got every Good Friday off — providing it fell on a Saturday.

It was pretty full on, and I loved it. I came to appreciate the camaraderie and generosity of colleagues both on *The Australian* and elsewhere; while the competition for an exclusive was always fierce, reporters would unhesitatingly cover for colleagues or rivals who missed a story through no fault of their own, and money was lent and drinks were bought with an abandon I had never seen in England. Within a year I identified totally with the industry. I hadn't yet found my specialisation, but I knew I was a journalist.

Unfortunately I was no longer a husband and father. It is fashionable to say that the 1960s didn't really come to Australia until the 1970s, and in a political sense that is true. But the sexual and chemical revolutions that drove them were certainly emerging by 1965, and both provided temptations and opportunities I found impossible to resist. I was only ever a casual user of drugs – I discovered that I couldn't really work stoned while I could work drunk, so alcohol remained my stimulant of choice. But I revelled in the promiscuity. I usually maintained some kind of more or less stable relationship, but within that there was room for a little on the side, as the saying went. The terrace house opposite the City Council rubbish truck depot in Ultimo I shared with a couple of other desperates became mildly notorious; interestingly it was known as 'The Ferret's Nest', although this was many years before Michael Leunig invented the ferret as the logo for *Nation Review*.

There was, however, *Oz* magazine, then being run more or less as a hobby by Richard Walsh and various mates. One of the spin-offs of working for a real newspaper was the gossip; inevitably I learned a great deal that I couldn't print in *The Australian* but which I felt deserved – no, demanded – a public airing. I happily passed this on to *Oz*. Since much of the best of the scurrilous stuff was political, or at least concerned politicians, over time I became the de facto anonymous political correspondent for the magazine. My vocation had thrust itself upon me, although I took a long time to recognise it.

I also kept up my connection with Sydney University in a somewhat desultory way; this gave me entree into the burgeoning protest movement as Australia was sucked further and further into America's maelstrom in Vietnam. In 1964 Washington claimed that North Vietnamese forces had attacked American naval units in the Gulf of Tonkin. Hanoi had a different version. Whatever the truth of the incident it became the excuse for a massive escalation from the American side. For the first time large numbers of regular troops (as opposed to so-called specialist adviser units) were sent to the aid of the regime in Saigon. At the same time, overtures were made to America's more malleable allies to come and join in the fun. Australia was top of the list.

The rhetoric from Canberra had always been big on the threat from the north, although exactly how an independence movement in a former French colony in Indo-China constituted a danger to Australian democracy was never spelled out. There was always a mention of the international communist conspiracy, with the implication that Vietnam was the first stage of a move by China for world domination; the clear historical fact that China and Vietnam were traditional enemies with no common interests whatsoever got lost in the tirade. Some genius invented the domino theory, by which the countries of South and South-East Asia would fall one by one to China, or Russia – well, to communism anyway, who cares? – and then the dominoes would leap the ocean and engulf Australia as well. The decision to send troops to Vietnam was explained not just by the fairytale that we would save the gallant little regime in Saigon for democracy, but by the still more preposterous fiction that we were acting in self-defence.

To their eternal shame, not one member of the Menzies cabinet believed this for a moment. A few years later in Canberra I bailed up John McEwen, who had been deputy prime minister at the time and in fact still was, and asked him whether he really believed the hogwash he had spoken at the time and in fact still was. Of course not, Black Jack admitted cheerfully, no one ever had. The only reason the decision was made was to suck up to the Americans. Giving them aid and support at such a critical time meant they owed Australia a big one, and the time might come when we needed to call in the debt, if not in terms of defence, then perhaps in terms of trade … His old eyes lit up at the prospect. What was a little war with your mates compared to the prospect of massive exports of beef …

On the day the announcement of Australia's entry to the war was to be made, the story broke in the early morning. But there was a hitch. The only request for military aid had come from Washington. While this certainly reflected the reality, there was feeling in Canberra that it would be nice to have a similar request from Saigon; after all, it was still nominally South Vietnam's war. The catch was that Australia didn't have anyone in Saigon with sufficient clout to get the job done as a matter of urgency. Washington was called to act as an intermediary. In the meantime I, together with a number of other reporters, had been sent to Sydney's Victoria Barracks, home of the Royal Australian Regiment whose 1st Battalion troops were to be the guinea pigs. We, and they, knew it was on; but everyone had to wait until the farce was complete and Menzies could solemnly announce that he had indeed received a request from the government of the Republic of Vietnam, and after deep and prolonged consideration in cabinet, the decision had been taken, etc etc. The troops we saw were relieved the die was finally cast, but it was a relief mixed with considerable apprehension. They didn't know what they were getting into. They weren't Robinson Crusoe. Nor did anyone else, and that included the all powerful Prime Minister, who was to retire covered in honours six months later – comfortably before the awful consequences of his sycophancy began to appear on television.

Chapter Eleven

POLITICS IS WAR WITHOUT BLOOD. WAR IS BLOOD WITHOUT POLITICIANS.

In my capacity as a junior reporter I met Menzies just three times. It would be fair to say that he treated my nervous questioning with benign contempt. This was no particular reflection on my youth, or even on my profession; he treated everyone in much the same way. When Harold Holt sat down after presenting the 1965 budget, his last as treasurer, Menzies approached him from behind and ruffled his hair in an avuncular fashion. The daily press reported that Holt blushed with pleasure; well, he certainly blushed. My own feeling was that he was probably thinking, as I had frequently done in my own encounters with the great man: what a pompous old fart. This, incidentally, was a view shared by many of the great man's colleagues. During one encounter with the irascible Archie Cameron, later to become speaker, Menzies snapped: 'Archie, I do not suffer fools gladly'; to which Cameron responded: 'It might be news to you to know that bloody fools have a lot of trouble putting up with you too.'

Nonetheless, this pat on the head was taken to signify that Holt was confirmed as the heir apparent, and so it proved. He was probably the pick of the bunch, but this is not saying much. Over the years Menzies had rid himself of any potential rivals. Some, like Percy Spender, Richard Casey and Garfield Barwick had been given diplomatic posts – Casey in fact ended up as Governor-General and Barwick as Chief Justice. Other lesser lights had simply been crushed. Those who remained were either yes-men or honest toilers who had learned to keep their heads down. Few had much of a public profile; Paul Hasluck was probably the best qualified, at least in his own eyes, but remained an aloof figure, although his wife's entry in *Who's Who* gave her hobby as searching country graveyards. Allen Fairhall was almost invisible in the Department of Supply. David Fairbairn was of impeccable background but little noticed, John Gorton was still an unknown quantity in the Senate and no one trusted William McMahon. The Country Party ministers over whom Menzies had no direct control were a far more colourful mob: the towering figure of Black Jack McEwen and his formidable enforcers Doug Anthony and Ian Sinclair were a major force on the political landscape. But they remained the junior partners in the coalition. The prime minister had to be a Liberal, so in 1966 we ended up with Harold Holt.

Wisely, Holt did not seek to fill the boots of his predecessor. He announced that his role would not be a domineering one, but that of *primus inter pares* – first among equals. His proudest boast was that he had achieved his position without having to walk over any dead bodies to get there, which was true up to a point; Menzies had already disposed of the political corpses on his behalf. He was comparatively youthful and likeable, with an outgoing wife and three attractive stepdaughters, and he smiled a lot, even if he displayed rather more teeth than normal in the process. There was a widespread feeling that he was probably more sizzle than sausage, but at least he was a fresh face. The public was prepared to give him a go.

The same could not be said of his Labor opponent. Arthur Calwell had been an imposing figure in his day, but his day had been almost twenty years ago. Since then he had lost two elections and become infected with the bitterness that attacked many of the older generation who believed, with some justice, that they had been denied power by the great split and were more intent on avenging that loss than presenting a palatable image to the electorate. Much of the bitterness was directed at his deputy, Gough Whitlam, who made no secret of his belief in his own destiny as a future prime minister and showed increasing impatience with the old guard who stood in his way. The relationship between the two was always strained and often poisonous. Their rivalry also produced some strange consequences. Calwell, naturally a conservative in the party – at one stage he was seen as a possible recruit by the DLP – became a captive of the left-wing Victorian branch, which was his home power base. Whitlam, whose instincts were invariably radical, was tied to the New South Wales right. Even for insiders the position was confused; for the electorate at large it was close to incomprehensible. In the context of the Vietnam War it became unacceptable as well.

Holt faced an election at the end of 1966; Menzies had left him about nine months to prepare for it. It was an awkward time frame, too long for a honeymoon but too short to establish himself as a settled prime minister. But he had an issue. Just six months after the troops had been committed and with the casualty list still insignificant most Australians were pretty gung-ho about the war. What protests there were came mainly from university students worried about the impact of national service, devout pacifists and the extreme left; these could be dismissed as dupes, idealists and traitors, and the government proceeded to do so. By extension the ALP, which opposed the commitment with varying degrees of enthusiasm, could be portrayed as the party of dupes, idealists and traitors. It was an unpromising position from which to launch a campaign.

However, Calwell was determined to make Vietnam the central issue; in practice it became the only real issue as the year progressed. It was a lonely crusade; even his long-term press secretary, Graham Freudenberg, deserted him although he found a handy part-time replacement in a senior journalist from *The Australian,* John Stubbs, and thus the catchphrase 'this filthy unwinnable war' was coined. *The Australian* was of course against the war, but was not at all keen on Calwell, who had been seen as an enemy of the media since his days as wartime and postwar censor. The rest of the media were locked into a patriotic fervour. Even the use of conscripts for service in Vietnam was widely applauded, at least until the first bodies began to come home. In 1966 the rights and wrongs of the conflict were rarely mentioned and in any case were considered irrelevant. The decision had been taken, our boys were over there fighting for freedom and it would be positively unAustralian (then, as now, the ultimate putdown) not to give the whole exercise unequivocal support.

In case there were any lingering doubts, Holt visited Washington where he assured his beaming hosts that Australia was 'all the way with LBJ'. This piece of grovelling was too much even for some of the patriots; when I met Holt at Sydney airport on his return, it was in the company of a small group of demonstrators, one of whom was waving a banner which proclaimed: 'Frogman Does the Australian Crawl' – a reference to Holt's liking for scuba diving. Undeterred, Holt announced that LBJ himself would make a return visit later in the year, and definitely before the election. Social climbers throughout the land went into a frenzy. A huge security operation did likewise; reporters covering the visit were briefed by tight-lipped Americans determined to reveal as little as possible. At the end of one unproductive session a disgruntled tabloid editor snarled: 'Well, we're obviously going to be all at sea with LJB, or whatever the cunt's name is' – a remark which caused more than one steely jaw to drop. A master of ceremonies was appointed to coordinate Sydney's ticker tape parade who announced his intention of releasing a flock of white doves symbolising peace as the President drove past – a singularly inappropriate display for what was, after all, nothing more than a massive pro-war election stunt. At least he promised to starve the birds for a couple of days in advance so that they would not crap on the joyful throngs.

But if the pigeons didn't rain on LBJ's parade, the protesters did. For once the left got itself more or less organised; in spite of a huge police presence reinforced by a squad of brutal and fanatical American security goons, a number of demonstrators got through the cordon and flung themselves in front of the car in which Johnson and the NSW Premier, the sleazy Robin Askin, were travelling. Askin, notoriously, snapped at the driver: 'Ride over the bastards,' to which Johnson is alleged to have replied: 'You're a man after my own heart.' Such was the commitment to democratic dissent among the allies.

All this, of course, did Holt's election campaign no harm at all; as the war itself escalated, so did the jingoism at home. While some conscripts burned their draft cards and had to be dragged to the barracks by sometimes reluctant police, other young men bragged that they would return from their stint in Vietnam with a pocketful of Viet Cong ears, a popular souvenir of the times. An Australian soldier named Kevin Wheatley received a posthumous VC, and was rechristened by the press, equally posthumously, as 'Dasher'. Eventually during the campaign proper, a deranged youth took a shot at Calwell after a meeting at Mosman Town Hall, providing the ultimate nightmare for reporters already on a deadline and with only one public telephone in sight. I have often thought that recreating this situation should be a compulsory exercise in any journalism course. Even Calwell's opponents regarded the bungled assassination attempt as a bit unAustralian; fortunately the perpetrator turned out to have the name Kocan, definitely not one of us in that pre-multicultural age.

I was of course opposed to any war as a matter of faith, and the more I learned about Vietnam the more convinced my opposition became. I was also appalled by the conscription of voteless eighteen-year-olds on the random basis of their birthdates (Holt's death lottery, as the protesters put it) for an undeclared war. More disturbing still was the public's ready acceptance. During World War I Billy Hughes as prime minister had lost two bitterly contested referenda seeking to use conscripts on overseas service and in World War II John Curtin, who had opposed Hughes twenty-five years earlier, had agonised through many party meetings before reluctantly accepting the need. And these were real wars, wars when Australian (or at least British, which in those days was the same thing) interests were genuinely threatened. In 1966 the debate seemed to have evaporated; apparently principle no longer counted, especially in an election year. As a result I found myself irrevocably drawn towards the Labor Party. I could no longer avoid party politics.

It was not easy. Calwell, for all his righteousness on Vietnam, still seemed hopelessly old-fashioned, a relic of the bad old days of the White Australia policy, which he still proudly espoused. Whitlam in those days seemed a bit sneaky, too willing to leave himself a lawyer's out if he did not like the policies of his party or his leader. I had met Lionel Murphy, the leader of the leftist anti-Whitlam faction in New South Wales, and found him a bit too unctuous; I had also met Ralph Marsh and John Ducker, the hardline controllers of Whitlam's own rightist faction, and found them less than idealistic. The idea of a closer association with either group was not tempting.

I could, however, do a little bit on a personal level. I was introduced by my wife, with whom I remained on reasonably good terms, to a Labor lawyer named Jack Grahame, who had gained preselection for the Liberal seat of North Sydney. The sitting member, Billy Jack, better known as Silent Billy for his reluctance to speak in parliament, had just retired. Despite his taciturnity, Billy Jack had acquired a large personal following because of his willingness to do things like rescue his constituents' cats from trees. Labor did not really see the seat as winnable, but it was thought that a good campaign could make a bit of a dent in it, thus setting it up for next time. Grahame was keen to try something a bit different. I was only too happy to help. I hired a jazz band, designed a pop art pamphlet and wrote a campaign song which was recorded by a local Bob

Dylan impersonator; the theme of it all was: Jack Grahame will make North Sydney swing.

It did absolutely no good; a combination of pro-war enthusiasm and a feeling that Calwell was well past it produced a record win for Holt and the coalition, and North Sydney, like scores of other seats, was buried in the landslide. But there was one curious corollary. Grahame's winning opponent was an RAAF veteran named Bruce Graham, who had lost a leg. He became mildly famous in Canberra for his habit of drinking a lot, then ringing his Liberal colleagues at random and scream-ing insults and obscenities at them in incomprehensible German. I was once treated to such a display, and asked why people put up with it. Well, one replied, you had to make allowances; the poor chap had lost his leg during a fire-bomb-ing raid on Dresden, and the horror of it had haunted him ever since. Hang on, I said, he lost his leg when he was run over by a tram in Sydney; this had come out during the election cam-paign. He was never anywhere near Dresden. Well, no, admitted the Liberal, he wasn't; but he thinks he was. Often in these drinking sessions Graham would pass out. Self-styled wits like Jim Killen would then remove his artificial leg and hide it. Sometimes when they returned it would be full of beer bottle tops so Graham jingled as he walked. Like his silent predeces-sor he achieved nothing of note during his parliamentary career and retired in 1980 on a full pension. He was not untyp-ical of the Liberals who came in on the landslide of 1966 – Holt's own war babies.

The election delivered to Holt what he wanted – legiti-macy as a prime minister in his own right. With the largest parliamentary majority since federation he looked, and indeed should have been, unchallengeable. And at first it seemed that he was. He was able to use his authority to push through the official abolition of the White Australia policy, albeit in a somewhat half-hearted fashion; many winks and nudges in the direction of the conservatives, particularly in the Country Party, made it clear that the switch of policy was designed largely for overseas consumption and that there would be no instant influx of the yellow peril. Any such arrival would, after all, have looked rather odd at a time when the government was hell-bent on scaring the pants off Australians with horror stories about the ongoing threat from the Asian dominoes to our north. It was not until the Whitlam government confirmed with much trumpeting a non-discriminatory immigration policy some six years later that White Australia could be said to be finally dead and buried. But Holt made a start, and received less credit for it than he deserved.

Far more importantly, he carried the referendum on aboriginal affairs through to an almost incredibly successful outcome. My uncle Bill Wentworth had proposed the idea to Menzies in 1965; his aim was to allow the Commonwealth to share in the powers over aborigines then held by the states. He argued that the states, even in the brief periods when they were well intentioned, did far too little and even then it was generally misguided. A national approach, or at least the opportunity to set guidelines, was needed, both for the tribal people in the outback and for the mixed bloods in their city ghettos. Menzies agreed – well, sort of. But he saw it as a difficult and divisive issue, and he didn't want his final years in office disturbed. The referendum stayed on the backburner until Holt decided to put it to the test. But he teamed it with another referendum aimed at increasing the size of the House of Representatives to more than double that of the Senate –

the kind of proposition that is invariably shot down in flames by a populist campaign screaming no more politicians and no more power to Canberra. Although there was general support for the question on aborigines (except from the Packer press, which said it just wasn't worth bothering about) there was a near universal outcry against the question on parliament. The fear was that people would fail to differentiate, and vote no to both.

But they didn't. The freedom rides organised by Charles Perkins and his fellow student Jim Spigelman may have contributed; the enthusiasm of the younger generation in ensuring a big turnout certainly did. The referendum passed overwhelmingly in all states. Contrary to popular belief it did not give aborigines the right to vote, which they already had, or make them full citizens, which they already were – although it did, for the first time, include them in the national census. But by focusing attention on their needs, and permitting – indeed, requiring – the Commonwealth to legislate on their behalf, it was a truly historic breakthrough. Uncle Bill had a moment of glory which was quickly forgotten; in 1992 on the twenty-fifth anniversary of his referendum, he did not even receive an invitation to the celebrations, a piece of mean-spiritedness for which Paul Keating and his government should have been thoroughly ashamed. But the legacy endures. While aboriginal issues have remained controversial and progress has not always been straightforward, never since 1967 has it been possible to ignore them. The Holt tenure was not memorable for very much; indeed, in retrospect most of that brief twenty-two months was mildly embarrassing. But that one act will always remain to salvage Harold Holt's somewhat tattered reputation. I applauded mightily, both as a citizen and as a journalist.

Becoming a member of Rupert Murdoch's workforce meant one instant lifestyle change: everyone had to wear a suit during duty hours. Well, for almost all of them anyway. There were exceptions. To illustrate a feature on the opening of the TAB I had to dress up as a pantomime horse – at least I scored the front end. When the conductor Richard Bonynge took exception to the way he and his wife Joan Sutherland were greeted on their arrival in Australia and made a brusque remark about 'the apes of the press', I found myself standing at the ticket office of the theatre where they were performing tastefully clad in a monkey suit – a real one, not a dinner jacket. But in general we were expected to conduct ourselves with dignity.

We were also expected to be extraordinarily versatile, quite unlike most of our colleagues on other papers. They specialised from an early age, which meant they quickly became expert in one very narrow field but pitifully ignorant about everything else. The airport round was a prize example. The correspondents who haunted the vast spaces out at Mascot were brilliantly well informed about the aviation industry, but quite hopeless when it came to interviewing celebrities who had jetted in (as the buzz phrase was) from overseas. I was actually present when one asked Frank Sinatra how he spelled his name, when a second asked Cardinal Gilroy if he had taken his family to Rome with him, and when a third, having established that Bill Waterhouse was a bookmaker, led off his copy by announcing the return of Mr W. Waterhouse, the well-known publisher. The benefits of a tertiary education enabled me to avoid such gaffes, which was just as well: at various times I was required to review light entertainment, fill in for the religious columnist when he was on holiday, and knock out the tips for Randwick when our racing writer failed to return from the pub.

But the best thing about those early days was that even as a very junior reporter I was sent out on important stories, simply because *The Australian* seldom had the space or the manpower to cope with run of the mill stuff. We were, after all, a national paper; Sydney had to compete for space with the rest of the country, which was not the case with the rival *Herald* and *Telegraph*. But the shortage of staff meant that time was seldom wasted; the vast majority of what I wrote actually got into the paper, not usually the fate of copy submitted by junior journalists. The first time I was sent to state parliament it was for a major crisis involving the expulsion of two members of the Legislative Council. The first court case I covered was the immensely complicated hearing in equity resulting from the collapse of the H G Palmer group. The first time I answered a police rounds call it involved the shooting of a major criminal as part of a gang war. One evening in the pub our chief of staff asked casually if anyone understood how the proposed reserve price scheme for wool, in which Murdoch had a special interest, was supposed to work; I unwisely replied that I did more or less, and was promptly despatched on a tour of graziers' meetings, one of which censured me for writing that the federal Minister for Primary Industry, Doug Anthony, had looked rather bored during the chairman's address. After sitting through a dozen or so of them, I could understand how he felt. Murdoch was a great advocate for the scheme, but the first time around it failed to get up.

I masterminded another loss when I persuaded the paper to take up the cause of Joern Utzon. He had been forced out of his job as architect of the Opera House by one of Askin's more philistine ministers, a man named William Davis-Hughes, who admitted in parliament that he had falsely awarded himself a Bachelor of Science degree. With the aid of some arty friends I rang Utzon in Denmark and cajoled him into offering to return and sort out the mess which had developed since his departure. It was a reasonable scoop, and Murdoch himself poured me a glass of whisky in the executive suite. He also spared no effort on the campaign to convince Askin to accept the offer, which was totally ineffective. Fortunately he blamed Askin rather than me.

The other most vivid memory of those years was that the paper was always facing a crisis of some kind: if it wasn't financial it was logistic. I remember an awful night when the solution to the previous day's crossword failed to arrive, and I was given half an hour to solve the bloody thing and provide one. When the time came to celebrate the paper's first anniversary, which we did in a dingy room of the pub over the road, we were all exhausted. But we also felt that we had done something rather special, and had heaps of fun in the process.

Chapter Twelve

TO LOSE A PRIME MINISTER MAY BE
REGARDED AS UNFORTUNATE. TO
REPLACE HIM WITH ANOTHER LOSER
IS JUST PLAIN BLOODY SILLY.

Apart from the triumph of the aboriginal affairs referendum, 1967 was just not Harold Holt's year. The voters clobbered his other referendum – the one about enlarging the House of Representatives. A clique of backbenchers took him to pieces over the sinking of the destroyer HMAS *Voyager* in a collision with HMAS *Melbourne* and forced a new and humiliating inquiry. And his wife Zara's taste was held up to public ridicule after she redecorated the Lodge with a display of antique euphoniums hung like china ducks in the stairwell.

But his real problem was the appearance of a cloud no bigger than a largish Member for Werriwa sitting opposite him as the Leader of the Opposition. The crushing election defeat of 1966 had inevitably meant the end of Calwell as leader of the Labor Party and just as inevitably prompted the accession of Edward Gough Whitlam; although there were still many of the old brigade and quite a few on the left who distrusted the smooth talking lawyer, he was so obviously the outstanding candidate for the job that there was very little open dissent. Whitlam proved his supporters right by quickly and effortlessly taking control of parliament and establishing a clear ascendancy over Holt. Sympathisers said that Holt was simply too nice a man to play the game hard; that he lacked the killer instinct. This was probably true, but he also lacked the quickness of mind and powerful debating skills that made Whitlam so formidable an opponent. By midway through the year Holt was complaining to anyone who would listen that it just wasn't fair, that as soon as he came to terms with Whitlam's argument the sneaky bastard would change the subject and be off on a fresh track. He sounded more and more like a leader who was not only out of his depth, but something of a wimp to boot. Whitlam proceeded to boot him.

Outside the big white wedding cake in Canberra things were not going so well either. The anti-war movement was steadily gaining strength. Casualties and conscription had both begun to bite; most people by now had at least a nodding acquaintance with a family affected by the involvement, and it was becoming obvious that the opposition was not composed entirely of ratbags. It had not yet reached boiling point, but the demonstrations were becoming bigger and more representative. In Melbourne, always a more passionate political climate than Sydney, Holt's election meetings had been generally rowdy and at times verging on the violent; one had involved an ugly clash between demonstrators and police which had led to the more excitable media gasping about threats to democracy and had given Holt's campaign a welcome boost. From a political point of view the protests were still counterproductive; public sympathy remained on the side of the government and its war effort. But they could no longer be ignored.

I had now become *The Australian's* senior demonstration correspondent, partly as a result of my student contacts; knowing my own sympathies, they kept me up to date and fed me minor scoops from time to time, always, of course, favourable to their cause. It was not always a cosy job; on one occasion I was walking beside a street march when it suddenly surged onto the road, pushing me into the waiting police cordon. A grinning constable punched me viciously in the stomach. As I recovered he noticed belatedly that I was wearing a suit and carrying a notebook. His finely honed investigative mind went into overdrive. 'Are you a reporter?' he asked hesitantly. 'Yes I bloody well am, and you're in trouble,' I gasped back. His face became a mask of concern. 'Gee, I'm sorry, mate,' he apologised. 'I thought you were one of them fuckin' students.' I looked at him speechlessly, then realised that he, like the rest of them, had removed his police number to make identification impossible. At that stage the police, as much as the government, were seen as the enemy.

By now some of the troops, both regulars and conscripts, were coming home. Some did so with bravado: the army, they said, had made them feel like real men. They did not, however, hand out gifts of Viet Cong ears. But many others were obviously victims. They talked of the frustration of fighting guerillas in a country where you could not tell allies from enemies, of the incompetence of the overbearing Americans and the untrustworthiness of the corrupt Vietnamese. Few of them thought they were achieving anything worthwhile; they did not understand what the war had to do with Australia, yet they were puzzled and hurt by the lack of enthusiasm from civilians for their cause. Very little of this got into print but the overall feeling of frustration made itself felt in every pub in the country. Then there were the Americans on leave, lonely, homesick and bewildered, squandering their pay on lavish gifts for barmaids and prostitutes. They looked more like lost children than fighters for democracy. Television has been blamed (or praised) for causing the eventual disillusionment with the war. But for those with eyes and ears, it had already begun to set in on the streets of Sydney in 1967.

My own position was also hardening. I had become an active and committed trade unionist and a firm Labor supporter, although I never seriously contemplated joining the ALP or any other party. I used to talk loftily about intellectual independence and the freedom to express my own views without hindrance; in fact I was simply too lazy to face the discipline (and the tedium) of meetings run by those whom I secretly considered less bright than myself. I did, however, offer my services to those in charge of Labor's campaigning and was rather hurt when I was unceremoniously rejected.

The Ferret's Nest, or rather its floating population, had now moved from Ultimo to the more salubrious neighbourhood of Birchgrove. Next door, Balmain was in the process of being taken over by the hippy-yuppie groups who are now firmly established, and their central meeting place was a pub called the Forth and Clyde. Here a number of self-styled revolutionaries held sway on Friday nights, not infrequently ending up at our Birchgrove abode after closing time. Most called themselves Marxists of one kind or another: Trotsky and Mao were favoured. There was no sign that any of them had ever read *The History of the Russian Revolution*, let alone *Das Kapital*, but some carried copies of the *Little Red Book*. Their enthusiasm was infectious even if their knowledge was scant. We had long discussions about the Cultural Revolution, then being widely if confusingly reported in the Australian press. The general view was that it was an unfortunate necessity; every ongoing revolution needed an occasional Robespierre to kick it along when things got dull. We were particularly intrigued by the story of Old Shih, a septuagenarian night carter who had been singled out by the Red Guards as a working-class hero embodying all the true revolutionary values. Meanwhile, of course, they were demolishing China's heritage and humiliating the intellectuals who were the country's only hope. Still, you couldn't make an omelet without etc, etc.

My own career was flourishing. Although technically still only a C grade I was now regarded as one of the more capable writing journalists in Sydney and was rewarded with many of the plum assignments from *The Australian*. My prospects improved further with the arrival of Adrian Deamer as the new associate editor – in practice the boss, a position in which he was soon confirmed. Our Sydney chief of staff, Hal Lenzner, whom I credited with the same omniscience as his namesake, the all-seeing computer in Stanley Kubrick's *2001*, warned us that Deamer had a reputation for being a touch difficult; we were all to be on our very best behaviour when he came to inspect the Sydney bureau next day and absolutely no drinking beforehand. At our sober and impeccable best we awaited the appearance of the great man. And awaited. And awaited. The word came through that he was over the road in the Fairfax building, renewing acquaintances at the *Sydney Morning Herald* where his father had worked. Then it appeared he had gone to lunch with friends. Eventually, at around four o'clock, the summons came: he was ready to meet us at the pub across the road. Like schoolboys on an excursion we trooped over and lined up at the bar. A quite short, very drunk man leered up at us, clearly dismissing us individually and collectively. Hal introduced us. When it came to my turn Deamer glowered with even greater contempt. 'So,' he snarled, 'you're fucking Mungo MacCallum. Isn't that funny? You're a tall man, and I'm only a little man. But I can still call you a cunt.' I barked back 'And you can go and get fucked,' and stormed out. From that day forth we were friends.

Deamer remains, to my mind, the best editor of his generation and possibly the best ever. He was fearless, innovative and full of ideas. He drove hard, but he had the knack of getting the very best out of those who worked with him – and they always felt it was with, not under. If I was ever stuck for a subject or bogged down in a story I could always go to him, and after a few moments of furious argument the problem would be solved. His period in charge of *The Australian* was all too brief, but it remains the paper's glory days. I have particular reason to be grateful to him; he was not only a mentor and friend, but a protector in hard times, when Murdoch wanted to swing the paper around to the right. After George Johnston, Deamer became the second of my big brother substitutes. He could indeed be difficult, particularly after a few drinks; it was said that spending an evening at the Deamers' was like being in a perfomance of Edward Albee's play *Who's Afraid of Virginia Woolf*. But by golly he was good.

By the end of 1967 it was clear that the balance of political power was swinging, perhaps decisively. Whitlam, now solidly embarked on his long fight to reform and modernise the Labor Party's structure in ways that would make it electorally acceptable, was clearly the coming man. Whitlam had already shown his voter appeal; he had masterminded and won three by-election campaigns, taking two seats from the government in the process. The half-Senate election at the end of the year also produced a big swing against the coalition. Even to his closest supporters Holt was starting to look like a loser. A tougher leader – a Menzies – would have faced down his critics. But of course Menzies himself had made sure that there was no one with his sort of clout left in the party. The innate ruthlessness of the Liberals came to the fore. Only a year after Holt had delivered them a record majority his rivals, red in tooth and claw, were unsheathing their knives.

In the normal course of events the plotters would probably have struck early in 1968; history suggests that their first attempt would not have been decisive and Holt would have faced a long period of destabilisation with the party badly damaged in the process. But fate decided otherwise. Holt and his wife were members of what was known as the Portsea set – a group of rich and feckless Melbournites who spent their weekends being playboys and playgirls around the beaches of the Nepean peninsula. Morals were loose and affairs common; Holt had been involved in several, one involving a neighbour named Margaret Gillespie. On the morning of December 17 the two were part of a small party walking on Cheviot beach. The sea was rough and dangerous, but Holt decided to show off to his mistress by going for a swim. He dived into the surf and was never seen again.

As it happened I was acting as chief of staff at *The Australian* on the day the news started to trickle through. It was a Sunday, which meant only a few junior reporters were actually on duty. Fortunately a number of others were alerted by radio reports and got on the job. I spent much of the afternoon on the phone trying to find the rest. The job was made more difficult by my leftie friends, who constantly rang in to confirm what to them were the glad tidings. Inevitably the conspiracy theorists had a field day. Their most unkind scenario was that Holt had suicided because of his political troubles, the most bizarre that he had been abducted by a Chinese submarine. The absence of a body gave the latter proposition more legs than it should have had.

Holt's press secretary, Tony Eggleton, an urbane Englishman nicknamed the Maltese Falcon by a press gallery wit, took charge of the public relations side of things and became briefly famous as a result, but there was little he could add to the bald facts. He was, however, fairly successful in covering the scandals surrounding the Portsea set. A memorial service was held in Melbourne; I was sent to write the lead story, which was mainly a national morale booster about how many world leaders had seen fit to come and honour a man who, even in Australian terms, had been a pretty unimportant politician. Johnson was there of course, to be greeted by demonstrators who rather tastelessly suggested that he should 'Do A Bolt Like Harold Holt'. So was Harold Wilson, looking very surly at having been dragged halfway round the world to the funeral of a man with whom he had disagreed about just about everything. But, of course, if the USA was to send its president, the mother country could hardly refuse its prime minister. Zara Holt played the grieving widow (definitely not the wronged wife) to perfection, and became something of a national figure, at least until she was sprung having an affair with a somewhat bedraggled member of parliament called Jeff Bate, and was embarrassed by the resulting publicity into marrying him.

And, of course, the rejoicing of the left was misguided, even in its own terms. In fact Holt had been something of a moderate over Vietnam; his closeness to Johnson (by no means a fanatic himself, although he had been influenced unduly by the hawks who were still claiming the war was being won) had given the impression that he was far more militant on the subject than was the case. If anything his demise meant that the hardliners in the party had another opportunity to move one of their own into the top job. But for the moment that was a secondary consideration. What was needed was a winner – at the very least someone who could take on Whitlam with some hope of success.

At first glance the prospects were not promising. The arguments against the front runners in the House of Representatives – Hasluck, Fairhall and Fairbairn – which had been persuasive two years earlier when Menzies retired still applied. Hasluck made it clear that he considered himself the only possible choice, but refused to campaign; his colleagues were not impressed. The lugubrious Les Bury threw his hat in the ring at the instigation of the Fairfax press, which wanted a Sydney candidate; the only other possibility, McMahon, was already regarded as a captive of the rival Packer organisation, and had in any case been the subject of a thunderous veto by McEwen on behalf of the Country Party. Although the veto was almost certainly bluff – the Country Party relied on its position in government to deliver goodies to its supporters, and even if it had moved to the crossbenches was hardly likely to vote to replace a Liberal government with a Labor one – the Libs caved in with surprising alacrity. Privately, many were glad of the excuse to rule out McMahon, who even though he had reached the position of deputy by sheer persistence, was widely loathed. His habit of retailing party business to the Packer press had earned him the name of Billy the Leak; Hasluck privately referred to him more bluntly as 'that treacherous little bastard'. The only other candidate, the very junior Billy Snedden, did not rate serious consideration.

Faced with this unappetising line-up the instinct of many Liberals was to write 'none of the above'. But someone had to take the chair, so they were drawn to the only other possibility: the government leader in the Senate, John Grey Gorton. Gorton had gained some brownie points the previous year by short-circuiting a developing scandal over the use of VIP aircraft, but he was still largely an unknown quantity; few members of the House of Representatives took much notice of what went on in the far more restful chamber on the other side of King's Hall. Gorton's fellow senators, however, provided a solid base of support ; they rather liked the idea of elevating one of their own to the top job. And in the end there wasn't much alternative. Holding their noses and closing their eyes, the Libs took the plunge: what was to become known as the Gorton Experiment had begun. It was to be one of the more turbulent periods of Australian politics since federation, and one that the Liberals, and more particularly the conservative old guard, were to bitterly regret. It was the Gorton years rather than the brief McMahon interregnum that followed which made a change of government inevitable. The Establishment was appalled; the general public was entertained. And the media, of course, loved every minute of it.

Chapter Thirteen

WILL SOMEONE PLEASE EXPLAIN TO THE PRIME MINISTER THE DIFFERENCE BETWEEN LIBERAL AND LIBIDO?

Gorton's win was good news for me personally; I had run an office book on the result with the senator as a short-priced favourite and most of my colleagues had taken the more generous odds offered about Paul Hasluck. It was also a fillip for the anti-war movement, as Gorton installed Phillip Lynch as his new Minister for the Army while leaving Leslie Bury as Minister for National Service. The streets soon resounded to a new chant: 'Lynch Bury!' which was, of course, answered by the antiphonal: 'And Bury Lynch!'

There were other changes as Gorton, in the time-hon-oured tradition of Liberal leaders, refashioned the ministry to reward his supporters; Uncle Bill finally made it to the outer, although he was never to realise his ultimate ambition to enter

cabinet as Minister for National Development. One change
Gorton could not make at the time was to demote McMahon;
his colleagues, perhaps feeling guilty at the manner in which
they had edged him aside at McEwen's behest, had reinstalled
him as deputy, thus giving him the traditional right to select his
own portfolio. He naturally chose to remain in Treasury, which
gave him the most powerful base from which to undermine his
leader, a task he pursued diligently for the next three years. But
the rest of the Libs, like the public at large, seemed inclined to
give the new man a go. In practice they had very little choice.

In Sydney things were finally hotting up; the demonstrations were becoming more frequent and much better
organised. Covering them was something like a full-time job,
but one with which I increasingly identified. By now I was on
first name terms with most of the principal activists, both student and union, and also with Sergeant Fred Longbottom, the
special branch man who was appointed by the state government to stand between it and anarchy. Fred, a staunch
Presbyterian with a dry sense of humour, was in fact not at all
what the government led by the corrupt Robin (call me Bob)
Askin had in mind; Askin, whom I was later to rechristen the
Filthmaster, believed that the more violent the protests the
more his government and the conservative side of politics ben-
efited, and the hell with both the democratic process and the
public interest. He was widely believed to have planted a
network of agents-provocateurs in the anti-war movement to
ensure maximum disruption. While this was never proved, I
was certainly aware of unfamiliar faces which would appear
to urge demonstrators on to confront the police and disappear
just as quickly afterwards. Longbottom, on the other hand,
saw himself as a mediator whose job was to keep the peace

rather than encourage riots. He went to great lengths to avoid inflaming situations; at one demonstration on the grounds of Sydney University he sat stoically in an unmarked police car for over an hour while students surrounded it, banged on the roof and finally turned it upside down. As a result Longbottom was regarded by the demonstrators as something like an impartial judge: firm but fair. He was never seen as an enemy in the way the uniformed police, the government and the Packer press were.

By now the protest movement was becoming avowedly political. Although the vast majority of the tens of thousands who appeared on the streets simply wanted an end to the war – more specifically an end to conscription – ideological considerations were coming into it, with the leadership identifying more and more with the extreme left. There were divisions of course, but they tended to be differences of degree rather than of direction. Following the lead from America, they saw the conflict in neo-Marxist terms, articulated in the chant: 'One side right, one side wrong, victory to the Viet Cong.' Nothing appeared sacred: during a ceremony involving the Sydney University regiment the NSW Governor, Sir Roden Cutler, VC, was struck by a tomato. My contacts led me to the girl who had thrown it; when I asked if she thought the publicity was helpful to the anti-war movement, she replied simply: 'Fuck the anti-war movement,' and proceeded to give me a lecture on the need to overthrow the entire capitalist system. I had some sympathy with her aims, but increasingly doubted whether they were achievable in a country like Australia and even if they were, whether salad vegetables were sufficient weaponry.

However, there was certainly a story in the fact that the

student protest leaders now saw themselves as revolutionaries rather than pacifists, and I persuaded a rather dubious Adrian Deamer to run a series of interviews with the most prominent. In Sydney the Trotskyist Bob Gould was the most dogged and Mike Jones of the US-style Students for a Democratic Society the most pragmatic; in Melbourne the Maoist Albert Langer was the most doctrinaire and in Brisbane Brian Laver of Students for Democratic Action the most passionate and committed. But in terms of Australian society as a whole, they were all way off the visible spectrum. Jones later tried to link up with sections of the union movement, but was seen as both opportunistic and impractical by those seriously interested in the industrial scene. Still, the student–worker alliance did produce one memorable moment. After a prolonged industrial dispute the secretary of the Tramways Union, Clarrie O'Shea, was sentenced to jail for refusing to pay fines or disclose the whereabouts of union funds. The judge who sentenced him was, of all people, Sir John Kerr; but the law which made the sentence possible was a Commonwealth one, staunchly defended by Gorton and his Industrial Relations minister, Bill Snedden. As unionists marched through the Sydney streets in protest, students unfurled a gigantic banner with the message: 'Cut Off Gorton's Penal Power.' It had a huge resonance with those in the know and an increasing one with the public at large.

However, this was in the future. The early worries about Gorton centred not on his womanising but on his apparent inability to concentrate his mind on the job. This was the period during which *Oz* magazine christened him Bungles, as in the Air Adventures of Bungles; Gorton had been an RAAF pilot before being badly disfigured in a crash. His rumpled features, repaired by plastic surgery, seemed to sit well with his casual and outgoing personality. Men were usually comfortable in his company and women (including, to my dismay, the left-wing types with whom I generally associated) invariably charmed by him; political opponents were disarmed. His political honeymoon lasted the best part of six months, but when it ended it ended with a bang. He made the ritual trip to Washington demanded of all conservative prime ministers, and made the right noises; his reprise of Holt's 'All the way with LBJ' was 'We'll go a-waltzing matilda with you.' But when he was cross-examined at a press conference about details of defence arrangements – the ostensible reason for the trip – he was all but incoherent. Critics pounced.

A couple of weeks later an advertisement appeared in *The Australian* calling for serious Liberals to urge the parliamentary party to get rid of Gorton and install Allen Fairhall as prime minister. The ads were authorised by a group calling itself Businessmen for Democratic Action. It seemed something of an overreaction – after all, Gorton had only been in the job for less than six months – and also a naive one; of all the possible contenders for the job Fairhall was the most colourless and most reluctant. But the advertisement had cost real money, so there was obviously a story in it.

I was deputed to track down the mysterious businessmen and eventually the trail led me to a bespectacled man in import-export named Patrick Sayers. What, I asked, had set him on this course? And to my surprise and delight he produced a copy of *Oz*, and opened it to a longish article I had written (anonymously, of course) which concluded that Gorton was the worst prime minister in Australian history, indeed in that of the world. The list of gaffes it enumerated was impressive, but really hardly rated my conclusion. However, Sayers was taken by the polemic and had decided to do a little stirring. It quickly became clear that this was all it was; Sayers and a few friends had got together one evening and concluded that this was the best way to make the Libs pull themselves together. And it had the desired effect: Gorton's opponents inside and outside parliament now had something to focus on.

In the years that followed Sayers came right over to the Labor side, but at the time he was certainly a genuine businessman and genuinely concerned about the way the government was starting to drift out of control. Gorton had been planning an early election to confirm himself as the new prime minister and to capitalise on the new tensions within the Labor Party which had developed as a result of Whitlam's attempts at reform; the Sayers intervention marked the first check in the process. Eventually the DLP was to veto it altogether, although Gorton always denied that this was the case. The delay gave Whitlam the time he needed to crash through and consolidate. My moonlighting had paid an unexpected dividend.

Apart from *Oz*, I had also become executive editor of *Quest*, the rather flaccid organ of the New South Wales Credit Union League. The basic idea was to produce a quarterly record of the goings-on of this worthy, if dull, organisation, but the board had no objection to me jazzing it up a bit. With the aid of contributions from colleagues at the *Australian* and other dailies I turned it into a readable kind of journal which contained about six pages of credit union news and another eighteen on social issues such as environmental pollution, violence in sport and censorship. It was never overtly political, but had a general lean to the left nonetheless. For two years running it was adjudged the best publication by the credit union movement anywhere in the world; hardly a Nobel Prize, but satisfying to its associates.

By this time I was firmly committed to the Labor Party; I had met Cyril Wyndham, the national secretary who was working with Whitlam on structural reform, and had become something of a convert. I was still not totally convinced by Whitlam's sincerity on Vietnam – to my mind his speeches still had too many ifs and buts. However, I was now certain that the only way out of the mess was to elect a federal Labor government and that the only Labor leader who had a hope of being elected was Whitlam. Thus I was firmly in the Whitlam camp when he put his leadership on the line as the only means of bringing the organisation to heel. His opponent was the charismatic Jim Cairns, who had risen to national prominence through his leadership of the anti-war movement and its street protests. While I thoroughly approved of the cause, I was dubious about the politics; it seemed to me that the protest movement in its more extreme form was more likely to keep Labor out of office than to win the hearts and minds of swinging voters. I also agreed with Whitlam and Wyndham that reform of the party machine and giving more power and flexibility to the members of parliament was essential if these votes were to be won and that Cairns was unlikely to have either the will or the clout to implement such reforms.

But there was no doubt that Cairns had immense appeal to Labor's rank and file. His campaign was run by Phillip Adams, a Melbourne advertising man who was (and remains) a political groupie with a frantic desire to be seen as a kingmaker, especially within the Labor Party; at various times he has supported Arthur Calwell, Jim Cairns, Gough Whitlam, Bill Hayden, Bob Hawke, Paul Keating and God knows how many others. According to party insiders whom I know and trust there is no evidence that his support or otherwise has had any discernible effect; while Adams is (or at least used to be) regarded as helpful in shaping public opinion on some issues his influence within the party has always been negligible. Certainly in this case he backed a loser, although Cairns ran it rather closer than Whitlam would have liked. The old guard in the organisation still had plenty of clout, as was to become obvious as the battle dragged on over the next three years. But Whitlam had won they key engagement of 1968. Ironically, while across Europe and America the left was pushing the barriers towards revolution, in Australia the world's oldest Labor Party was preparing itself for parliamentary government.

The Libs, on the other hand, seemed intent on preparing themselves for defeat, with Gorton himself leading the charge. One of Labor's shrewder apparatchiks remarked to me later that he regarded Gorton as a very near miss: had he been shifted out of the indulgence of the Senate a year or two earlier and had a less frantic period in which to slot himself into the Reps he might have made a formidable prime minister. I disagreed; my view is that even if Gorton had been able to control his private life and embrace the work ethic, his politics – specifically his centralism – would have eventually become too much for his colleagues and the Libs would have torn themselves apart, which is essentially what happened anyway. Gorton's personal habits were really just a sideshow; but what a sideshow. At a time when politicians were being scrutinised more closely than ever before, Gorton seemed intent on defying all the conventions.

Rumours about his drinking and skirt-chasing started to circulate very early in his term as prime minister, starting with some salacious gossip about his relationship with his private secretary, an attractive young woman named Ainsley Gotto. A joke of the time was that Gorton's favourite spot in Canberra was Mount Ainslie. From time to time he missed appointments; his press secretary, Tony Eggleton, inherited from Holt, used to explain that the Prime Minister had a touch of the flu. 'Gorton flu' quickly became a euphemism for becoming tired and emotional. Around the Sydney pubs this was all treated as good clean healthy fun; no one took it terribly seriously, and if it made people start to doubt that the Liberal Party was composed entirely of celibate teetotallers, well, it was about bloody time.

But in the Establishment clubs of Sydney and Melbourne it was a matter of serious concern: perhaps Gorton (or Jolly John, as he had been nicknamed by the Canberra press gallery) was not quite the sort of person they wanted to lead the party of the sainted Sir Robert. Holt and his philandering had been reprehensible, but at least young Harold had the sense not to do it in the street and frighten the voters. Gorton seemed to have no sense of what was proper. If a man had to drink, let him do it among his peers in the privacy of his club, like Leslie Bury or Jim Forbes, two ministers who shared a flat in Canberra and were stonkered for most of their waking hours, but at least had never been known to burst into a chorus of 'Waltzing Matilda' in an RSL club, still less invade a nightclub singer's dressing room. Gorton had done both, and although he had escaped at the time with a minimum of publicity, few doubted that such incidents were being filed away for use when the time came.

But perhaps more important than the wine, women and

song was the underlying fear that Gorton might not be altogether sound on such Liberal Party shibboleths as states' rights. The 1968 Premiers' Conference had been reasonably straightforward, if more than usually tense; the two key figures, Askin from New South Wales and Sir Henry (known as the Hangman for his relish for capital punishment) Bolte were still convinced that they could handle Gorton, who was relatively uninterested in the finer points of economics, as long as they had McMahon on side, which they did. Premiers' conferences had long been a ritual in which the premiers (I coined the collective noun 'a penury of premiers') arrived in Canberra clad in sackcloth and ashes, whinged like mad at the Commonwealth's first offer of tax sharing and then, when the Commonwealth upped its offer as everyone knew it would, joyfully claimed victory and rushed home to tell their various states that they and they alone had been responsible for saving their constituents from starvation. But Gorton refused to play the game; he was unwilling to be portrayed as a sucker by the newspapers of Sydney and Melbourne, and while the premiers got more or less what they expected in terms of cash, they missed out on the usual triumphant headlines. Askin and Bolte tried to repair the damage with a special meeting to which the Commonwealth was not asked and at which the question of tax sharing was broadened into a more general complaint about the erosion of states' rights.

But for all but the most dedicated political observers, this was pretty eye-glazing stuff; a debate over states' rights generated about as much excitement as a Senate committee discussing the cellulose flake acetate bounty bill number two. Much more to the point were the increasing scurrilous stories about Gorton's private life. I got a few bits and pieces into *Oz*, which kept the gossip mill churning. But it was another fringe publication that really raked the muck, a scandal sheet named 'Things I Hear' written by Frank Browne, who had already been jailed for breaching parliamentary privilege in the reign of Menzies. Things Browne heard were almost invariably wrong, and his story on Gorton was no exception. But there was just enough in it to persuade the Labor Party that it deserved a wider audience.

We were just about to put *The Australian* to bed one evening in March 1969 when Canberra got on the phone to say hold the presses: the Prime Minister's private life was about to go on the parliamentary record. The job was done very sancti-moniously by Labor's resident bucket-tipper, Bert James, a man known for possessing the most noisy and noisome farts in par-liament. Under normal circumstances the combined reputations of James and Browne would have ensured that the story got a run only at the bottom of the funnies page, if at all; but Gorton himself had spent the previous year making everyone aware that these were not normal circumstances. That night at *The Aus-tralian*, no one had the slightest hesitation about turning the story into the front-page lead. The other papers agreed.

On the night of James's speech, which basically regurgi-tated the bar room gossip collected by Browne, the Libs had been caught short; their attempts at defusing the situation were panicky and ineffective. Next morning they regrouped behind their leader; for their own survival they could hardly do any-thing else. Well, almost all of them did. There was one dissenter, a man with whom I had had enough previous deal-ings to know that I would have hated to have him as an enemy: Edward St John, QC, champion of civil liberties and the world's worst practical politician.

Chapter Fourteen

IN THE GOOD OLD DAYS A SAINT WAS SOMEONE YOU BURNT AT THE STAKE

St John's enemies called him a bloody wowser; but in fact the urbane North Shore lawyer belonged to a much earlier tradition. He was a puritan, a zealot, a sea-green incorruptible, and like his illustrious predecessors he set himself impossibly high standards and then expected everyone else to live up to them.

In our previous encounters he had been on the side of the angels, which to me meant pushing for civil liberties and opposing censorship. I first met him shortly after I joined *The Australian* when an enterprising publisher named Alec Sheppard decided to get around Australia's draconian provisions against importing foreign filth by printing a local edition of D H Lawrence's *Lady Chatterley's Lover*. The book had only recently been cleared in the United Kingdom after a celebrated court case during which the prosecutor had asked a bemused jury of ordinary Poms: 'Is this the kind of book you would want your wife or your servant to read?' Sheppard now arranged with the English publishers to mail him the book chapter by chapter thereby ensuring that he was not importing a banned publication intact. Having thus circumvented federal legislation, he put the book back together, ran off a few hundred copies and invited the state authorities to prosecute. I covered the story, and in the process met Sheppard, whom I grew to admire greatly; he had been a resistance fighter in Greece during World War II and later organised Australian protests against the fascist regime under the colonels.

St John was a passionate supporter of the cause, which he regarded in the nature of a crusade; his style was to take no prisoners. Over the years I was to meet him several times in this kind of role. He was also a friend of Richard Walsh, having been a witness in the earlier trials of *Oz*; this made him a useful contact for the magazine. He was, by definition, a man of influence; but he was far too pure for politics. Nonetheless he gained preselection for the safe seat of Warringah and arrived in Canberra in the landslide of 1966.

He made his position clear in his maiden speech, an occasion normally devoted to giving a glowing description of the member's electorate, thanking the voters and humbly promising to work in the interests of party and country. St John did none of the above. Instead he launched a swingeing attack on the government's handling of the *Voyager* disaster, castigating all concerned. It caused a sensation and led to the setting up of a new Royal Commission which more or less vindicated St John's complaints. But while this may have endeared him to the press and to sections of the public, it made him highly suspect within the party. Bright young backbenchers are supposed to exhibit their brightness by taking on the Opposition, not their own leader. St John was marked down as a man to watch, but not with a view to promotion.

Things did not improve with the advent of Gorton: the two men were total opposites in their approach to public life. The fact that St John was something of a fan of McMahon, who cultivated the new member assiduously, didn't help either. From the beginning St John expressed doubts about the new prime minister's suitability for his high office, buttonholing colleagues and then, when that didn't work, journalists, among whom he found a much more attentive audience. The day after Browne's speech Gorton called a party meeting to demand a vote of confidence. St John said: 'Sir, I don't agree ...' but was shouted down. That night he finally burned his boats by rising on the adjournment debate to complain about Gorton's conduct in general and specifically the fact that the Prime Minister had taken a young female reporter from the press gallery dinner to the American embassy late at night and had proceeded to dance with her.

Put like that, it was all fairly innocuous stuff, but at the time it seemed real shock-horror material. The point was that the muck-raking was not only coming from dubious newsletters and Opposition shitkickers but from a man of impeccable virtue on Gorton's own side of politics. Now the door was open others from the McMahon camp started giving journalists their own opinions of Jolly John. Of course they did so off the record; they were not ready for political martyrdom. But St John was. He happily accepted exclusion from the party room and then resigned from the Liberal Party altogether, continuing to sit as an independent until his inevitable defeat at the next election. While interest remained he carried on his crusade with a series of talks at universities and interviews with student newspapers, all of which were predictably anti-Gorton; for him, this was safe and familiar territory. I saw him on one such occasion on the Sydney campus; he greeted me somewhat feverishly as a long lost friend (which I wasn't) and informed me that his crusade was gathering strength (which it wasn't). If people had their worries about Gorton, they found St John altogether too good for this world, let alone the steamy stews of politics.

However, he had left his mark; the opinion polls showed a marked fall in Gorton's standing over the time of the fracas. It remained very good by today's standards – well over 60 per cent on average – but the drop would normally have been seen as a warning. Instead, it only made Gorton more determined to carry on regardless; it was around this time that he adopted as his theme song Frank Sinatra's 'I Did It My Way'. Most of his colleagues didn't like Sinatra much at the best of times. Labor was of course delighted by Gorton's discomfiture but understandably reluctant to be associated with St John's wowserism. Whitlam more or less ignored the whole affair. A couple of members of the left, notably the Senate leader Lionel Murphy and the anti-war activist Tom Uren openly backed Gorton against his critics but by and large the party was preoccupied with its own problems.

As always, the ALP presented its internal struggles as being about great matters of principle and differences of ideology; but as always, they were really about power. In 1969 the question was whether control of the party's heart and soul would remain with the traditionalists, who held that the self-evident truths of the past (white Australia, no state aid for private education, and members of parliament as simply the voice of the organisation, which in turn was the voice of the unions) were always more important than gaining political power or pass to the new generation. This was symbolised by Whitlam, who believed in a broadly based left party with flexible and pragmatic policies and leadership coming from the elected politicians rather than the industrial wing. Whitlam had been pushing for a showdown since well before he became leader, but so far progress had been frustratingly slow. While the parliamentary leadership had finally gained seats on the all-powerful federal executive, the old guard still had the numbers.

For Whitlam, facing an election at the end of the year, it wasn't good enough. Once again he prepared to crash through and his chosen ground was state aid. Whitlam pre-empted the debate by unilaterally promising a package of assistance for all poorer schools, both public and private, and challenged the party to disown him. A few years earlier it probably would have; there might even have been another 1950s-style split. But now some of those who had hung around on the Opposition benches for twenty years were getting the hitherto unimaginable sniff of government in their ageing nostrils. From the moment of Menzies's retirement the balance had started to shift; now, although the coalition was still sitting on a record majority, it was showing unmistakable signs of decay. Possibly, just possibly, victory was in sight − if not at this election, then at the next. And there was no longer much dispute that Whitlam, whatever his lack of ideological soundness, was the best person to secure it. The anti-state-aiders thundered, but in the end they compromised. Reluctantly and still somewhat indecisively the numbers swung Whitlam's way.

But there had to be a *quid pro quo*, and one turned up fortuitously in the figure of Brian Harradine. Harradine has since become famous as a so-called independent senator; I use the phrase so-called because it has long been apparent that Harradine sees his primary role in politics as representing the views of the more conservative wing of the Catholic church. He has used (or misused) the times when his vote has been crucial to the government of the day to secure such legislation as the removal of all forms of birth control from Australia's foreign aid program, and governments from both sides, to their shame, have given in to his pressure more often than not. In 1969 this was still well in the future. But he was already a sanctimonious and much avoided character with the knack of infuriating his enemies and making his allies (he had few friends) thoroughly uncomfortable. Harradine was a supporter of Whitlam on the state aid issue (of course) and had been selected as a Tasmanian delegate to the ALP's biennial federal conference. This caused considerable angst among the crustier lefties, who suspected Harradine of playing footsy, if not something more, with the DLP, still seen as untouchable rats. In return for acquiescing on education policy, they demanded Harradine's head on a platter.

This put Whitlam in an uncomfortable position. There is little doubt that he would eventually have sacrificed Harradine anyway, but Harradine virtually hung himself by announcing that 'the friends of the communists' were seeking to have him barred from the conference. This was not only grossly insulting to the left; it was extremely silly. The CPA had lost most of its members and nearly all its friends when Russia invaded Hungary in 1956; the few that remained had drifted away when Russia invaded Czechoslovakia in 1968. Some of the more hidebound Libs were still carrying on about communist influence in the Labor Party, but you had to expect that kind

of nonsense from them. However, coming from an insider —
one who claimed to be a delegate on the ALP's highest policy-
making body — it was not to be tolerated. A vote to exclude
Harradine was carried on the voices with Whitlam studiously
looking at the ceiling. The old guard had received its pound of
flesh, and made no serious trouble for the remainder of the
conference. But the Victorians, in particular, made it clear that
they were a long way from accepting Whitlamism.

I had watched this political mini-series from the Sydney
office, which I was starting to find a little claustrophobic. I certainly couldn't complain about the way I was being treated; I
was regularly getting the plum assignments, and had become
the automatic choice for anything that was seen as needing a bit
of extra writing. I was probably rather underpaid for what I was
doing; as the bureau's top gun I was still only on a B grade salary
and was regularly competing against super-As; indeed, I had
been since my first days as a lowly D. But I had a good deal of
latitude about what I did and even where I went. This involved
a certain amount of travel within Australia, and one brief excursion to Norfolk Island where some colourful locals held me
down on a table and threatened to shave my beard off with a
broken beer glass. Deamer had also given me a weekly satirical
column, which I enjoyed enormously but which was to prove
a major headache for him as I used it increasingly to take the
piss out of the government in general and the Prime Minister
in particular; Murdoch, although he had begun sucking up to
Whitlam as a form of insurance, was still keen to be in the good
books of the government of the day and constantly asked
Deamer to pull the column. Deamer replied spiritedly that he
would not indulge in political censorship. The column continued until I left the paper.

But in spite of the enjoyment I still got out of the work and the camaraderie and lifestyle that went with it I was feeling restless. I felt that I had done just about everything journalism in Sydney could offer; I needed a fresh challenge. This may sound excessively immodest coming from a 27-year-old who had only been in the game for a bit over four years, but it remains true; my meteoric career had left me prematurely jaded. I thought about going overseas again, but I had no particular aim in mind. This, of course, was the story of my life; I had never made plans, things had just happened to me at the right moment. And so it was to prove again. I told Deamer I was thinking of resigning and went to Queensland for a short holiday. While I was there Deamer contacted me through the paper's Brisbane office: he couldn't offer me an overseas post, but he could offer me the number two position in the Canberra bureau under my old university mate David Solomon. David would, of course, continue to cover the main political stories of the day while I looked after parliament and other peripheral issues; he mentioned trade, a prospect that filled me with dread. At one stage in Sydney I had been despatched to unearth the inside story on roll-on, roll-off shipping, perhaps the most tedious job of my entire career. But there was bright side: I would be able to keep my weekly column and, said Deamer meaningfully, it would be a good place from which to continue my other work: with a sinking feeling I realised he knew about *Oz*. Murdoch obviously didn't or I would have been out on my ear. Once again Deamer was looking after me.

I still hesitated; while I was increasingly fascinated by politics, I wasn't sure I wanted to make it a full-time job. Also I had my doubts about Canberra, which I had visited rarely and found unwelcoming and basically uninteresting. Apart from that it was a long way from the beach. But what the hell; if I didn't like it I could always resign, which was what I was planning to do anyway. With some trepidation I packed a survival kit of books, records and winter woollies (it was the end of July) and headed for the bleak south-west. By Wattle Day – August 1 – I decided that the place might have been designed specifically for me. I was to stay for nearly nineteen years, most of which replaced my time at the university as the most satisfying of my life. I had discovered the delights of the Great Game – politics.

> Polynomial polyhedrons all have polygons to boot
> While polyanthus pollinates and polymers pollute
> And when the polysyllables get rather too prolix
> It all comes down to polling day and poli-tics.
>
> Polymaths use polyesters, also polyurethane
> Polygamists face polygraphs, policemen on the brain
> There's polylingual polyglots in polytechnics
> But policies still polarise with poli-tics.
>
> There's polliwogs and polyps in the Polynesian seas
> And poliomyelitis is a polyphase disease
> While polyandrous pollsters look for polymorphous
>   pricks
> The polecats still all polka on to poli-tics.
>
> There's pollywaffles neatly wrapped in polypropylene
> And pretty Polly Perkins from the Paddington Green
> There's polly wants a cracker and there's polly needs a fix
> But all a real pollie gets is poli-bloody-tics.

Chapter Fifteen

CANBERRA USED TO BE A SHEEP STATION. THEN THE POLITICIANS MOVED IN. FROM BAA TO HUMBUG

I had first visited the national capital as a child, before the lake had been filled; in those days the south side was dominated by the old Parliament House, which I recall thinking looked rather like a newly excavated tomb. In my brief return visits since that time I hadn't paid much attention to the place, never imagining that I might actually have to live there. Now I gazed on it with a more proprietorial air.

The invasion of public servants had given birth to numerous sprawling suburbs and also to a variety of office blocks of almost Stalinist ugliness. But the south side – the parliamentary triangle, as it was called – now had its own melange of styles. To the west was the neo-classical library, a reasonably harmonious structure reflected in the muddy waters of the lake. But then, cutting the skyline like a giant decaying tooth, came the new High Court, a monument to the Brobdingnagian ego of the Lilliputian Chief Justice, Sir Garfield Barwick. Beside it the National Gallery was rising from a mountain of builders' rubble. Parliament was still the focus, but it was now reduced to a little white wedding cake framed, or rather overwhelmed, by the newcomers. Nonetheless, this was where I was to spend most of my working, and a good proportion of my leisure, hours from here on in, so I set out to master it.

I quickly discovered that, in all its unhealthy, overcrowded confusion the building was a fine allegory for a politician's mind. Corridors led round a series of bends to bring you back to where you had started. There were countless dead ends and blind alleys; there were nooks and crannies ideal for conspiring or for merely looking as if you were. There were rooms which were never used and doors which were never unlocked. There was a windswept and mildly dangerous catwalk across the roof, and rumours of bomb shelters and secret tunnels underneath. For the public, restricted to the spacious foyer of King's Hall and the galleries overlooking the well-appointed chambers of the upper and lower houses it all looked honest and open; little did they know.

The media were accommodated, if that is the right word, on the topmost of the three floors of the building, in conditions which would have had the RSPCA demanding prosecutions if they had been applied to battery hens. *The Australian*, being a relative newcomer to the scene, was squeezed in with Murdoch's other principal publication, the *Sydney Daily Mirror*; fortunately, the fact that this was an afternoon publication meant that the *Mirror* mob were generally out of the way and into the turps by the time we started serious work.

We, facing a late evening deadline, seldom started our serious drinking much before lunchtime. But drink we did; during non-sitting weeks, of which there are more than the general public realises, our brisk working lunches frequently dragged on towards sunset. The time, we assured each other, was not wasted; much valuable information was exchanged and many profound insights mused upon. It was thoroughly worthwhile, or at least it would have been if anyone had remembered any of it later.

Even in those days Canberra had half a dozen reasonable eating spots, so at least our gastronomic meditations took us around the city. There was a canteen in Parliament House itself, but few serious lunchers used it except in emergencies. Known variously as Hepatitis Hall because of the food or the Sheltered Workshop because of the staff, its one and only concession to epicureanism was an apparently inexhaustible supply of pickled walnuts; the conventional wisdom was that there must have been a glut in the electorate of the deputy Prime Minister, Black Jack McEwen, and the caterers had been cowed into buying them.

Next door to the canteen was the nerve centre of the building, the non-members bar; I was to write later that if King's Hall was the building's heart, the chambers its lungs and the corridors and lobbies its veins and arteries, then the non-members bar was its liver. This sordid venue was where the day's nourishment was digested: the good bits were absorbed and the waste rejected. It was frequented mainly by the house staff, but used as a meeting place by reporters and political staff, and not infrequently by the politicians themselves; late at night they were likely to admit that the non-members was the only place they could ever find out what was really going on.

The place was run by a little man named Dick, who regarded it as his personal fiefdom; he was no respecter of persons. On spotting Bill Hayden, later to be a minister in two governments, a party leader and ultimately a governor-general, attempting to help himself to some ice for his whisky, Dick screamed: 'Get your fucking cunthooks out of my ice bucket.' On non-sitting days the bar was supposed to close at 4.00pm; if Dick was feeling sociable he would invite selected cronies to stay behind and have a free one on the Prime Minister, then one on the deputy Prime Minister, one on the Minister for Defence; on a good day he could work his way through the entire cabinet and well into the outer ministry. Dick was also the resident SP bookie. The non-members bar was a homosexual affair; if women wanted a drink they were relegated to an even more revolting hovel next door, known as the Snake Pit. Drinks would be passed through a serving hatch or not, as Dick's fancy took him.

Official after-hours drinking took place mainly at the Wellington, a pub down the road. It was here I re-met David Solomon on the night of my arrival to discuss my role in the office. As I have mentioned, I was not keen on the trade round; we agreed that I would have to go through the motions, but that it was to be secondary to anything more interesting that might come up. David also suggested that I should spend as much time in parliament as possible to get a feel for the place and to get to recognise the members; this was good advice and I was happy to take it, even if many of the debates were pretty boring and very few yielded anything like a news story. But the best bit was David's disclosure that while he would continue to cover the government and the various announcements that flowed from it, he would hand over the principal responsibility for covering the Opposition – the Labor Party – to me.

This was an extraordinarily generous offer. In the other offices in the gallery at that time the bureau chief – 'our political correspondent', as he was known – reigned supreme. The rest of the staff had their assigned rounds – defence and foreign affairs, for instance, or health and education – but as soon as a good political story developed in the area, OPC snaffled it for himself. For the chief to hand over a whole political domain, and one which was increasingly overshadowing the troubled government as a source of major stories in an election year, to a blow-in was unprecedented. I grabbed it with both hands, but assured David I would always keep him informed, come to him if I needed advice (which in the early days I very often did) and would never work behind his back to try and knock him off, the constant fear of senior journalists. I think I can say the arrangement worked splendidly in every way; we both produced lots of good copy, with my somewhat flamboyant style complementing David's more academic approach to the satisfaction of head office.

There were formalities to be gone through; I needed to introduce myself around the place. I had met Gorton's chief minder, Tony Eggleton, a few times after Holt's death, but I had only seen Gorton himself once. In a typically unconventional gesture he had decided to return from an appointment in Perth on a cruise ship, and to give a press conference on its arrival in Sydney. I was sent to cover it and found the Prime Minister genial but largely incomprehensible; it was as though he was talking in some kind of jargon which could only be decoded by an inner circle. I was pleased to discover that it wasn't just me; senior Canberra journalists who had flown up for the event were similarly bemused. As time went on Gorton's speech patterns were to become increasingly convoluted and a fertile area of parody. At that stage, however, I was more interested in trying to figure them out. Eggleton reintroduced me to the PM, who was, as always, dishevelled but charming; as I recall we found common ground in our liking for native plants, with which he was keen to replant the gardens at the Lodge. As parliament was not then sitting (thank heavens) other ministers and the Opposition front bench had to wait for a couple of weeks.

This gave me time to make a somewhat unnerving discovery. I had thought myself to be a fairly keen observer of federal politics; I had covered a fair few important stories and had been careful to keep in touch through a variety of media. I considered myself, if not an expert, at least a reasonably well-informed layman. After a few days in Canberra and particularly chatting to my new colleagues in the non-members bar and the Wello, I realised this was emphatically not the case; in fact, I knew three-fifths of five-eighths of fuck-all, and precious little of that. I had no real idea of the cabinet hierarchy or the mechanics of the Labor caucus. I didn't understand the importance of the committee system or the tensions that operated between the Senate and the House of Reps. The role of the public service and the interaction between it and the political staff of ministers was a complete mystery. In short, I was a fairly full bottle about what came out of the process, but I had no idea at all about the mechanics of the process itself. I knew what happened, but not how or why it happened. And if I, who had actually made some attempt to study the subject, was as pig ignorant as it now appeared, where did that leave the average newspaper reader, who was probably pretty pissed off with the whole idea of politics?

From this revelation came a conscious decision: as much as I could within the constraints of the job, I was going to use my time in Canberra to try to demystify the system. I would try and get down to the most basic explanation of the way things worked and lay it out as simply as possible. I would do my best to find out how and why decisions were made and take the reader through it step by step, humanising it as much as possible on the way. I would, in short, try to cut through the bullshit.

This probably sounds somewhat pompous and pretentious; all I can say is that it isn't, and wasn't, meant to be. I have always considered politics important – it is, after all, the basic framework by which people's lives are governed. To a large extent politics determines our priorities; it decides whether we spend our resources on building schools or buying submarines. In a real sense a world without politics would be a world without civilisation. But most Australians regard politicians with contempt, and extend that feeling to the process itself. I felt that they shouldn't, and if they understood it a little better they would be less inclined to do so.

But there was a catch: first I had to get them to read about politics, something they were traditionally loath to do. Hence conscious decision number two: the pill would have to be sugared. Politics must be made entertaining; it should look not just important, but fun. This required an unconventional approach to writing about it; it meant including jokes, reporting gossip, incorporating visual images and a good deal of vernacular to replace the usual jargon. It would also require a fine balance; the last thing I wanted was to portray politics as a series of blunders and politicians as a mob of drongos. But I did want to make the process accessible and the participants human. That way at least some readers might get to understand and appreciate the value of politics and, with a bit of luck, get involved in it themselves. Democracy, as they say, would be the winner. I apologise for the apologia; I'm not trying to set myself up as some kind of preacher. But I would like it known that there has been a method in my madness.

The other move I made in those early days was to resurrect the press gallery cricket team. The ostensible reason was simply to get the odd social game going on a sunny Sunday; a number of the public service departments ran teams, so there would be the bonus of developing some useful contacts. But the real purpose was again one of political reform, this time within the gallery itself.

Among the hundred or so journalists in residence at that time there were quite clear divisions. First came what might be called the old guard; a small but solid group whose origins went back to the early days of Menzies and in some cases far beyond that. Its doyens were Don Whitington, who ran his newsletter *Inside Canberra* from an office on the comparatively isolated Senate side of the building, Ian Fitchett of the *Sydney Morning Herald* and Alan Reid of the *Sydney Daily Telegraph*.

Reid was already a legendary figure, purveyor of numerous political scoops, the majority of them to the detriment of the ALP. His book on the manoeuvring to succeed Holt, *The Power Struggle*, was already a classic, by far the best written and most absorbing work on Australian politics yet produced. It was also a highly judgmental piece, pro-McMahon and anti-McEwen. On Gorton it was fairly neutral, but Reid was already working on a sequel which was to be rather less so. Known in his youth as the Red Fox, in later years he remained impressively vulpine. Reid liked to warn young journalists to keep their distance from politicians; a favourite line was 'Just because you work in the zoo it doesn't mean you have to socialise with the animals.' He himself, however, was very much a part of the menagerie, working tirelessly on behalf of his proprietor, Frank Packer. Fitchett referred to him scathingly as 'Packer's creature'.

Fitchett, a huge man with a booming voice and an intimidating manner to those who did not know him, was close to McEwen, but remained a reporter of the old school – first and foremost a news man who distrusted the increasing tendency to include comment in political reportage. In private he was less restrained: his clashes with various politicians, up to and including Menzies, were spoken of in awed tones by newcomers. And plenty of newcomers there were. In the post-Menzies years a group of younger, university-educated journalists had arrived, impatient with what they saw as the restrictions of the past and anxious to broaden political coverage beyond straight reportage.

Many were already heads of bureau, among them Max Walsh at the *Financial Review*, Allan Barnes at the Melbourne *Age*, my own boss David Solomon and the most recent arrival, Laurie Oakes at the Melbourne *Sun-Pictorial*. Other formidable figures included Eric Walsh at the Sydney *Daily Mirror*, who moonlighted for *Nation* magazine, his opposite number at the Sydney *Sun*, Neil O'Reilly, and the *Canberra Times* John Bennetts, who was suspected of being the ASIO man in the gallery. These were the OPCs, the main men; they preferred to socialise with each other, although of course they were in constant touch with the other members of their individual offices. These were clearly regarded as the junior division; some were more junior than others, but all were at a lower rung on the hierarchy. The radio and television contingent included some good journalists, but they were seen as second class citizens by the print people. They tended to form a pack by themselves.

I found these class distinctions a bit hard to cop; in Sydney, and particularly at *The Australian*, things had been a lot less structured. I looked for something that would break down the barriers to some extent and mix the groups in a more egalitarian manner. The obvious answer was sport, the great leveller. Hence the press gallery cricket club. A mad politician named Douglas Darby had once had a vision of 'civilising' the Chinese by teaching the entire nation to play cricket. My ambition was more modest: to democratise the press gallery. I took the idea to David, and he was enthusiastic; he was, after all, a much better off spinner than I was a leg spinner. We decided to approach Max Walsh to be captain; he wasn't much of a cricketer, but he regarded himself as the elite head of an elite publication, and would take such an invitation seriously. We also brought on board, at first in an honorary capacity, a real cricketer: Jack Fingleton, the great opening batsman from the Bodyline series. Fingo, as he was universally known, was the stringer for the *Argus* group of papers in South Africa; he was at first somewhat sceptical and mildly amused by the whole idea, but he quickly joined in the spirit of the thing and even played a few games. Then in his sixties he retained a sweet sense of timing and bowled a well-flighted off break.

We made him honorary captain for the first of what became an annual match against a politicians' XI, for which Gorton himself played; the Prime Minister's bowling was as erratic as the rest of his behaviour, but I regret to say he had me caught on the fine leg boundary as I tried to hit a long hop out of the ground. He would probably rather have had Eric Walsh, who was being particularly nasty about him in *Nation*; Gorton was later to complain pointedly about the little white frog-bellied creatures who spread their libels under cover of anonymity. Still, I made a fair substitute victim. In the early days Gorton had referred to me as the Pard, as in Shakespeare's warrior in the seven ages of man: 'Full of strange oaths and bearded like the pard'. Now, as a result of my writings both in *The Australian* and *Oz*, I had become Mungo MacCalumny. What was to become a strange kind of love-hate relationship was starting to blossom.

Chapter Sixteen

EVEN IF THERE'S NO ONE YOU WANT TO VOTE FOR, YOU CAN STILL ENJOY PUTTING SOMEONE LAST

Many years later Bob Hawke's Foreign Minister Gareth Evans was to say of his *bête noire*, the Liberal Bronwyn Bishop: 'Why do so many people take an instant dislike to Mrs Bishop? Because it saves time.' The same gag could never have been applied to John Gorton. He might have been eccentric, difficult, infuriating, at times just plain silly, but he was never hateful. Even the most fanatical Labor supporters agreed on this. Jolly John was a bit of a clown, and Whitlam would beat him like an egg, but he wasn't a bad bloke.

It is said that in politics there are no friends, only temporary allies, and by and large this is true. But it must be said that Gorton's allies, while some did in fact prove to be temporary, comprised the best and brightest of the new generation of Liberals, while those of his less-than-loyal deputy, McMahon, were among the worst. Not only were they the kind of conspiratorial conservatives who would probably have been more at home in the DLP than the Liberal Party – they were spoilers to man – but they were horribly sanctimonious in their undermining of their leader. Coming from St John this was tiresome but acceptable; St John himself was, as he kept telling us, above suspicion. But some of the others were blatant hypocrites. The fact that Gorton was openly enjoying the kind of lifestyle they practised in guilty secrecy made it easy to discount much of their criticism.

Moreover, Gorton's independence was a refreshing change in a party that had a tradition of kowtowing to the Establishment, most notably the Packer press. One McMahon supporter, Les Irwin, used to go directly from the coalition party meeting to the office of the *Daily Telegraph*, where he would dictate the details of the supposedly secret gathering from the copious notes he had made. Such was the fear of Packer (and of his hatchet man in Canberra, Alan Reid) that no one was prepared to take Irwin on; indeed McMahon, whom Packer described with contempt as 'Our man in Canberra', actually proposed him for a knighthood, a proposal which was voided by the 1972 change of government. Whitlam described it as the most extraordinary suggestion since the investiture of Sir Toby Belch.

By contrast, Gorton's brigade was the nearest thing the somewhat jaded Libs could provide to a breath of fresh air; it included Tom Hughes, Andrew Peacock and Don Chipp. As Gorton supporters they were naturally worried about the growing feeling that he was losing touch, not only with the electorate, but with the party; they sent him a friendly signal by forming a dinner group called the Mushroom Club, the name signifying that they were kept in the dark and fed on bullshit. Gorton took the hint and insisted on joining; he was given the honorary title Chief Spore.

I particularly liked Chipp, who, like me, had a passionate dislike of Establishment snobbery; but while mine came from the inside, his was a result of rejection, real or imagined, from the outer. He would complain that he had never made the university football teams because he had not attended a private school, and that he was shunned by the rich and powerful within his own party. He was particularly bitter about McMahon; as a professional runner Chipp had been good enough to contest the Stawell Gift, but he claimed to have been robbed of victory in a charity race at the Gold Coast by the bias of McMahon, who was the judge. I tried to convince him that it was more probably myopia than malice, but the chip, as it were, remained on his shoulder.

Ideologically we had our differences; he was a convinced free-enterpriser, while I was a somewhat wishy-washy socialist. But I admired his liberal approach to censorship and his open-mindedness in most other areas, although I could never convince him of the need to review the drug laws. I also enjoyed our meetings on the cricket field where he was, predictably, a ferocious competitor. Fortunately his sledging was usually confined to the failings of his own team rather than the manifest incompetence of ours. Over the years I like to think we became friends; certainly he accepted an invitation to become a godfather to my second daughter. Gail's other godfather was Gough Whitlam; when he learned that my own godfather had been the high Tory editor of the *Sydney Morning Herald*, Guy Harriott, Whitlam drew himself up to his full height and thundered: 'I will be the godfather of the next MacCallum.' Considering that we were still fairly recent acquaintances, I regarded this as an impressive vote of confidence. Or something; with Whitlam it was often hard to tell.

Oddly enough I had never even seen him in the flesh before moving to Canberra; for some reason our paths had never crossed. As I have mentioned before, I was somewhat wary of his commitment to the anti-war cause, which for me remained absolutely paramount. I liked what I knew of his domestic policies, especially the idea of a free and compulsory health system. But these were secondary; if he was not absolutely committed to getting out of Vietnam he was still part of the problem. After he became leader of the party I gave him the benefit of the doubt; there was, after all, no alternative. Only Whitlam could win an election for the ALP, and only a Labor government was pledged to oppose the war. But until I met Whitlam face to face, I was not sure he could be trusted.

Five minutes changed that. I asked to interview him about his problems with the left; he gave me ten minutes, which turned into over an hour. He clearly regarded me as someone worth cultivating; I emerged a fervent disciple. Many people have found Whitlam to be insufferably arrogant and intolerant, and personally too prickly to make a comfortable companion. From the start I found him rather shy, pleasantly self-deprecating and hugely eager to communicate on every level. The fact that I had a broad education and could even recognise some of his Latin tags undoubtedly helped, but I always found him a thoroughly decent human being – larger than life, certainly, but not in any sense intimidating. Without quite realising it at the time, I elected him as the third of my big brother figures. From that day the imperative was not the long-range aim of ending the war in Vietnam; it was the more immediate goal of getting Whitlam up as prime minister. Everything else would then follow.

This, of course, meant getting rid of Gorton. Theoretically I had embarked on this course long ago; I had been a Labor supporter (or at least against the conservatives) since gaining political consciousness. But now I found many things to admire about him: he may have been on the conservative side, but in the context of the coalition in 1969 he was definitely at the progressive end of it. This probably made him, in the words of an American leftie, no better than a guy who stumbles forward every time someone shoves him; but looking at the alternative – McMahon – Gorton had a bit going for him. I had long ago abandoned my harsh judgment of him as the world's worst prime minister.

I liked the way he stood up to the premiers, and particularly his attempts to wrest control of the Great Barrier Reef from the rapacious Queensland government. I applauded his tougher approach to foreign investment, and his efforts to involve the federal government more directly in the development of remote Australia. So, of course, did the Labor Party; it was precisely this interventionist approach, the essence of what became summarised as 'Gortonism' (meaning centralism, which was dangerously close to socialism) which was getting him into so much trouble with his own party.

I was also grateful to Gorton for his fairness; I was attacking him openly in *The Australian* and anonymously in *Oz*, but he never to my knowledge complained about me to Murdoch or tried to freeze me out of the government information process. On the contrary, he seemed to enjoy our occasional encounters. In retrospect I think this was because although I satirised him mercilessly and was ruthless in retailing whatever scurrilous rumours I could pick up, I never questioned his integrity. The only time he ever sued a journalist was when Max Walsh accused him of being disloyal to his ministers. The fact that I presented him on a weekly basis as an incoherent, lecherous, drunken buffoon genuinely did not seem to worry him; he accepted it as part of the game.

And even he would have had to admit that he made an easy target. After a hard night at the office he sometimes did not make it back to the Lodge; the early morning cleaners would discover the Prime Minister parked unconscious on a couch in the lobbies. Further, Eric Walsh had a contact in the firm which cleaned the Lodge itself, who regularly passed on terrible stories of the state of the master bedroom. Gossip from the diplomatic circuit was also useful: I was able to recount the tale of how at one reception Gorton bailed up the wife of the Ghanaian ambassador and informed her that he had always had a hankering to carve himself off a slice of black tart. These stories and others had, of course, to appear in *Oz*, as did the splendid headline: 'Official: Gorton is a bastard', which we ran when an enterprising biographer revealed that the Prime Minister was what was euphemistically described as 'a love child'. By now it was an open secret that I was the *Oz* correspondent; in the hothouse atmosphere of the press gallery it would have been impossible to hide it. I am pleased to say that my colleagues, with commendable loyalty, never dobbed me in to anyone at head office. But some politicians, including Gorton, certainly also knew, which gave me a few worried nights. I knew my days at *The Australian* were coming to an end: Deamer informed me that Murdoch had taken to stamping around the Sydney office shouting that he had not started the paper as a refuge for soft, bearded lefties with suede shoes. I could hardly deny the description. But I was not ready to jump ship yet, and if I were to be thrown over the side there was no obvious life raft.

Nonetheless I persevered in *The Australian*, especially in sending up Gorton's speech patterns. This was not easy: there were many times when they defied parody. What, for instance, was the satirist to do with this summary of the government's alternative health scheme? 'On the other hand the AMA agrees with us, or, I believe, will agree with us, that it is its policy, and it will be its policy, to inform patients who ask what the common fee is and what our own fee is so that a patient will know whether he is going to be operated on, if that's what it is, on the basis of the common fee or not.' Or with the definition of an operational air base as one where 'planes can fly in, or planes can fly out, or they can stay there all the time'? Better, perhaps to do what Whitlam and his speech writer Graham Freudenberg did and simply quote verbatim. Certainly the audiences loved it, as the 1969 election campaign was to show.

Gorton would have liked to have gone to the polls earlier and probably would have done better if the chance had been there; but circumstances largely beyond his control had made him hold off. The DLP, which he detested but could not do without, had prevented an election at the end of 1968. Now, twelve months later, both the standing of his government and his own position had deteriorated sharply. The satirists and the cartoonists, led by the incomparable Bruce Petty, had done their damnedest; Gorton was in real danger of being seen as a clown in charge of a party of squabbling incompetents. Moreover, the ALP had gone a long way towards cleaning up its act; the recalcitrants of the Victorian left remained in the category of unfinished business, but the party was in a fair state to present itself as an alternative government and Whitlam had certainly shown the credentials to be considered an alternative prime minister – and a better one than the incumbent. At the start of the campaign the polls still gave the government a comfortable lead, but the next three weeks showed just how tenuous the advantage really was.

Solomon decided that the way to cover the campaign was week by week; for the first week he would travel with Gorton and I with Whitlam, for the second week we would swap around, and for the third, including election night itself, we would swap back. This would give the readers different perspectives from time to time and perhaps more importantly would stop either of us from getting too one-eyed, a real danger as we were both Labor supporters – although David was far more discreet about his politics than I was. It suited me fine; after Labor's official opening (which Solomon covered) I hitched myself to the Whitlam bandwagon and did some barnstorming around the suburban town halls of Sydney and Melbourne.

It quickly became obvious that this was going to be a real campaign; the voters were turning out in large numbers and a solid core seemed genuinely uncommitted; they wanted to hear what Whitlam had to say. And what he had to say about free health care and free university education struck a chord. While Gorton continued to rely on the conservative stand-bys of foreign policy and defence, the punters on the ground seemed far more concerned about domestic issues. Gorton, who spent much of his first week campaigning on television, missed this feedback; Whitlam grabbed it and thrived on it. He also had some very good groundwork to rely on. In the weeks before the campaign proper he had done an extensive tour around the marginal electorates in the back-blocks to pick up whatever support Labor could garner in the bush. There was an element of cynicism about it; his staffers would take a quick look out of the windows of the plane as it landed at each centre. If they saw a river, Whitlam would promise to build a dam; if they didn't he would promise to build a College of Advanced Education. But although Whitlam's record in regional by-elections in Dawson, Capricornia and Bendigo was a good one, no one really expected much return from these trips; in those days the Country Party still held their rural community in a tight grip and in the last budget McEwen and his colleagues had been into the pork barrel even more deeply than usual. The real battle would be in the suburbs, and that was where Whitlam was to spend the last vital days.

But Gorton, as I saw when I switched planes, was much more laid-back. He was still treating the whole thing as a bit of a junket. From time to time he would make a desultory attempt to explain his hastily cobbled-together health scheme to increasingly bewildered journalists; the media eventually christened it 'The $5 heart transplant plan' and left it at that. But much of the week was spent visiting mates in the outback, some of whom were in plainly unwinnable seats. I accompanied him to the opening of the annual show at Yallunda Flat, a hamlet at the tip of the Eyre Peninsula on the outskirts of the sprawling South Australian electorate of Grey. It was a pleasant enough way to spend the day, but it seemed that the time could have been used better. Alan Reid, who spent most of the day asleep under a tree, commented sagely that Gorton had performed very well. I, who had actually watched him in action among the pigs, goats and somewhat sullen constituents, did not believe he had won a single vote. Still, he probably hadn't lost any either, and if the polls were right that was going to be enough; even a moderate swing to Labor would only dent the record majority he had inherited.

Back in Adelaide we were greeted by Andrew Jones, the youngest member of parliament and a man of some notoriety. Jones had been unexpectedly elected to the normally safe Labor seat of Adelaide in the landslide of 1966, and had distinguished himself by making a speech in which he complained that many members of parliament were half drunk half the time. If anything this was an understatement, but in an act of monumental hypocrisy the party bosses got together and forced him to make a grovelling apology. As a result Jones had apparently decided that if he couldn't beat them he might as well join them; he spent most of the rest of his term very drunk much of the time. He was approaching that state in the bar of the hotel where we were staying; some Labor-leaning journalists including myself encouraged him to do a thorough job on himself. Later that night he was arrested for drunk driving. A sympathetic magistrate agreed to suppress his name, but the beak's writ ran only to the South Australian border. Next morning the Melbourne *Age* ran the triumphant poster: 'Andrew Jones's name suppressed'. It should be stressed that Jones was not Robinson Crusoe; at Gorton's public meeting that night (itself a rare event) Jim Forbes fell off the stage. When I rejoined the Whitlam camp I told them to expect a big swing in South Australia.

The polls were now showing that the swing was definitely on; some brave souls were openly whispering that there was a chance, just a chance, that Labor could win government this time around instead of simply laying the ground for a victory three years later. The conservative press was openly concerned; the *Age* exhorted the real John Gorton to stand up. And belatedly the old John Gorton, if not the real one, did so. He resumed holding public meetings, and his reappearance brought out the demonstrators. The protests were no longer as massive as they had been earlier in the year; Gorton had given a commitment that Australia would not increase its commitment to Vietnam and in America the tide was starting to turn. The election campaign itself had helped to dampen things down; the more thoughtful left, including the majority of the unions which had given the movement their organised numbers, realised that violence in the streets would do Labor's cause no good and had stayed at home. But that still left enough to make a lot of noise at a televised meeting or two, and Gorton grabbed the opportunity. He baited the hecklers by talking about the need for more, not less, emphasis on defence; they roared back and he talked tough. For the first time in possibly months he looked like a man in control of the situation. It was enough.

Whitlam did a last blitz through the Sydney suburbs, but it was clear that Labor had lost the momentum. I wrote that it had been a closer run thing than most had expected but in the end the result would be pretty much what Labor had been planning for almost three years: a decent sort of swing which would set things up for next time. And so it proved. I spent election night at Whitlam's home in Cabramatta; for one mad moment it looked as if he had got there, but the later results showed he hadn't. Once again Victoria had been the stumbling block. The party was still a celebration; after all, Whitlam had given Gorton a hell of a fright. Still the post-mortems started early. A disappointed staffer turned to me and said, only half jokingly: 'If you'd managed to keep your mad leftie friends under control we might have made it.' I felt this was unjust, but I took it on board for next time. If there was any of the left still around in 1972, I would ask it politely to behave.

Chapter Seventeen

ARE THEY RESTING BETWEEN ELECTIONS OR IS IT JUST POST-POLLING TRISTESSE?

In the meantime Gorton savoured his win. To any other politician the loss of sixteen seats would have been seen as something of a setback, even a near disaster; Gorton chose to regard it as a vindication of his approach. After all, as he pointed out, the vote in his own electorate of Higgins had actually increased; therefore if the overall coalition vote had plummeted, it could not possibly be his fault. Rather than adopt a position of humility himself he took the opportunity to humiliate his remaining rivals.

Hasluck had already gone; tired of waiting to be handed the leadership by those he considered his inferiors, he had somewhat ungraciously accepted Gorton's offer of the governor-generalship, thereby fitting into a tradition that had begun with Menzies and Casey and was to continue with Hawke and Hayden. Fairhall had not contested the last election; tired and disillusioned with the whole business of politics he retired into even deeper obscurity. The only serious contenders still on their feet were Fairbairn and McMahon. Fairbairn was not a real threat; a gentlemanly conservative, he disapproved of Gorton's politics and style and finally refused to serve in another Gorton ministry. His wife Ruth, of whom it was said that if she had been a man she would have been prime minister, persuaded him to stand for the leadership, but he never had more than a handful of votes from those anti-Gorton forces who could not stomach the idea of McMahon. McMahon remained the only real alternative; Gorton was determined to bury him at the crossroads with a wooden stake through his heart.

I saw McMahon in the week before the election; I had flown commercial to Brisbane to catch up with the Whitlam caravan and had a couple of hours to kill before it arrived. Knowing that McMahon was ensconced in the Commonwealth office block I decided to pay him a call; he courted me as much as any other journalist who was perceived to be anti-Gorton and could always be relied on for a spot of malicious gossip. But that day he was not in a scandal-mongering mood; he was as angry as I had ever seen him. 'Look,' he hissed, throwing down the morning's paper, which I had not read. 'Do you think the bastard would dare?' The offending story claimed that 'according to well-placed government sources' Gorton intended to replace McMahon as treasurer with Les Bury. Having planted innumerable such leaks of his own, McMahon was in no doubt about who the well-placed sources were. I replied truthfully that I hadn't heard the story but that it was certainly plausible; however, assuming McMahon was re-elected as deputy, surely tradition demanded that he could choose his own portfolio. McMahon muttered that Gorton had never hesitated to breach tradition in the past. 'But if he does it this time, he'll be sorry,' he snarled. Clearly it was the wrong time to ask him about other aspects of the campaign. I beat a hasty retreat.

But the bastard did dare, and there was no sign that he was in the least sorry. McEwen had withdrawn his veto on McMahon running for the leadership, but against the combined opposition of Fairbairn and McMahon Gorton won easily on the first ballot. He obviously considered himself invulnerable; although McMahon was re-elected as deputy he had to be content with external affairs. Later in the year Gorton agreed to change the name to the more modern-sounding Foreign Affairs; I remarked to Whitlam that all Gorton ever gave McMahon was FA. It became another Whitlam one-liner.

Ominously the previous external affairs minister, Gordon Freeth, had actually lost his seat at the election; with Gorton's approval he had put out a statement playing down fears about the Russian fleet entering the Indian Ocean. This enraged the hardliners, especially the DLP and McEwen, who believed that the whole basis of Australian foreign policy was to slavishly shadow Washington's lead in the Cold War; it was in this context that McEwen admitted to me that this was the real and only purpose of our commitment to Vietnam. Freeth's statement was only commonsense, but Australian politics was not yet ready for it. One of McMahon's first acts in his new job was to put out a statement repudiating Freeth and warning the Russians to stay clear not only of the Indian Ocean but the Pacific as well. It sounded rather as though he was preparing to blockade Vladivostok. McMahon's successor as treasurer, Les Bury, was a loyal Gorton follower, but even had he not been he constituted no threat. A heavy drinker with few close friends he appeared in parliament only when he had to, and even on those occasions seemed to spend most of his time asleep. Because of his unvaryingly lugubrious approach to politics he was known to his colleagues as the Brontosaurus, or as Eeyore.

What Gorton consistently failed to acknowledge was the closeness of his win. Two things saved him: the fact that Victoria did not swing with the rest of the country and the persistence of the DLP. There was little he could do to preserve the former: if the ALP managed to clean up its act, as it quickly moved to do, his problems could become terminal. Thus it was all the more important to keep the DLP on side. McMahon in external affairs was a good start. To drive home the message that there would be no more playing footsy with the Russians he elevated another right-winger to defence: Malcolm Fraser, who had been one of his earliest supporters. The irony is that although the pair did no discernible damage to the Soviet cause, they eventually blew Gorton himself right out of the ministry.

But this was still a long way in the future. In the meantime the Gorton government drifted on seemingly to little purpose. The new health scheme failed to eventuate. Other election promises were similarly forgotten. Apart from a few personal obsessions – the film industry was one, as Phillip Adams noted to his advantage – Gorton seemed mostly interested in trying to neutralise Whitlam, who, after a few false starts, had now comfortably got his measure. Harking back to his success with the demonstrators in the last week of the election campaign he decided on a good old-fashioned appeal to law and order.

The protests were now of two distinctly different kinds. On the one hand were the moderates who simply wanted an end to the war, and especially to conscription; they were not interested in either ideology or history. On the other hand the radicals had swung sharply to the left. Like their American counterparts they had taken to chanting 'Ho, Ho, Ho Chi Minh' rather than the simpler 'No Conscription'. They were also more sophisticated about publicity, targeting government offices and ministers' homes rather than simply taking to the streets. On one memorable occasion a small group invaded the front garden of the Attorney-General, Tom Hughes; the doughty first law officer was filmed driving them off with a child's cricket bat.

Gorton's aim, of course, was to link Whitlam and the ALP with this latter group; to suggest that the Opposition was once again in the grip of the subversive, un-Australian mad left. He was not overly scrupulous in his approach. On one occasion Whitlam came out of parliament to address a group of demonstrators and, unknown to him, someone behind him started waving a Viet Cong flag. Photos taken on the government's behalf managed to suggest that he was actually speaking under the flag. The coalition, with McEwen in the lead, had a field day, accusing Whitlam of downright treachery to his country. I managed to put together a collection of pictures taken by the real media which showed Whitlam's actual distance from the offending banner; by the end of the day the Opposition was out of trouble. But the incident showed that the gloves were well and truly off. Later McEwen, who had announced his intention to retire before the next election, professed to be deeply hurt when Whitlam referred to him as a lame duck minister; he had, he said, been a friend of Whitlam's father. It occurred to many of us that if this was the case he should have hesitated before describing the son as a traitor. In the days that followed, the law and order campaign gathered momentum, with the government hinting at draconian penalties for demonstrators who trespassed on private or government property. But when the bill was finally produced it was pretty feeble stuff; the law'n'order legislation turned out to be more about lawn order – keeping people off the grass. I parodied the whole debate as a soap opera centring on the eternal conflict between the lady with the whip and the long black boots, Laura Norder, and her sworn enemy, the mysterious Anna Key. It was considered to be one of my more successful pieces; the campaign swiftly died away, and the Labor people gave me a slice of the credit.

I was happy to accept it. With Whitlam's party reform process entering its last and most difficult phase, I needed all the contacts I could get. The 1969 election made one thing abundantly clear: if Labor was to win government, things had to change in Victoria. The garden state had delivered only about half the national swing and just one seat to the ALP. The problem was to persuade the party machine to take action. Some progress had already been made; the all-powerful federal executive was a very different beast from the twelve witless men Whitlam had castigated a few years ago. With the aid of the now ex-secretary Cyril Wyndham, Whitlam had secured seats for the parliamentary leaders, and the Northern Territory was also represented: the executive now numbered seventeen. The political balance had also shifted; the grip of the Victorians and their allies from the left was far more tenuous. But things were far too delicate for a head-on approach. Negotiations began.

The key to the operation was the veteran South Australian MP Clyde Cameron, a powerbroker far beyond his own state. Cameron was always a man of the left; a bitter anti-state aider and anti-grouper who liked nothing better than a good feud with the right – notably with the rulers of the Australian Workers' Union. But the prospect of finally realising his dream of becoming Minister for Industrial Relations had softened him up. Whitlam held out the carrot; he could have the job if he would help fix up Victoria. Cameron agonised but eventually agreed on one condition: if there was to be intervention in the left-wing Victorian branch, the same must apply in right-wing New South Wales. The federal president, Tom Burns, and the federal secretary, Mick Young, must be empowered to put the cleaners through both. And so it was agreed. The New South Wales hierarchy was told, and reluctantly accepted its role. The Victorians were not. Supremely confident that they could win this one as they always had in the past, they prepared a list of complaints of their own for the next meeting, including, absurdly, one against Whitlam himself. Those whom the gods seek to destroy they first make mad.

For reasons which at first appeared to be purely sentimental Young, an ex-shearer from the district, had arranged to hold the crucial meeting at Broken Hill. A second reason for his choice became clear when he took the travelling pack of pollies and journos to the town park, in the centre of which was a memorial to, of all unlikely things, the band of the good ship *Titanic*. Young let us note for ourselves that the name of the unfortunate bandmaster was William Hartley, which was also the name of the state secretary of the doomed Victorian branch. Naturally the media could not resist the comparison. It was a neat scene setter for the week which followed. The extant Hartley and his fellow delegate Bill Brown put on a fine show of bravado, drinking with their fellows long into the night at the Socialist National Hotel, a name which demanded some care.

The drinking was truly prodigious; when I went for a leak the man beside me at the urinal turned round and complained: 'It's a real bastard, isn't it?' What was, I wondered. 'Well, a man's missing a round stuck out here,' he shouted, explaining the obvious. Next morning I found that the motel where I was staying did not serve breakfast and repaired to the local milk-bar. The waitress asked if I wanted anything to drink with my eggs; I ordered tea. A man seated further down the counter yelled: 'And I'll have a schooner.' Certainly, she said, producing a bottle from the ice cream container. To add to the general inebriation the town mayor, Shorty O'Neill, made his official suite, including the permanently stocked mayoral fridge, available to the visitors. He did, however, cancel the town's permanent two-up game for the duration, fearing adverse publicity. Noting our disappointment the local cops came to the rescue and organised a new game especially for us.

There was one major hitch at the meeting itself; when the motion for intervention in the two states was moved and the New South Wales delegates agreed, the Victorians realised they had been ambushed. Brown turned on an old style thundering denunciation of the duplicity of his colleagues and the collapse of traditional loyalties, and Cameron, momentarily abashed, watered down his demands for direct intervention; he would be satisfied with a general inquiry into the affairs of the branch. Typically Australian, Brown couldn't wait to tell his mates and made a call to Melbourne in which he boasted of how he had called the silly old bugger's bluff. Unfortunately he left the door of his room open; Cameron heard every word. From that day forward he dropped the idea of intervention altogether. The word now was execution. There were plenty of happy assistants; a group of moderate Labor lawyers had spent years preparing dossiers against the undreamt-of day when they would have the numbers. Close to half a ton of documentation about the branch's abysmal record of ignoring the federal policy, especially on state aid, and of its domination by an outside body known as the Trade Union Defence Committee was produced for scrutiny. And although the numbers on the executive were now locked in at ten votes to seven in favour of knocking over Victoria, it was regarded as essential (especially by one delegate, Kim Beazley Sr, whose unswerving morality had led to comparisons with Edward St John) that everything be done in a fashion so proper that no accusations of haste or bias could ever be levelled at the party.

So there we were back in Melbourne, stuck in the St Kilda Travelodge (enticingly opposite the Golden Hands Massage Parlour) writing the same story day after day: Labor's federal executive was poised last night to declare that its Victorian branch no longer exists … With a final dotting of i's and crossing of t's it eventually did so; Young marched across the road and ordered a bucket of beer and a well-wisher told Whitlam he could get Margaret to start redecorating the Lodge. The left snarled that he'd have to live with his conscience; from his unusually broad grin it appeared that would be no trouble at all. In a sense it was a historic moment; Whitlam nearly made it more so by almost stepping under a tram. But the biggest sense was one of relief. The first of the two big blocks identified in 1969 was out of the way; now it only remained to neutralise the influence of the DLP.

At the end of 1970 this looked as if it might be a difficult task. Because of Australia's peculiar electoral system an election for half the Senate had to take place at the end of the year. The result was not going to change anything and for serious politicians it was a bloody waste of time, a silly sideshow that distracted everyone's attention from the main event. However, the constitutional rituals had to be observed and the party leaders flogged their various ways around the country talking to small and bored audiences and trying to pretend it all mattered. For the travelling press it was just an excuse for a holiday; there was even more drinking done than is usual on such junkets.

Nor was the Prime Minister immune. On one memorable occasion he left Canberra by VIP aircraft to address a dinner meeting in Melbourne. It had been a long hard day in parliament, and naturally he used the trip to unwind with a few drinks. Arriving at the Sheraton he found himself among friends, so a few pre-dinner drinks were in order; then there were the wines and a glass or two of port, and of course it would have been impolite to refuse a palate-cleanser or several later. Eventually they wheeled him back to Tullamarine and poured him onto the plane which was to take him back to Canberra. Sensibly he decided to take a refreshing nap, but when he was woken by the thrumming of the engines some time later he felt decidedly queasy; so much so that he leaned into the aisle and threw up. A stewardess came to clear up the debris, and Jolly John thought he had better make the best of it. 'Well,' he said, switching on all his charm, 'I suppose you're surprised that an old RAAF man like me still gets airsick occasionally?' To which the stewardess replied: 'Well yes, sir, I am actually, because the plane hasn't taken off yet.' She dined out on it for weeks.

Whitlam's campaign produced similarly amazing scenes. I was on his plane when bad weather diverted it from Melbourne to Hobart. Like many of my colleagues I had made various sybaritic arrangements for the evening and complained long and loud. Whitlam came down the back to cheer us up. 'Never mind,' he said encouragingly, 'there's one thing about Tasmania. With all that inbreeding, there's always the chance of picking up a bit of double-headed fellatio.' Presumably he, too, missed out; ambushed next morning by an enterprising local reporter who wanted to know what a Labor government would do for Tasmania, the Leader of Her Majesty's Opposition replied tersely: 'Well, what can anyone do for Tasmania? I mean, the whole place is fucked.' Fortunately the reporter did not have a tape running at the time. Both incidents would have made marvellous stories for *Oz*, but alas, *Oz* was defunct. The magazine had long since been scaled down to a subscriber newsletter, but even this finally withered away for lack of support.

The Libs were no doubt grateful; but they may also have known how *Oz* and its supporters felt. The results of the half Senate election, when they finally emerged, were just awful. As often happens in Senate elections voting for both major parties was down, but it was down much further for the coalition than for Labor; the primary vote had sunk below 40 per cent. It proved beyond doubt the hollowness of Gorton's triumphalism; he could never win a second election against Whitlam and probably shouldn't have won a first one. From that time Gorton was effectively political dead meat; the Libs can put up with a lot from their leaders, but losing elections is not tolerated. The sentimentality that gives Labor leaders a second or even third chance is not part of the conservative make-up. The prospect of Gorton's replacement was not necessarily good news for Labor. But worse was the DLP vote, which was above 11 per cent nationally and for the first time elected a senator in the previously quarantined state of New South Wales. Yet again, Margaret Whitlam put the interior decorators on hold.

Chapter Eighteen

IF A DOG CAN BECOME A FERRET WHY CAN'T A RAT BECOME A PRIME MINISTER?

My own career had also moved into something of a hold-ing pattern. David Solomon had now moved to the *Canberra Times* to give himself more time at the university, where he was planning to complete a degree; since this process had been going on sporadically since 1954 his friends were not exactly dusting off their mortar boards. His replacement was Ken Randall, who spent much of his time amassing honorary positions within the journalists union and the press gallery. Deamer told me later that he had seriously considered pro-moting me to the senior position but had decided reluctantly that Murdoch would never have let him get away with it. I can honestly say that I never considered myself a chance; I was still too new to Canberra and too much of a maverick to fit into the illustrious title of Our Political Correspondent.

In fact I was rapidly becoming too much of a maverick for

The Australian in any capacity. Murdoch was moving decisively to the right; he had long since abandoned his student flirtations with socialism and was now deserting the classical liberalism of the Brass era as well. Some observers thought he was attempting to please his mother, Dame Elisabeth, a doyenne of Melbourne society who had exhibited a regal ability to close her mind to her son's vulgarities such as the Melbourne *Truth* and the Sydney *Daily Mirror*; she was reported to be rather more concerned about *The Australian* cocking its snoot at the verities of the golden age of Menzies. Others believed more cynically that Rupert was just trying to slime his way into the Establishment temples which had never really treated him as one of their own. But for whatever reason, his tolerance level for the excesses of his staff was becoming lower by the day. Deamer warned me that he himself was now having frequent clashes with the boss, and that sooner or later there was going to be a showdown; and of course if he went, I would be a nanosecond behind. He suggested that I should start looking for a parachute.

At first glance the prospects were grim. The other dailies all had their own staffs in the press gallery and their own methods of operation. Even if one were to be charitable enough to pick me up it was unlikely that I would have the same kind of beat, let alone the same freedom, that I had enjoyed in *The Australian*. I could no doubt find plenty of work back in Sydney, but I had been there and done that, and besides, I was now thoroughly hooked on politics. Anything else would be a severe anti-climax. In hindsight I think I may have been unduly pessimistic; while *The Australian* was still well ahead of the pack in its innovative approach to political coverage at the time, the rest were pushing to catch up and there may have been a slot for me in papers like the *Age* or *The Financial Review* – in the years to come they both saw my liking for pushing the barriers as a potential asset. But at the time I believed my only chance was to find something outside the circle.

As usual I was lucky; something turned up just when I needed it. The idiosyncratic millionaire Gordon Barton was once again broadening his horizons. Barton was a peculiarity in Australia, a highly successful businessman who had retained his youthful idealism. As a broke university student he had bought a half share in a truck as a way of financing himself through his course; his natural entrepreneurship quickly turned this into a medium sized transport empire. He was, of course, a private enterprise man and his natural instincts were towards the Liberal Party. But he became totally disillusioned with the Vietnam adventure and in 1966 formed the Liberal Reform Movement, a breakaway group to oppose the war. This had grown into the Australian Reform Movement, and later became the Australia Party. For a few dizzy moments it appeared that it could become a sort of DLP of the left, directing its preferences to Labor and cancelling out the effects of the DLP itself. This never happened; it never had the purpose or discipline of its rival and only became a marginal nuisance to the conservatives. Critics pointed out that you couldn't really form a political party without a socio-economic base; Barton famously retorted 'I'll be its socio-economic base.' He refused to be convinced that politics, even in Australia, had to be something more than a rich man's hobby.

The media, however, were something else. Barton bought himself an offset press in Melbourne and opened a weekend paper called *The Sunday Observer*. It was a worthy, if rather dull, publication, and the heavies at the *Age* and the *Herald and Weekly Times* thought it would be easy to knock off, particularly as they owned the newsagencies. Besides, Melbourne had never had a Sunday paper; why should it start now? But in fact Melbourne rather liked the idea and *The Observer* clung to its corner of the market for long enough to persuade the big boys that perhaps it would be worth running a real Sunday paper; so they did and *The Observer* eventually folded. But in the meantime Barton's press was idle for most of the time it wasn't printing *The Observer*, and he looked for something else for it to do.

The result was *The Sunday Review*, a weekly which appeared in October of 1970 under the editorship of Michael Cannon. Its model appeared be the London *Spectator*; it was heavily weighted towards the arts and its social commentary was of the generalised, academic kind. Topicality was scarce; it was clearly a magazine rather than a newspaper. But it usually ran a political column somewhere and was looking for a Canberra correspondent, at least on a part-time basis. Randall picked up the job, but was not always available to do it. On his off weeks he passed it over to me. Cannon liked my style which in those days was chatty but reasonably restrained; I took the role of the informed insider prepared to offer the reader a few stories to enliven a staid Toorak dinner party. It was apparently what was required. A few weeks later Cannon rang and offered me a permanent job. I said I'd think about it and rang Deamer. He urged me to jump.

True, it was a risk; *The Review* was bound to lose money, at least for a while, and no one knew how long Barton was prepared to prop it up. I was also bound to lose money; although my salary would nominally be the same, there would not be extras like my column, there would not be expenses and there would not be any perks such as travel. On the other hand it was an opportunity to let myself go; at the very worst I should have a few weeks of uninhibited fun. And besides, what was the alternative? Deamer felt the final crunch with Murdoch was now very near. In fact it turned out to be still some months away; things came to a head not over Vietnam but over the South African rugby tour. Nonetheless I decided not to wait. I rang Cannon back and accepted the job; my first report appeared the following week.

Then, for reasons which have never been clear to me, Cannon resigned. Somewhat to my alarm, his replacement was announced as Richard Walsh. Was *Oz* to be reborn as a tabloid? While I had always got on with Richard, we had never been all that close; I was never quite sure what his real commitments were. He could be cheeky, irreverent, even outrageous but he was certainly no revolutionary. In those days his politics were conventionally left but not passionately so; he was certainly not interested in changing the world. I still was, and I wondered how we would fit together.

As it turned out there was no need to worry. Walsh let me have my head, and concentrated on rejigging the paper into the larrikin gadfly it became. Whatever misgivings I had were swept away; if nothing else, Walsh was a superb organiser. He quickly cemented a solid core of established writers of hugely varying styles and opinions; what we had in common was a healthy scepticism about conventional wisdom and a burning desire to push back the barriers. Most if not all of us were already reasonably well known in our fields; it is a myth that *The Review* produced a new generation of writers. But it certainly offered us a freedom which, at that stage, didn't exist in any other commercial publication. Where *The Review* did break new ground was with its cartoonists; apart from the wonderful Leunig the paper was the proving ground for Patrick Cook, Peter Nicholson, Ross Bateup, Victoria Roberts and a great many others. For this alone Walsh deserves a place in publishing history.

He also showed an enormous flair for making the best of what were always limited resources. For all of its short life *The Review* depended largely on casuals and freelancers; while many of these were professionals working for other publications who moonlighted for their own reasons (and, like most media leaks, many of these had more to do with revenge than with the public's right to know) a lot were enthusiastic amateurs attempting, usually without success, to imitate the paper's freewheeling style; a common failing was that they said a lot about the writer but very little of interest to the public at large. Walsh winnowed them brilliantly; every edition of the paper produced something new and unexpected.

Another innovation was frank and often embarrassing discussion about the role of the media, something that no other publication had been able to attempt. Unlike our rivals, we had no vested interests, no interlinked connections and no axes to grind. Under the entirely fictitious byline, C M Evans, *The Review* collated insider gossip about the way the industry ran from around the country. The paper became a must-read in journalist circles, in political circles and to some dedicated outsiders. I have frequently been told that it, and the radio broadcasts I did on 2JJ (later JJJ) in Sydney, brought a new generation into politics. I'm flattered, of course, because this is how I had dreamt of my role in Canberra. But in fact the paper's overall effect was marginal; we became The Ferret, an image Walsh's marketing genius drew from a Leunig drawing which was actually meant to be a dog. We were a cult beast lurking around the fringes of the media industry. If we had any lasting effect, it was to chivvy our larger cousins into action.

But that was in the future. At the start of 1971 the imperative was simply to get the show on the road. At a safe distance from the chaotic head office in Melbourne, I collected my thoughts about the Gorton government and let fly. It was a good year to do it. The forces that controlled the Liberal Party had finally embraced the Labor slogan of 1969, which was 'Gorton's Got to Go'. (Bruce Petty had turned this into a badge with a cartoon of the Prime Minister as a firework and the caption 'light blue touch paper and retire quickly'.) The Melbourne Club, the Liberal premiers, the business Establishment and Sir Frank Packer agreed that the time had come. McEwen was ready to accept McMahon. All that was needed was a crisis. Gorton's enemies set out to manufacture one.

Ironically enough when it came the instigator was Malcolm Fraser, who had been one of the team responsible for installing Gorton in the first place. Gorton had treated him well, moving him up through the ranks to his present portfolio in defence; but Fraser, a man of limitless ambition, was not satisfied. He was also a proud man; he felt that the Prime Minister was paying him and his views insufficient respect. And above all he was a man in love with power. He saw the forces massing against Gorton and determined to get with the strength.

The crunch, when it came, emerged from a row within the Defence Department itself. The details were complicated, involving the civil aid program in Vietnam, the Joint Intelligence Office and even an alleged call-out of the army in Papua

New Guinea; but as usual the real motivation was a power struggle, this time between the civilians and the military within the department. Fraser was on the side of the civilians, Gorton and his army minister Andrew Peacock backed the military. Fraser briefed journalists on his side of the row; stories appeared, especially in the Packer press, confirming the rift. Gorton ordered Fraser to deny them; he did so. But in the meantime Alan Ramsey in *The Australian* published a story implying that the army chief of staff, General Thomas Daly, had accused Fraser of gross disloyalty to the forces and Gorton had backed him. At the urging of the Packer press Fraser resigned from the ministry and in turn accused Gorton of gross disloyalty for not killing Ramsey's story when he had the opportunity. It should be noted that the truth or otherwise of the whole incident had long ceased to be an issue: what mattered was the politics.

Next day in parliament Fraser, from the backbenches, made a statement and Gorton replied, saying that he had refused to confirm Ramsey's story and that Ramsey had accepted this. From the press gallery Ramsey yelled: 'You liar.' Arthur Calwell, never an obsessive defender of the freedom of the press, screamed back: 'Jail the mongrel.' Before he could be dragged to the bar of the House Ramsey sent an apology and a withdrawal – well, sort of. But now things were clearly out of control. Whitlam gave notice that next day he would move a motion of no confidence in the government. Gorton's enemies were now faced with a stark choice. Either they could vote to support a prime minister they now considered an irretrievable disaster or they could vote against him and bring down the government, precipitating an election in circumstances where they were almost bound to lose it. The corridors of the House were full of Liberals shaking with rage and fear; they were, as Whitlam was to remark in another context, caught in a classic conflict of disloyalties.

But fortunately there was time for a circuit breaker. A party meeting was called for next morning at which Gorton could be disposed of once and for all. It says much for the air of unreality that hung over the Gorton years that there was any doubt at all about the matter. Before the meeting the Gorton forces were still confident – so much so in fact that they didn't even bother to summon one of their number, Duke Bonnett, from Townsville where he was recovering from a minor operation. Part of the reason was undoubtedly a fairly general dislike of Fraser, an aloof pseudo-aristocrat whose idea of a joke consisted of filling his colleagues' pockets with pickled onions from the members bar. And, of course, the alternative to Gorton was stunningly unattractive in his own right. McMahon remained the only real possibility, although Fairbairn and Snedden both let it be known that they would throw their hats in the ring if it came to a vote. There was also a reluctance to fall for what a number of Liberals believed was a Packer plot; while they were used to being pushed around by the big end of town, this time it seemed a bit too blatant altogether. So in spite of the fact that the logic of the situation demanded a swift, clean kill – something the Libs would traditionally accomplish with no qualms whatsoever – there were few in the crowd that assembled in King's Hall next morning prepared to put large sums of money on the result.

And, of course, what should have been a landslide turned into a cliffhanger. In spite of the rhetoric of the McMahon supporters – 'If a man has a cancer, at least if he cuts it out he gives himself a chance,' cried Harry Turner, who had occupied the safest seat in the country for untold years without leaving the slightest trace upon the body politic – the Libs prevaricated. And the final irony is that if Gorton had played it to win he would have won, even while he was a number short. He allowed his supporters to move a vote of confidence in him: he should have insisted that his opponents show their hand by moving for a spill. Then he agreed to a secret ballot; he should have forced his enemies to declare themselves publicly. And even then the vote was tied; he could have toughed it out and forced his opponents to choose whether to be loyal to their leader or bring down the government on the floor of the house. Instead he chose to end the whole schemozzle by using his casting vote against himself. From Gorton's point of view the meeting was a long drawn-out political suicide. It is hard not to feel that he was sick of the whole bloody business.

But he wasn't too worn out to miss out on one final piece of mischief. To the astonishment of the crowds assembled outside Gorton stood for deputy and in an incredible rush of idiotic sentimentality his colleagues voted him in with a very handsome majority. There is no record of McMahon's immediate reaction, which is probably just as well. What is known is that the ALP president, Tom Burns, and secretary, Mick Young, caught between disbelief and hilarity, were prepared to shout the non-members bar for as long as it stayed open. Certainly it took the gloss of McMahon's long overdue (in his mind at least) accession to power.

My first reaction to the result was that it was still, on the whole, a plus for the Libs; after all, the Labor whip, Gil Duthie, had said publicly just the other day that Labor regarded Gorton as its greatest electoral asset. With McMahon there the Opposition would have to stop coasting; at least he would make

Whitlam work for victory. I mentioned this view to an old and wise Labor apparatchik, who simply looked at me quizzically. He was totally unruffled, and of course he turned out to be right. But for the moment, McMahon was in the ascendant. His look of completely unfeigned delight as he emerged from the party room made it hard to begrudge him at least a moment of triumph after all those years of struggle, however unedifying they had been for those around him. I wrote a long and thoughtful piece for *The Review*, but Leunig summed it up best. He pictured a tiny McMahon safely inside the prime minister's office, his back against the door, screaming: 'Yahoooooooooo!' The caption was: 'The Mouse That Roared'.

Chapter Nineteen

HE PROMISED TO FIGHT TO THE LAST MAN – UNFORTUNATELY HE WAS THE LAST MAN

But right from the beginning the problem for McMahon was that he was seen less as a mouse than as a rat. His colleagues had elected him not as a saviour but as a last hope, and they never made much secret of the fact that they thought it was a pretty slim one. On the whole they neither liked nor trusted him, a sentiment which turned out to be mutual.

As prime minister McMahon was even more of a loner than he had been in the past. Like Boxer, the horse in George Orwell's *Animal Farm*, he believed that the secret of success lay in constantly increasing his personal workload; forests were felled to provide the endless stream of paper that crossed his desk, a stream which apparently served no purpose whatsoever. Not only was it impossible for one man to keep track of all the riffling and shuffling which went on; such was the pressure of work that he began fantasising about having done even more.

On several embarrassing occasions he was to claim to have processed documents he had never seen, or written letters that existed only in his imagination.

McMahon boasted frequently of his phenomenal memory, but like most things about him, this was fraud. As treasurer he had gained a reputation in question time for always having the figures at his fingertips; what in fact happened was that he would quote with great authority the first number that came into his head and his staff, listening anxiously to the proceedings in his office, would check what it should really have been and insert the correction in Hansard. But McMahon grew to believe his own publicity; what made him slightly dangerous instead of merely silly was that he genuinely considered he had the talent and ability to run the government as a one-man band. Repeated experiment showed that this was not the case.

But even if he had placed more faith in his ministers it probably wouldn't have helped all that much. In the great tradition of Liberal prime ministers he surrounded himself with his supporters, most of whom were the kind of people you would cross the street to avoid; many of their colleagues in fact did so. One appointment I especially deplored was that of Peter Howson to the aboriginal affairs portfolio, which he held together with the arts and the environment – surely one of the strangest grab-bags ever assembled. Howson was a pukka sort of Englishman with an irritating accent and a marked contempt for his less well bred associates. He was also a permanent member of my Unctuous Bastards XI, a team which was a regular feature of *The Review*. Howson was known as a pain in the arts for his general philistinism and as Peter Howson-Garden for his apparent lack of environmental credentials but his olde worlde, culturally superior approach to the aborigines was particularly distressing: his view appeared to be that they should assimilate into the lower end of white society and it was high time they got on with it. Neville Bonner, the indigenous Queensland Liberal who entered the Senate in 1970 and who was always ready to give his fellow Libs the benefit of the doubt right up to the time they withdrew his preselection, found him insufferably patronising.

The elevation of Howson and others like him of course meant the demise of several Gorton supporters. Tom Hughes and Jim Killen were particularly bitter. On one occasion when McMahon was giving one of his regular homilies to the party room he remarked that he sometimes thought he was his own worst enemy; Killen snarled from the back of the room 'Not while I'm alive.' He used to describe McMahon's appearance as a Volkswagen with both doors open. But while McMahon could shuffle and riffle the pack to neutralise most of his perceived enemies (Bury, for instance, was moved from Treasury to Foreign Affairs and dropped altogether six months later) he couldn't eliminate them completely; to do so would have involved a wholesale massacre not only in the ministry but through the party room. The cabinet room in those months was not a nice place in which to be.

And in the background loomed the king-makers: McEwen and the Country Party and Vince Gair and the DLP. I have said before that I always regarded McEwen's threats to leave the coalition as largely bluff; under almost any circumstances the government seats were more comfortable than the crossbenches, and actual opposition was unthinkable. The same reasoning applied to Gair; he might mutter about switching his party's preferences, but in practice the sole reason for the DLP's existence was to keep Labor out of office. If it failed in that, it would inevitably disappear, as actually happened a few years later. But McMahon seemed transfixed by the formidable pair. And then of course there was his deputy: Gorton. He had demanded the defence portfolio simply in order to get Fraser out of it and McMahon, who in similar circumstances had been denied his beloved Treasury by Gorton, had meekly acquiesced.

At about this time I wrote a song for him, to the tune of the old jazz standard 'Balling the Jack':

> I'm the sort of thing you dream of on a real bad night
> As I knife my former colleagues with both skill and spite
> Some people think I'm really a hermaphrodite
> Because I sneak around and squeak around and scratch
>   and bite
> I look as if I've just dropped in from outer space
> And I tell my dreadful lies as if I'm saying grace
> And every time you hear me speak
> You know why I'm called Billy the Leak.
>
> My chances of survival on my own are slight
> So I kowtow to the morons on the loony right
> And when I get in trouble or I think I might
> I turn around and squirm around and duck the fight
> I usually negotiate from on my knees
> I grovel and I slobber and I oil and grease
> They used to say that piss was weak
> Until they heard of Billy the Leak.

Richard Walsh said that it was too unkind to publish and in any case it wasn't all that funny; he was right, of course, but it captured the mood of the time. When I distributed a few copies around parliament house the Libs loved it.

By now it was becoming obvious that while getting rid of Gorton might have been a necessity, his replacement by McMahon was not much of an improvement, if indeed it was an improvement at all. Gorton and his convoluted speech patterns had become a national joke, but McMahon's choice of words, not to mention his chee-chee accent, were just as funny. He had particular trouble with his r's and l's, which came out as d's. Once his speech writer made the mistake of giving him a sentence which began with the word militarily; it came out as miditiditadiddy.

This was bad enough when it was limited to an Australian audience but it became numbingly awful when taken to the world at large, as happened when McMahon paid the ritual visit to Washington to be given the once-over by President Richard Nixon. McMahon had married late; his tall, blonde wife Sonia was still a bit of a novelty and she occupied a prominent position in Sydney society. She was seen as McMahon's greatest political asset, a compliment that was rapidly losing its value. However, at the grand White House dinner she was to be exploited to the hilt. Wearing a dress with slits up to the armpits, she descended the staircase to a chorus of approval; the president himself said 'ravishing', while others contented themselves with gasps of 'phwoar', or 'hubba hubba hubba'. The band played 'Fascination'; McMahon confessed that, on proposing to Sonia he had sung it to her not just once, but maybe ten times; he knew how to wear her down.

Then came the speeches; McMahon was so overcome by the occasion that he threw away his notes and decided to extemporise. What he actually said was: 'I take as my text a few familiar words that there comes a time in the life of a man in the flood of time that taken at the flood leads on to fortune.' In the room where the Australian and American press were watching the event on closed circuit television an Australian reporter groaned: 'God, I wish I was Italian.'

Fortunately McMahon made no other major appearances on the world stage; he was too busy riffling and shuffling at home. But even in Canberra he still managed to be an embarrassment on foreign policy. The South African rugby side – the Springboks – toured Australia and the protest movement, which had been fairly quiet as it became obvious that the war in Vietnam was being wound down suddenly revived in its full fury. While there may have been shades of opinion over the politics of Vietnam, the question of apartheid was quite literally one of black and white; massive demonstrations took place everywhere the bewildered Springboks appeared. The conservative state premiers, delighted to be presented with a good old law and order issue, let their police forces loose with predictable results.

Once again the country split apart. Australian policy was nominally anti-apartheid; McMahon regularly rose in parliament to wring his hands and say how abhorrent he found the system. But for most of the right South Africa was still a brother country, staunchly anti-communist and with a few trifling internal problems it should be allowed to solve in its own way. And, of course, politics should be kept out of sport. Indeed, McMahon too could have been kept out of it; there were no national security issues involved and controlling the demonstrators was strictly a matter for the states. But incredibly he offered the beleaguered rugger-buggers the use of

RAAF aircraft and crew to transport them between engage-ments. Not only the left found this outrageous; it was a blatant and calculated misuse of the armed forces for domestic politi-cal purposes. Adrian Deamer wrote a swingeing editorial for the front page of *The Australian*; Murdoch objected, and the ensuing row led to his sacking the best editor in the country. In the media world it was considered a tragedy. The general view was that Murdoch had gone mad, a view confirmed by his choice of Deamer's successors. Deamer himself, resilient as ever, supported himself by subbing on *The Financial Review* while doing a law degree. He graduated with great distinction and ended up as Fairfax's in-house defamation lawyer. We remained friends; indeed he launched my first collection, *Mungo's Canberra*. Murdoch later acknowledged that he was the best editor *The Australian* ever had, which made his sack-ing all the more reprehensible. It would have happened sooner or later anyway, but that left me no less furious. It was another score for which McMahon was to be paid back.

Encouraged by what they saw as official endorsement at the highest level of government, the South African sporting authorities now began preparations for a cricket tour. The mere idea was madness; it had been all but impossible to pro-vide security for ninety-minute games of football. To do so for a five-day Test was simply out of the question. And yet McMa-hon dithered and temporised and mumbled about sport and politics not mixing and ultimately refused to take a decision. It was left to Sir Donald Bradman as chairman of the Australian Cricket Board to show some leadership by cancelling the pro-posed tour. The next South African sporting team to visit Australia did so when Nelson Mandela was president.

In effect McMahon had left a foreign policy vacuum; into

it, with considerable audacity, stepped Whitlam. His greatest coup emerged oddly enough from what was traditionally Labor's area of least competence: agriculture. In 1971 the party had just one MP with the slightest expertise on the subject, Rex Patterson from Queensland. For reasons which were not clear at the time China had suspended its regular orders for Australian wheat, causing something of a panic among growers. The government was unsure how to react; the ALP, seeking to steal a quick political march, cabled Peking seeking an invitation for Patterson to go and discuss the impasse. To everyone's surprise the reply was swift and favourable; Patterson was welcome to lead a delegation in July. Whitlam swiftly gazumped Patterson as leader and Young and Burns leapt on the bandwagon, as did a large contingent of Labor-friendly press – not, alas, myself. From being a modest attempt to talk trade the project had turned into a major diplomatic mission run not by the government but by the opposition. The Chinese were obviously treating it seriously; the climax was a discussion between Whitlam and Premier Chou En-lai which was open to the press.

Back in Canberra McMahon argued that Chou had Whitlam on a hook and was playing him like a trout; but when you're hot you're hot and when you're not you're Billy McMahon. Twenty-four hours later it was announced that US secretary of state Henry Kissinger had paid a secret visit to China at the same time as Whitlam's public one and that Nixon would follow shortly. Neither Whitlam nor anyone else had any knowledge of the American about-face; Whitlam had just followed his political instinct and it had proved sound. The ALP issued a triumphant press release headed, at my suggestion, 'I wonder who's Kissinger now.' Probably the only person more pleased than Whitlam himself was that old Cold War stalwart John Gorton. He turned on the drinks in his office for those of us who had missed out on the trip and we toasted McMahon's discomfiture. Such was the morale in the Liberal Party in 1971.

The one bright spot for McMahon was that Gorton was now out of the ministry altogether. The appearance of Reid's book *The Gorton Experiment* had prompted him to write a series of newspaper articles defending his own record and in the process querying that of his successor – in so far as Reid's book had a hero, McMahon was definitely it, and Gorton, with typical bravado, felt he had to set the record straight. Unsurprisingly he was forced to resign from the ministry as a result. As he was now working for the media, I mischievously invited him to join the Press Gallery XI for our next outing against the pollies; he accepted and performed better than he ever had for the politicians' side. Critics drew their own conclusions. McMahon also turned up to bowl an exhibition over of lollipops; he claimed to have been up all night practising by bowling a squash ball to Sonia down the hall of the Lodge. He swiftly retired to do more riffling and shuffling.

In the meantime the Whitlam camp was cruising towards government. A group of subversives from within the public service formed a dinner club which met regularly at a restaurant called the Shepherd's Hut in Queanbeyan, just outside the ACT; prominent among them were Peter Wilenski and Jim Spigelman, both of whom I had viewed with some contempt as student politicians, an occupation which I had always regarded as a contradiction in terms. Now, preparing to take over the reins of government, they were much more impressive. They were accompanied by a number of politically committed academics from the Australian National University, among them Stephen Fitzgerald, who had been on the Whitlam trip to China. There was also a sprinkling of journalists, of whom I was often one. We ate lamb cutlets stuffed with avocado and dreamed our dreams of power.

There was one minor hitch; Whitlam's staff had decided to run what they called a mid-term campaign simply to keep the momentum gained from the last election alive. The agency employed for the task decided the theme would be explaining Whitlam's ideas to the general public: it asked a series of questions along the lines of 'Does Gough Whitlam believe that universities should be free?' and answered them with emphatic, if somewhat vague, assurances that he did and they would be. The ads were mostly on this level of motherhood statement, but one nearly got through the system asking if Whitlam believed Australia should have its own nuclear weapons, and replying that indeed he did. When appalled Labor staffers confronted the agency, the admen replied aggrievedly that all their research had shown this was a popular position so they just went ahead with it. The fact that Whitlam would have been instantly expelled from the party if it had appeared was, to them, a side issue. It was a problem which was to recur during the campaign proper when an advertising man named Paul 'Very-big-Stateside' Jones took credit for the famous 'It's Time' slogan (a shortened form of the New Zealand Labour Party's 'It's Time For a Change') and claimed to have introduced Whitlam to the pleasures of reading. No one was prepared to admit that the ALP was winning on matters of substance rather than style.

But basically, as Graham Freudenberg pointed out in his record of the times *A Certain Grandeur*, the McMahon months were happy ones, simply because they were seen as leading up to a new dawn. It was obvious to all but the most hidebound Tories that the government was doomed, and by all but the most purblind that this was seen as not a bad thing. After twenty-three years, the coalition had finally run out of puff; at the very least it needed a bit of down time to recharge its batteries. Moreover, Labor under Whitlam didn't look too threatening; from time to time the man talked tough, but then he had to do that to satisfy his own rag-tag troops. There was still a feeling around the Establishment that he was really one of them, a bit of a sheep in wolf's clothing who would, when it came to crunch, do the right thing.

Even Sir Frank Packer gave up; his media interests had been McMahon's last real bastion, but now Packer decided to sell his newspapers to, of all people, Rupert Murdoch. At a meeting sealing the deal between the two moguls someone suggested that Packer should inform McMahon; he rang the Prime Minister, whose wail of despair at the bad news was audible across the room. Packer handed the phone to Murdoch, who promised formally to treat the McMahon government with the utmost fairness. Packer interjected: 'If you do that you'll crucify the little bastard.' Unlike the more sanctimonious media critics, Packer understood what fairness entails. It is unrealistic to demand that the media be objective: the journalistic process is by its nature a selective one, which involves value judgments. It is plain silly to demand what is normally referred to as balance; no one treats the flat earthers with the same credibility as Nobel Prize winners, and the views of Adolf Hitler do not deserve an equal hearing with those of Jesus Christ. But the media can be fair, which means that they are open to all the evidence and that they assess it without fear or favour. There are times when the assessment will come down against a particular group or individual; well, tough. That's what journalism should be all about.

At least it's what my journalism was all about. There were times when it took me a little too close to the Labor Party; in some ways I became an insider, a player rather than an observer. Richard Walsh occasionally warned me against what he termed my Whitlamolatry, and fair enough. But I had no doubt my judgment was correct: the election of a Whitlam government would not only be a good thing, it had become a desperate and long overdue necessity. If this required aggressive and partisan journalism, then so be it; the times demanded such an approach. I should add that the vast majority of my press gallery colleagues shared these views and envied me the freedom I enjoyed on *Nation Review*. As had been the case with *Oz*, they assiduously fed me the scuttlebutt their own papers would not print.

The Murdoch campaign against McMahon went well beyond what would normally be regarded as fair. It was real boots and all stuff. At *Nation Review* we had been pretty ruthless, but I like to think we stopped short of becoming downright vicious; the word McMahon himself used on the rare occasions he mentioned the publication was 'unkind'. Murdoch went for the jugular. I had contributed a number of scripts to a revue called *Misrepresentations* which was performed with great panache by an amateur company in Canberra; interestingly the roles of McMahon and Whitlam were both taken by members of the Philosophy Department at ANU. Some of it was fairly close to the bone. But compared to what appeared in the Murdoch press it was almost flattering; Rupert was taking no prisoners. It was a performance unequalled until he was to turn on Whitlam with even greater venom in 1975.

It was nasty stuff, but, like most media onslaughts, it made little difference to the overall result. The writing was on the wall for McMahon and the coalition from the moment Whitlam got on top of him in parliament, which was within the first few days of his leadership. In a rather pathetic interview with the Englishman David Frost, McMahon confessed that he had prayed for victory. Long before the campaign proper began it was clear that his prayers had been answered and that the answer was no.

NEW BROOM

Chapter Twenty

HAIL TO THE CHIEF. ALSO RAIN, FROSTS AND FOGS, BRIEF SUNNY PERIODS AND A COOL CHANGE FOLLOWED BY STORMS, CYCLONES, EARTHQUAKES AND TSUNAMIS.

The 1972 It's Time campaign has gone into history as a kind of crusade – the Great Gough rampaging his way through hostile territory, taking town after town before winning the final victory on December 2, 1972. But in truth it was more like a Roman triumph; all the important battles had already been decided. Whitlam rode majestically to power through the cheering crowds with the enemy, totally disarmed, trooping dispiritedly behind. All that was lacking was the slave to whisper in his ear that he was only a man. In retrospect it was a significant omission.

By modern standards the whole thing was a bit of a shambles; while there were a few well-prepared headline grabbers (the legendary H C 'Nugget' Coombs emerging as a key adviser on the public service, the arts and, I was especially pleased to note, aboriginal affairs; a Catholic bishop endorsing the education policy; a dramatic commitment to open government) most of it consisted of the usual trudge from one suburban town hall to the next, with the same speech slightly rejigged in view of the day's news and local demands. Television was important for the official openings and for the closing addresses to the National Press Club, but the nightly ten-second grab was far from the be-all and end-all it has become today. This meant that the campaign was a bit more risky for the participants but a hell of a lot more fun for the observers.

I was a bit of both, starting by helping to set up the stage for Whitlam's opening at Blacktown Town Hall and finishing as a numbers man in the Labor bunker on election night. In the meantime I watched and chronicled the disintegration of McMahon from every possible angle. After one somewhat boozy lunch in Sydney I persuaded Whitlam to visit the headquarters of the Liberal Party in a gloomy office in Ash Street. The scene was Dickensian; under 40 watt light globes ancient and wizened ladies were mechanically stuffing envelopes with propaganda which, in some cases, had not changed since the Menzies years. And this was in the front room where the customers went; God knows what pitiful scenes were being enacted out the back. Whitlam was visibly shaken. His own team had its eccentrics, but it was a machine for the 1970s. The Libs still seemed to be stuck in a 1950s time warp.

And so it transpired. McMahon had decided not to brave a real crowd for his opening speech; instead he opted for a tele-vised policy speech in front of an audience of his ministers and other prominent Liberals. It was amateurish beyond belief; watching it in a hotel room I couldn't decide whether the fault was in the set or in the Prime Minister. I heard later that he had tried six times to record it, and when Sonia insisted on a seventh attempt he had responded: 'I might as well try it with my head down the toilet.' Well, yes. The Prime Minister would mention his government's fine record on roads; the screen would flash up a picture of a deserted country stock route. Cut to a shot of the ministry applauding politely. Move to transport in general; shot of an ancient steam train, etc etc. And it didn't get any better.

I had, as instructed, asked my leftie friends not to invade McMahon's public meetings but they were not to be denied a farewell appearance. As it turned out it didn't matter. In order to avoid distractions, McMahon's team had provided their boss with a new-fangled device called an autocue: an oversized lectern through which his speech scrolled in inch high capitals at a speed determined by a tech in a backroom. Thus there was no room for spontaneity, improvisation or answering hecklers; the tech ploughed on and McMahon was forced to plough on at the same pace. As it turned out the demonstrations at his meetings were more triumph than protest, but even so he could have followed Gorton's lead in 1969 and tried to turn them into a positive. Instead we had an endless drone about how Whitlam was a socialist and socialism was bad and McMahon wasn't a socialist so you had to vote for him. The negativity was summed up in the Libs answer to 'It's Time', which was 'Not Yet'. It must have been one of the most dispiriting T-shirts ever manufactured.

Unofficially Labor had its own negative campaign. Patrick Sayers had been unearthed to authorise a series of anti-McMahon ads which were prepared by Mick Young and Eric Walsh, who was now working openly for the ALP, in an apartment lent to them by the boss of Marrickville Margarine, Richard Crebbin. Crebbin was to get his payback when Walsh arranged the lifting of the restrictions on his product imposed at the behest of the Country Party. At the end of the campaign the apartment had to be cleaned with a flamethrower and firehose, but the ads effectively portrayed McMahon as weak and untrustworthy. When the Libs ran an ad purporting to highlight the demonic union control of the ALP, they showed a smiling Whitlam lifting his mask to reveal the sinister features of the ACTU chief Bob Hawke. The Young–Walsh team promptly replied with an ad showing Billy McMahon lifting his mask to reveal Billy McMahon. He had indeed become, as he had predicted, his own worst enemy. To clinch the image John Taylor, a friend I had known in advertising in London, produced a lapel badge which showed the outline of a big-eared, bald head and the slogan: 'Stop laughing at Billy'. It was totally devastating, and during the three-week campaign I must have distributed several thousand at the cost price of ten cents each. It was around this stage that the *National Times* planned a pair of articles under the headings 'Why I won't vote for Whitlam' and 'Why I won't vote for McMahon'. The idea had to be dropped; the paper could not find anyone of even marginal credibility to write the anti-Whitlam piece.

It ended, mercifully, on December 2 as the results from Western Australia began to come in. As numbers man I was privileged to say to Whitlam: 'Well, I think we can send the white smoke up the chimney now.' Freudenberg, on cue, responded: *'Habemus papam.'* And so we had – though not by anything like the margin the optimists had predicted. This was, of course, explicable; the big swing had occurred in 1969. 1972 was just a bit of catch-up, particularly in Victoria. The majority was a clear one, but it was no landslide. Even in what should have been the most unfavourable possible circumstances for the government, the punters would only reluctantly vote Labor. In a sense this was hardly surprising. Not only was Whitlam the first Labor prime minister since Ben Chifley lost office in 1949; he was the first Labor Opposition leader to win an election since James Scullin in 1929. People just weren't used to the idea. We should have been warned, but we weren't; we believed the world had changed forever. The celebrations went on through the night and for most of the next day as we made our boozy ways back to Canberra.

And then came the morning after. Whitlam had arranged to meet the key heads of the public service in his office at ten o'clock on Monday; although we didn't know it at this stage he had already decided to have himself and his deputy, Lance Barnard, sworn in immediately to begin the process of change. The hard heads in the party had always worried about Whitlam and the public service; his own father had been a great public servant and this had perhaps given the son an exaggerated respect for the integrity and impartiality of the service as a whole. It was, after all, an innately conservative body and after twenty-three years of unremittingly conservative government there was not likely to be a burning desire for change in its top ranks. Moreover, many of Whitlam's shadow ministers and staff had had their own dealings with the bureaucrats and had not been impressed. The general consensus in the ALP was that the higher levels, and especially the permanent heads, should be treated as potentially hostile until they proved themselves otherwise. It was therefore essential that as many of Whitlam's political inner circle as possible, including the Shepherd's Hut group, should be around to cushion the impact of the senior shiny bums.

But they weren't; in fact at 10.00am many of them were in the bar of the Canberra Rex drinking a peculiarly lethal brand of champagne cocktail called a Martin Collins. I know, because I was there too. By the time we staggered across the lake to Parliament House it was too late. Sir John Bunting of Prime Minister's and Cabinet, Sir Keith Waller of Foreign Affairs, Alan Cooley of the Public Service Board and Clarrie Harders of Attorney-General's had cemented their own positions and those of most of their colleagues. In the event only two departmental secretaries went, and even that was against Whitlam's wishes; Clyde Cameron replaced a particular enemy, Hal Cook, in Labour and National Service, and George Warwick-Smith had his Department of the Interior abolished altogether. As neither could be sacked outright, posts of ambassadorial rank were created for them in Geneva. To outsiders it looked like a pretty lavish golden handshake.

Another to achieve ambassadorial rank was the former Labor senator and Lord Mayor of Sydney, John Armstrong, who became the Australian High Commissioner in London. Although Armstrong, a man of independent means and something of a bon vivant, wasn't a bad choice for a job that had become more ceremonial than diplomatic there were the inevitable mutterings of jobs for the boys. But in the background there was a much more serious rumble. Although few people knew it at the time, Rupert Murdoch wanted the London job but at the same time to be allowed to retain and operate all his media interests. Whitlam regarded the demand as outrageous and refused point-blank, thus making a long term enemy. Like many before and since Whitlam had misunderstood Murdoch's role. The Dirty Digger has no allies, only enemies; he works on the principle that the enemies of his enemies are his friends for just as long as it takes to defeat the common foe, and then all bets are off. He sees himself as a king-breaker, not as a king-maker.

Like all media moguls he has an exaggerated view of his real influence, but since most politicians share that view it makes little difference in practice. Prime ministers now truckle to gain his favour, and most are far more accommodating than Whitlam was. But Murdoch is not for sale, he is only for rent and then only for as long as interests coincide. For Whitlam to have given in to him would have had far worse consequences than refusing him. When some time later the government knocked back Murdoch's request for favourable treatment for his mining interests in Western Australia, whatever remained of the temporary alliance was over. But it was never going to last anyway; in the end the only thing Murdoch had in common with the Whitlam ideal was a sense of nationalism and in time he was to shed even that in pursuit of wealth and power.

There were a few more controversial appointments; to the Queensland Labor heavy, Jack Egerton, who had proclaimed loudly 'to the victors the spoils', went a seat on the Qantas board. Stephen Fitzgerald was made Australia's first ambassador to China. But these were minor incidents in the rush of decisions that flowed from the offices of Whitlam and Barnard in the dramatic period of the duumvirate, as it became known. The rush of decisions was such that the daily papers started carrying boxes on the front page headed: 'What the government did yesterday'. They sometimes ran to half a broadsheet column ranging in scope from the withdrawal of military assistance to the government of South Vietnam to legalising contraceptive advertising in the ACT; what they had in common was that all were promises made at some time during the campaign. There were no tricks; the government could claim a mandate for each of the forty-odd decisions made in the hectic seventeen days. The rush was exhilarating to the young and involved, who found themselves referring, for the first time in their lives, to 'our government'. It was disconcerting and even alarming to others, who believed that on the whole the job of governments was to muddle along quietly and not disturb the voters between elections – after all, that's how it had usually been in the past. It was downright scary for the conservatives who had comfortably believed that Whitlam was all bluff and would never actually do what he had promised over and over again to do; damn it all, the man was a politician, wasn't he? He wasn't supposed to be honest. And for *Nation Review*, and especially for me, it was a big problem.

On the eve of the election I had a long and increasingly drunken conversation with Max Walsh of *The Financial Review* on the subject of how we were going to do our jobs under the new government. We both agreed that it was eminently desirable and we were both convinced of Whitlam's qualifications to be a good, even a great, prime minister. But we were acutely aware that it was going to be the most inexperienced government since federation; only two of those expected to make the ministry – Kim Beazley Sr and Fred Daly – had even been on the backbench in the time of the last Labor government and none had served as a minister. Moreover, there were areas where the talent was pretty thin; to fill the important portfolio of primary industry Whitlam was forced to turn to a former merchant seaman, Ken Wriedt, because *The Financial Review's* rural expert, Tom Connors, agreed to work for him but not with the rurally based Al Grassby. Connors, an unelected journalist, was to be the de facto minister.

In the circumstances there were bound to be a lot of mistakes made and probably some fairly major stuff-ups. Obviously when they happened they would have to be reported. Moreover, it was our duty as journalists to seek them out and to highlight them. But in doing so we would be helping to harm, perhaps even destroy, a government we both fervently believed was the best thing for the country. Could we honestly do our job as journalists if we followed our consciences on the national interest? Was there a way out of the dilemma? Not that night there wasn't; the argument drowned in the third or fourth bottle. But it explains why the election of the Whitlam government, while unquestionably good for Australia, was disastrous for *Nation Review*.

1972 had been a very good year; we had become firmly established among a growing and loyal following and we were being noted by the mainstream press. For the first and only time the paper actually made a profit. I had personally broken some new ground by writing the election campaign as an extended diary; 'Mungo's Magical Mystery Tours', as they were headlined, became required reading for all those interested in the background to the campaign and there proved to be a lot of them. I had also started 'Ferretwatch', a weekly critical review of the press coverage, which was extremely popular and became the predecessor for all the various Mediawatch-style writing and broadcasting that was to follow. As a recognised weekly correspondent I had even been invited on a government junket to Papua New Guinea for the opening of the 1972 parliament, an occasion I celebrated by sharing a bottle under a tree with the Speaker, Sir John Guise. We were on the way to becoming an accepted, if still larrikin, member of the media at large, and the merger with *Nation*, a magazine which took itself more seriously, had brought us added respectability. The future seemed bright – until December 2, 1972.

Almost from day one we were caught in a bind. Half our readers loved us for our fearless iconoclasm; they wanted us to get stuck right into the new government as we had into the old one, no quarter given and no holds barred. The other half regarded such attacks as the grossest disloyalty; they saw us as a paper of the left, and our greatest vindication the election of the Whitlam government. To turn against it now would be close to infanticide. Whatever we did would be wrong. Fortunately along with *Nation* we had inherited George Munster, one of the country's best investigative journalists and a man to whom governments of all shades were by definition the enemy. While I wavered from week to week and made few friends in the process Munster waded right in. The problem was that while his thoughts were invariably interesting, his prose was so turgid that few bothered to follow it through to the end. *Nation Review* types, as our readers now described themselves, liked a few laughs with their news; Munster gave them unalloyed gravity. The readers began to drop away. In a sense, *Nation Review* had served its purpose. It lasted for another seven years and had many high points over the time, but it is fair to say it never regained the carefree extravagance of 1972.

Typical of our problems was the raid the new Attorney-General, Lionel Murphy, launched on the ASIO headquarters in Melbourne in February. Murphy was worried about the impending visit of the Yugoslav Prime Minister, Dzemal

Bijedic; there had been serious violence in the past from the Croatian community in Australia including the bombing of the Yugoslav consulate. Security was obviously going to be a problem. One of Murphy's advisers, Kerry Milte, a former Commonwealth policemen with a grudge against ASIO, suggested that ASIO had files on the extremists involved; if Murphy hadn't seen them ASIO, for reasons of its own, must be concealing them. Murphy, who shared the belief of the left that ASIO was only ever interested in harassing himself and his mates and was secretly in cahoots with the right, was a receptive listener. Discussions about what to do continued between him and his staff well into the night; drink was taken. Milte suggested that a surprise visit to ASIO's Melbourne headquarters might be the go. By midnight this idea was looking even better.

Milte raised a force of Commonwealth police whose job it would be to cordon off the building and seal the files while Murphy arranged for a VIP plane to take him and his personal staff to the scene. His Press secretary, George Negus, alerted a few mates to the possibility of a story. The cameras were there in force when Murphy and his hit squad arrived at the building in St Kilda Road just as dawn was breaking. For the first time Murphy realised that he could perhaps have handled the situation more delicately. He turned deliberately to his press secretary. 'Jesus, George,' groaned the first law officer of Australia, 'what have you done to me?'

It was undeniably a great yarn, but how were we to handle it? Was Murphy a hero, moving against the entrenched forces of the hard right and striking a blow for civil liberties? Or was he a drunken buffoon, endangering the nation's security in a fit of paranoia brought on by a deranged staff member? Well, a bit of both, probably; politics tends to be like that. But our readers wanted a direct answer; the problem was that they didn't all want the same one. It was a problem which was to recur increasingly as the government started to go off the rails.

But for the present, my faith in Whitlam at least remained absolute. And as others jostled for positions on ministerial staff or other signs of gratitude I was not forgotten. On January 2, just a calendar month into the life of the government, my second daughter was born. True to his promise, Whitlam agreed to be godfather (in a non-believer's sense, he added firmly) and a simple but moving ceremony took place at the Lodge during which daughter Gail was presented with a set of rather ugly port glasses which had been a gift to the people of Australia from some obscure Asian potentate. But there was practical recognition too. Gail's mother Rosa was a public servant, and in Labor's platform there was a provision for extended maternity leave. In celebration of Gail's birthday, the legislation was made retrospective to January 1. To the victors the spoils indeed.

Chapter Twenty-one

EVEN 50 PER CENT OF QUITE A LOT IS MORE THAN ALMOST ALL OF VERY LITTLE

Rosa was not the only public servant to benefit. Clyde Cameron had long been eager to try out his package of workplace reforms and now he had a perfect laboratory in which public servants could be relied upon to behave like rats. He swiftly introduced a package of benefits crowned with the concept of flexitime, a system which allowed people to juggle their working hours to suit the needs of parenthood or other voluntary activities. Unfortunately he overlooked the Australian genius for turning a good idea into a rort. Within days the streets of Canberra (not to mention the slopes of Thredbo and the beaches of Bateman's Bay) were thick with crowds of bureaucrats informing each other that they had just flexed off for a few days.

Moreover, Whitlam's ambitious program involved huge increases in their numbers and with Cameron's utopian (by the standards of the day) working conditions there was no difficulty in attracting them:

> And day by day and constantly
> The shiny bums increase
> And all their ways are flexitime
> And endless morning teas.

The newcomers were by and large content to lie back and enjoy their new jobs, but among the old hands there was a certain amount of resentment; any change at all was to be greeted with suspicion. And then there was the ministerial staff problem. There is alway tension between the bureaucracy and the personal staff in ministers' offices; the former's priority is caution and constraint while the latter wants to act to maximum political advantage. But the lot that arrived at the beginning of 1972 was an even brasher bunch than usual. They were determined, in the words of their beloved prime minister, to crash through or crash and if the public service wasn't prepared to play the game the public service had better get out of the bloody way or else.

Not only was the Labor mob uncouth; it was also contemptuous of the old standards, especially where security was involved. Shortly after the ministry had been announced I went down to Bill Hayden's office to congratulate him. He wasn't there but his staff members were trying to get the office organised. Paddy McGuinness was struggling in the manner of Mr Bean to open the giant security safe; eventually he gave up. He passed me the combination and asked me to try, which I did successfully. A passing bureaucrat who witnessed this capital crime almost fainted on the spot.

Whitlam himself was reluctant to submit his personal staff to the rigmarole of a formal clearance; he announced grandly that he had cleared them himself. Lance Barnard's people were not so privileged; at the behest of the fearsome Secretary of the Defence Department, Sir Arthur Tange, better known as Sir After Dark, his two most loyal and senior advisers, Clem Lloyd and Brian Toohey, were barred from attending secret briefings. Since Tange was a leading figure in the group regarded as most hostile to Labor, this was seen as a submission to the enemy. Lloyd and Toohey resigned on the spot, depriving Barnard of political expertise he was to miss sorely in the troubled days ahead.

Foreign affairs was something of a preoccupation in those early days; apart from the ending of conscription, the preparations for the final withdrawal from Vietnam and the recognition of China, there was a certain amount of uneasiness with our great and powerful friend. At the end of 1972 Nixon had unexpectedly resumed the bombing of North Vietnam; it was his last desperate bid to prove that the unwinnable war could be won after all. The left went ballistic, with the usual suspects – Jim Cairns, Tom Uren and Clyde Cameron – leading the charge. The problem was that they were no longer just voices in the street; they were senior ministers in the government of a country that the United States had always treated as a complaisant ally. Nixon was apparently furious; there was a brisk exchange of cables between Washington and Canberra.

At the time it was thought that Whitlam had been placatory, and he did nothing to correct the impression. However, a year later *Nation Review* had a major scoop when I stumbled across, as they say, an almost complete set of the cables involved, many of them classified Top Secret. They showed that Whitlam had been very tough indeed, that he had told Nixon bluntly that his policy was unacceptable to the new government of Australia and that if it continued down the track he could expect more of the same. It was not only the Australian Establishment that was realising that Whitlam might prove much harder to deal with than had been anticipated. Nixon retaliated by sending a senior officer from the State Department, Marshall Green, across to keep an eye on things. In the past American ambassadors had generally been political bagmen rewarded for their support of the president; the posting was regarded as a bit of a holiday. Whitlam demanded a professional. At least it showed that we were finally being taken seriously.

At home the mood was less serious than bewildered. The pace of change was such that even the hardiest found it difficult to keep up; by the time parliament opened in February we were already exhausted. Next morning we were even more so; the ceremony had turned into an almighty binge, leaving King's Hall littered with empty bottles and more than one full member who had not quite made it home. My last coherent recollection was of staggering after Mick Young who, bottle in hand, was lurching out of King's Hall with the rallying cry: 'It's on in the Speaker's office!' But my best memory was of the Governor-General, Sir Paul Hasluck, proclaiming through gritted teeth that 'his government' was to embark on the most ambitious program of reform since federation, including land rights for aborigines, independence for Papua New Guinea, friendly relations with China and a communist Vietnam, the ending of appeals to the British Privy Council … All the things he had opposed throughout his deeply conservative political life. Even in politics, what goes around comes around

– eventually.

Whitlam's next outrage, as the Establishment saw it, was to augment his staff by the inclusion of a special adviser on women's affairs. The first wave of feminism was then nearing its peak; the Women's Electoral Lobby was becoming a significant political force and the push for equal pay, which Whitlam had publicly endorsed, was firmly on the agenda. A side effect of the rise of the sisterhood was the break-up of a great many heterosexual relationships, especially on the left; my own was among them. Coincidentally the decline of the left as a major political force also dates from that time – at least I hope it is coincidentally.

There was still some significant catching up to do; invitations to a reception for applicants for the job of what the tabloids insisted on calling Whitlam's Superwoman included the line 'Dress: lounge suit'. Infuriated, many of the women indeed appeared in lounge suits borrowed for the occasion. Others invaded the men's lavatories and covered them with lipsticked graffiti along the lines of 'Lesbians are lovely' and other less printable slogans. The job was eventually given to a local academic named Elizabeth Reid; she made no obvious impression. But everyone agreed that the symbolism was important.

Far more significant from my point of view was the handover of land at Wattie Creek to Vincent Lingiari and his Gurindji people. Again there was a bit of symbolism; Whitlam poured a handful of dust through Lingiari's hands, a gesture which puzzled the old man the first time around and even more so when it was repeated for the cameramen who had missed it. But it was the culmination of a long campaign by the Gurindji and a longstanding promise by Whitlam. At his campaign launch he had said: 'We will legislate to give aborigines land rights – not just because their case is beyond argument but because all of us as Australians are diminished while the aborigines are denied their rightful place in this nation.' The goodness and rightness of this sentence still moves me to tears.

Indeed, during that glorious false dawn a number of things went close to moving me to tears. There was a splendid camaraderie about the early days which I had not experienced since my time at the university – or perhaps it was closer to the feeling of togetherness of a crowd of schoolboys barracking for their team. Indeed John Button, who entered the Senate after the double dissolution of 1974, told me he found the place just like a boys' boarding school. I replied that he must have gone to a shithouse boarding school and he looked suitably abashed. But by then the gloss was wearing off. In the first year, it was all love and harmony. Like Dante, we had finally emerged and we saw the stars. We all called each other 'comrade', a half-ironic reference to the old union greeting 'Comrade brother fellow worker'. It seemed a harmless enough affectation, but as time went on it fuelled the worst fears of the conservatives that Labor, democratic socialism, was really just a euphemism for communism.

But in practice Whitlamism, in its ideal form, was precisely the opposite of the grey and secretive world of the totalitarian state. From early in his political career Whitlam had hammered the theme of open government; he was intent on dismantling barriers between the punters and the politicians. It was a mission very similar to my own, and of course I applauded; but, like my colleagues I had my doubts about whether it could actually be achieved. In fact Whitlam made a good start; he kept his promise to hold weekly press conferences, something unheard of in the modern era. These were relaxed affairs, often more like tutorials than inquisitions; at one Whitlam and a young hackette from Melbourne solemnly discussed the most desirable refreshments for cabinet meetings, coming down in favour of chocolate eclairs. Open government extended through most of the ministry; journalists were welcome to wander in and out of offices in a way they had never been in the previous government. There was a pervading sense of trust between the politicians and the press gallery; some of the old hands compared it to the atmosphere of the war years when John Curtin had taken the press into his confidence, a confidence which was never abused. Another symbol of the commitment to open government was Whitlam's decision to allow a debate on abortion. In a sense this was a deliberate gesture of defiance: in the last days of the election campaign Robin (the Filthmaster) Askin had dived into the gutter to accuse the ALP of favouring abortion on demand, a course he claimed would see thousands of babies ripped from their mothers' wombs, 'their little hearts beating and their little lungs breathing'. In fact, abortion, along with homosexuality and capital punishment, is one of those select matters on which Labor gives its members a free vote. Unlike such issues as declarations of war, sales of chemical weapons or the treatment of refugees, abortion is supposed to be a matter of conscience. Thus the party has no policy as such, a stance which infuriates the feminists in its ranks.

However, many of its members feel passionately one way or the other and Whitlam decided to allow two of the most outspoken, David McKenzie and Tony Lamb, to move a motion which would make abortion legally available under certain conditions. All members were to have a free vote on the issue, which made a lot of people on both sides of the chamber very uncomfortable because whichever way they went they were bound to offend a powerful and articulate pressure group. Predictably, the Catholic church pulled out its big guns: not one but two cardinals were despatched to Canberra to work on the consciences of honourable members. In full drag they appeared at the press club as a double act, which would have been more effective if they had read the proposed bill before attacking it; they were long on rhetoric but short — indeed, downright wrong — on facts. I felt a song coming on:

> Oh Cardinal Freeman, dear Cardinal Freeman
> What do you think we should do with Catholic semen?
> I know that you're a caution
> When you rave about abortion
> And a devil when you exorcise your demon.

> Oh Cardinal Knox, yes Cardinal Knox,
> It should firmly be implanted in a box
> And when it grows into a foetus
> I will write a learned treatise —
> Absolutely, Cardinal Freeman! Absolution, Cardinal
> Knox.

In the end prelate power carried the day and the vote. But it had been a useful exercise in airing a generally taboo subject — open government in action.

Of course, to some the government was more open than to others. Whitlam had made it clear that he was always available to the ALP federal secretary, Mick Young, and Young chose to take this literally. One night he appeared on the doorstep of

to spend very large sums of money on its programs it was potentially disastrous. In a mood of some desperation the government cut tariffs across the board in an attempt to reduce the price of imports, but prices continued to rise. This forced an increase in interest rates; what the public in general thought of that was shown by a 7 per cent swing against the government at a by-election in the litmus test seat of Parramatta. Admittedly, there is usually an anti-government swing in by-elections, and the situation in Parramatta was exacerbated by Whitlam's promise − or threat − to build an airport in the vicinity. It was a long overdue decision; Sydney had first been promised a second airport in 1945. But the rolling hills of Galston, alive with the sound of semi-rural retirees, made an unpopular choice. Whitlam tried to tough it out: 'You're getting Galston,' he bellowed regularly at bands of demonstrating landholders who arrived at Parliament House bearing fresh flowers, fruit and vegetables to prove their bona fides. It was a useful distraction; I usually managed to collect enough produce to save the weekly trip to the markets. The older style Labor men derided the crowd as 'silvertails' and seemed to feel that an airport would be an appropriate act of class vengeance against them. When I argued that this was an inadequate justification for the project I was attacked with some venom. Belatedly I realised that there were sections of the movement who would always see me as one of them rather than one of us, no matter how fiercely I protested my dedication to the cause; no matter how sincere, a class traitor is never quite the real thing. In the circumstances the result in Parramatta was only to be expected. But no one could pretend it was good news. For all too many voters the mood now was: stop the government, we want to get off.

Just how frantic the pace had been was illustrated when parliament rose for the Christmas break. Whitlam asked leave to incorporate a record of his government's first year in the parliamentary Hansard; it was an innocuous enough request, but Snedden refused leave. Whitlam, seriously miffed, announced that in that case he would read the whole thing out and have it incorporated that way. He proceeded to do so; in all there had been 1675 cabinet decisions, 254 bills had been presented to parliament and 223 had been passed and 39 reports from 94 different inquiries had been tabled. During this marathon performance Snedden sat ostentatiously writing Christmas cards; his was a nice safe family portrait. Whitlam's, on the other hand, was a reproduction of *Blue Poles*, the Jackson Pollock painting that had been purchased by the National Gallery amid huge controversy with his approval. Even for the season of peace and goodwill there was no let-up.

The new year dawned with both sides grimly determined to force a showdown one way or another. Whitlam had already made it clear to anyone who would listen that he had no intention of being a lame duck prime minister; he would rather go down in flames than simply occupy the chair and do nothing. Snedden and Anthony, however, were equally firm about blocking Labor's key reforms. Anthony in particular was terrified of Whitlam's proposals for one vote one value; he believed his party would be destroyed if the extra weighting given to votes in rural electorates was removed. Control of the Senate was of course the key. At present the Opposition, with the support of the DLP, had it; the government was desperate to gain it.

As it happened an election for half the Senate was scheduled for May 18. In normal circumstances this would have been a non-event, a big yawn; but it is fair to say that in the Whitlam years very little was normal and almost nothing was boring. Yet again he seized the opportunity to crash through or crash. If he could remove one of the DLP senators before the election, in one state six seats would be up for grabs instead of five. Even with Labor a bit on the nose, the senate's proportional voting system should give Labor that extra seat and, oh, joy, the numbers in the upper house to get the program through. It was too tempting a prospect to resist.

The obvious target was Queensland's Vince Gair. Gair, a former Labor premier, had never been an ideologue; he had ended up in the DLP as a result of losing a power struggle and he had never much liked the sanctimonious company in which he found himself. He liked it even less since he had been deposed as leader of the party (a position he had originally gained through the toss of a coin) by Frank McManus, who still saw the party as a religious crusade. Gair had also fallen out with Snedden, whom he insulted as a lightweight who couldn't make an impression on a soft cushion or go two rounds with a revolving door. Bored and lonely, he drifted more and more into the company of the knockabout Labor types with whom he shared a tradition. Sensing opportunity, they encouraged and cultivated him; Lionel Murphy in particular became a drinking companion, something Murphy was always good at. Murphy softened him up and wheeled him round to Whitlam; Whitlam offered him the ambassadorship to dear old Ireland and Gair tearfully accepted.

So far the soap opera was going according to plan, but the problem was that the Irish had to be told and they didn't like it at all. They were sick of being a dumping ground for superannuated politicians and Gair looked like the absolute last card in the pack. They leaked the story before Gair had resigned from the Senate; the Nationals, realising they were close to disaster, instantly grabbed Gair and kept him dosed up on beer and prawns till they could decide what to do. The solution came from a Queensland lawyer: that state could issue the writs for its own half Senate election for five seats before Gair resigned. It did so. This meant Labor's dreams of a sixth Queensland seat and consequent control of the Senate evaporated into thin air. Labor had been comprehensively outmanoeuvred by an Opposition far more skilled in the politics of deception. The press, which had initially been excited and impressed by Labor's audacity, now closed ranks with its traditional conservative allies to inveigh against the immorality of Labor in seeking to subvert a senator. The senator, whose political career had been built around betraying colleagues of one kind or another (and was now preposterously trying to take the credit for Labor's discomfort) set off for the fleshpots of Dublin declaring that he'd never doublecrossed anyone in his life.

And Snedden and Anthony decided the moment had come to force an election: the Opposition announced that in these circumstances of political corruption – 'the most shameful act by any government in Australia's history', Anthony called it with his usual hyperbole – it would defy all precedent and convention by blocking supply. McManus, on behalf of the DLP said he'd be in it, thereby signing his own and his party's political death warrant. This was to be Whitlam's consolation prize; in the double dissolution that followed he didn't win control of the senate but he did, finally, get rid of the DLP. Given the magnitude of the stuff-up, it wasn't such a bad result.

Chapter Twenty-two

THE TROUBLE WITH AIMING FOR THE STARS IS THAT IF YOU MISS YOU END UP NOWHERE

The 1974 election saw the emergence of what became known as the Rat Pack. While for some years most of the leading figures in the press gallery had clearly been pro-Whitlam, this would not have been obvious to the average punter. By and large journalists took pride in at least giving the appearance of impartiality.

Allan Barnes of the *Age* took it to extremes; he used to boast that he knew he was doing a good job if both sides criticised him equally. I always thought this was a fatuous cop-out; I believed we were there to make judgments, not to provide balance. I took no pleasure from the idea that I was equally in (or out of) favour with both the goodies and the baddies. But this did not prevent me, or any of my colleagues, from asking Whitlam the tough questions. Indeed, we probably took more pleasure in putting him on the spot than we did with Gorton or McMahon; he was, after all, a much worthier opponent.

But with the blocking of supply and the forcing of an election at the convenience of the opposition rather than the government things changed. A tight-knit team within the press gallery started to savage Snedden in a way that his predecessors had mercifully escaped; hence the name Rat Pack. This did not mean that Whitlam got off lightly; to that extent the old standards still applied. But the feeling was that Snedden had broken the rules and deserved no quarter. Also, there was the question of ability. The idea of replacing Whitlam with Snedden just as the government was getting into stride was clearly absurd – overseas journalists found it beyond their comprehension. Yet the polls suggested it was a real possibility. Some of us made it our business to try and neutralise the threat.

On paper it should not have been difficult: Snedden was clearly a boofhead – an amiable enough one, but a boofhead nonetheless. By the standards of the past decade this was no disqualification from high office; indeed, Snedden stacked up pretty well against McMahon. But those were no longer the standards that applied. Snedden should have been easy meat. But he turned out to be tougher than we thought. He gave us plenty of ammunition; the centrepiece of his policy was a prices and wages freeze to bring inflation under control. When the difficulties of such a course were pointed out he threatened to abolish the Arbitration Commission if it did not cooperate, a ploy which cost Stanley Bruce both government and his own seat in 1929. He simply refused to go into details; to every challenge he replied in increasingly strident tones: 'We can achieve it and we will achieve it.' He was equally impervious to logic, history and (when it was tried by an enterprising heckler in Adelaide who dressed up as Uncle Sam and announced that Billy wanted to sell him Australia) satire. You had to give him marks for persistence.

And in a sense this was what the election was all about: certainty, to replace the breakneck course of change. The central symbol of the campaign became, of all things, the national anthem. Whitlam had promised to give Australia one of its own to replace 'God Save the Queen' and had even initiated a national contest for words and music. It was not a success; when I asked one of Whitlam's staffers what the quality of entries was like he replied tersely: 'I cannot tell a lie. Ratshit.' In the event the matter dragged on until a plebiscite under the auspices of Malcolm Fraser's conservative government chose 'Advance Australia Fair', which is now being defended by so-called traditionalists in exactly the way GSTQ was back in the old days. All the tired old arguments which have since been used to uphold the monarchy and the flag were trotted out. This was the anthem for which our forefathers fought and died in two world wars. It provided security, stability and identity to our troubled nation. To abandon it would be to surrender to the dark forces of socialism, communism and anarchy. At Snedden's meetings the faithful roared out chorus after chorus of God Save; seldom can the monarch have felt safer. Labor crowds tried to reply with Advance Australia, but were hampered by lack of knowledge of the words. Snedden clearly won the battle of the music.

Indeed, he could easily have walked away with the glittering prize except for intervention by Anthony. Like the press gallery, Anthony had his doubts about the viability of Snedden's freeze, especially as it affected rural produce; he would not, he said loudly, accept a cheap food policy. Since cheap food seemed like quite a good idea to the people in the swinging suburban seats which Snedden had to win, this went down as an error. Whitlam, who had spent most of the campaign lecturing uncomprehending audiences about the Constitution (he had, against all advice, insisted on incorporating four referendum proposals with the election, all of which fell in a heap) finally pulled his finger out and took the coalition apart in the last week. This, combined with an underlying feeling that the new government really deserved a bit more of a go than it had received, probably saved the day. But it had been a narrow escape.

Back in Canberra Whitlam was briefly chastened; he even started consulting his cabinet. But not for long. During one interminable and indecisive debate over the economy, Clyde Cameron took a more than usually pessimistic view. Whitlam wheeled on him. 'What would a fucking ex-shearer know about economics?' the Prime Minister demanded. 'As much as a fucking ex-classical Greek scholar,' Cameron replied. In fact none of the ministers knew much; but in the circumstances they were hardly alone. Around the world Nobel Prize winning economists were arguing about how to react to the oil pricing crisis; checking out the various theories was like drawing numbers out of a hat. I wrote at the time that cabinet would have done better to have examined the entrails of a chook; at least that way they could have eaten the chook afterwards.

The government's spirits were revived by the prospect of the historic joint sitting of parliament; as a result of the double dissolution and a further rejection by the Senate of government legislation, the Constitution allowed both the Reps and the Senate to sit together and the government to use its combined numbers to pass its bills. This finally paved the way for

Medibank, arguably the most important of the changes Whitlam had been foreshadowing for more than five years; if ever
the dubious concept of a government mandate meant anything, surely it applied in this case. Given that the numbers
were now nailed down, the brief session in which the entire
parliament crowded into the chamber of the House of Representatives was more ceremonial than dramatic; as I pointed out
at the time the problem with the joint sitting was that there
was too much sitting and not enough joints. It was also yet
another precedent set by the Whitlam government, yet more
new and unsettling ground broken. Admittedly there wasn't
much choice if the government was to get even a portion of
its program through, but it was hard not to feel that a period
of good old-fashioned consensus, do-nothing-much government was long overdue.

Instead Whitlam soon resumed his habit of taking the
important decisions by himself; the next one was the appointment of a new governor-general. This is one of the few areas
where the prime minister has total discretion; the choice is his
and his alone. Whitlam's first thought was to offer the incumbent, Sir Paul Hasluck, a second term; since he regarded the
post as a constitutional irrelevancy he had no objection to
leaving it to a political foe, and in any case Hasluck had
behaved impeccably during his tenure. Hasluck declined; this
was a disappointment to the press gallery, who had enjoyed
photographing him looking ridiculous in vice-regal clobber,
particularly on horseback. Whitlam's next choice was the Melbourne businessman Ken Myer; he thought it would get up
the nose of the Melbourne Club if he appointed the first Jew
to the job since Sir Isaac Isaacs. Myer also declined. At this
stage various people were offering suggestions; my own was

Judith Wright, a great poet and a fervent advocate of aboriginal rights and environmental protection. Whitlam was tempted; he liked the symbolism of a woman and an artist. But eventually he decided to play safe with the Chief Justice of New South Wales, Sir John Kerr.

The choice was eminently acceptable to the public at large and to the Tories; but a lot of those on the left were dismayed and worried, even in those days. Kerr, it was recalled, was the judge who jailed the union leader Clarrie O'Shea. He had been a spook in the war years and was rumoured to have kept up a connection with the CIA through a body called Lawasia. Moreover his life was seen as a bit unstable; his sexual proclivities were reportedly both busy and confused and even by the standards of the legal profession he was regarded as a lush. Around parliament he was famous for his long lunches when he visited the capital in his capacity as chairman of the Government Remunerations Tribunal. On one memorable occasion he and his lunching companion Lionel Murphy were seen struggling to negotiate the steps of Parliament House while a Commonwealth car and its driver waited patiently at the bottom. A passing reporter charitably assisted them to the vehicle; at which point Murphy shook his head angrily. 'You dumb bastard,' said the Attorney-General of Australia, 'we were going up the stairs, not down them.' At least it was an improvement on the lunch where Kerr did not make it back at all; he slid gracefully under the table at the Lobby and remained there until extracted by the same long-suffering driver.

Thus there were misgivings; but Whitlam himself had none. He had no doubt that the role Kerr would play would be a purely ceremonial one or that he would act, when he acted at all, entirely on the advice of his ministers. When it came to matters of tradition and convention, Whitlam expected everyone to be as punctilious as he was himself. In his dealings with the Queen he always respected confidentiality; the most he would reveal was that her corgis farted constantly. During the otherwise uneventful royal visit of 1974 Whitlam was entertaining the Queen in Parliament House when a deputation of aborigines arrived at the front door demanding to talk to him about the lack of progress on land rights. They were met by the President of the Senate, Sir Magnus Cormack, who sternly informed them that they must wait their turn: the Prime Minister was engaged in a private meeting with her majesty. 'Well fuck the queen,' one of the delegates exploded. Sir Magnus, a royalist of the Menzies school, reeled back in horror. When Whitlam met the aborigines later he gently informed them that their suggested course of action would be seen as a serious breach of protocol.

Meanwhile Snedden huffed and puffed his way on, seemingly oblivious to the increasing discontent within his own ranks; his followers, he insisted, would walk over hot coals through the valley of death for him. In fact some of them would not have walked behind him into a pub that served free beer. Snedden had had his chance and failed; now, by the ruthless logic prevailing in the Liberal Party at that time, he must make way for someone else. There was no real doubt about who it should be; the towering figure of Malcolm Fraser had already proved to be the only threat – or even serious discomfort – to Whitlam on the floor of parliament. The problem was that Fraser was also hugely unpopular within his own party. A sizeable group had neither forgotten nor forgiven his execution of Gorton. Others were dismayed by his extremism; his favourite reading was Ayn Rand, whose pitiless philosophy of social Darwinism was too bleak even for the Libs. Fraser's sense of humour also left something to be desired; apart from the pickled onions in the pockets, he confessed on radio that the funniest incident in his life had been when his father let go of the shafts of a sulky and tipped his mother out into the mud. He was widely loathed and universally mistrusted. Nonetheless, he was the only real candidate for the job; it was only a matter of waiting until the party became desperate enough.

I found Fraser an intriguing figure; there was an awful fascination about him, as with a poisonous snake. He must have noticed my interest; at one stage he actually offered me a job writing speeches for him. I was so disconcerted that I almost took it. I had always supposed him to be an idealogue; now he revealed himself as a complete political pragmatist willing to use any means at his disposal. I was taken aback to realise he saw me in the same light. Fraser had his first crack at Snedden at the end of 1974 and lost fairly narrowly; even at the time it was obvious that he never really expected to win but was just setting the stage. Although both men followed the usual practice of saying that the matter was now settled, unity and harmony would prevail and so forth, there was never any doubt that there would be another, and decisive, round. Snedden continued to huff and puff and Fraser kept right on plotting. Some of my friends did a little stirring by producing a series of T-shirts with slogans like 'Put the value back in the pound, vote Malcolm Fraser' and 'Relieve Mafeking now, vote Malcolm Fraser'. Fraser professed to find them puzzling; perhaps, he opined, they were trying to suggest that he was a shade old-fashioned. However, he could hardly mistake the irony of the one which read: 'Support Bill Snedden, vote Malcolm Fraser'. I took to wearing it around late night parties in

Parliament House; Snedden supporters, which meant most of the more tolerable people in the Liberal Party, were a bit equivocal. The general view was that for a bastard like Fraser, there was no such thing as bad publicity.

Towards the end of the year there was that total waste of time, a Queensland state election. Apart from the fact that the local Labor Party had completely lost both hope and interest Joh Bjelke-Petersen had stitched up a gerrymander of such perfection that it would take something close to a revolution to dismantle it; such a revolution was still nearly twenty years in the future. There were electorates shaped like doughnuts, like pretzels; votes in rural areas were worth six or seven times as much as those in the cities. In case there was any doubt about just who was in charge, Bjelke-Petersen informed the citizens of Mt Isa that their water supply would be cut off if they voted for the Labor candidate. Into this fine example of the democratic process stepped Whitlam, whose denunciation of their sainted Premier as a bible-bashing bastard made most Queenslanders reach for their crucifix when they saw him on television. Since Bjelke-Petersen had based most of his campaign about demonising Canberra in general and Whitlam in particular this was not necessarily a productive move; but Whitlam refused to stay away. The local party retaliated by sending its leader, one Perc Tucker, to Thargomindah for the duration of Whitlam's Brisbane visit and confining the Prime Minister's appearances to surreptitious meetings with the faithful: a morning tea and a barbecue.

Together with a handful of other journos along for the ride I attended both functions and realised that Queensland was indeed different. More, it was hopeless. There was nothing to do but drink. Whitlam, with nothing better to do, joined us for a long lunch; he was so depressed that in spite of allegedly being on the Israeli Army grapefruit diet he demolished an entire wheel of brie. By the time we set out for the barbecue we were torpid, which was exactly the right condition. I have become convinced that there is a perpetual floating Labor barbecue which goes round the country dispensing warm beer, burnt sausages and raffle tickets for prizes like a night alone at Mermaid Beach. It was alive and well that night. Seldom has defeat been so palpable. We fled back to Canberra; on election day I was, surprise surprise, at a Labor Party barbecue as the results came through. Labor had been reduced to a team of eleven; Perc Tucker could not even field a twelfth man. We comforted each other with the thought that Queenslad was different. It had to be.

Meanwhile the Establishment had decided it had collectively had enough of the Whitlam aberration; it was time to get back to the eternal verity of power in the hands of those who were born to hold it. Queensland, of course, had declared the federal government an implacable enemy to be crushed at all costs. Victoria, under the moderate Liberal Rupert Hamer, was more cautious. But New South Wales, fortuitously, was in a position to strike the first blow. The Filthmaster, Robin Askin, had retired after a performance in the 1974 federal election which must still rank as the single most untruthful, vicious and downright disgusting by any politician since federation. The high point was an advertisement featuring an old and frightened woman from, I think, Estonia describing life under communism; starvation, torure, terror and the gulags. This was what we would get if Labor were to be re-elected. She feared for her home, her children, her very life … Several federal Liberals, including Chipp, publicly dissociated themselves. Askin called them namby-pambies and wimps.

His successor, Tom Lewis, was a pussy cat by comparison, but was happy to head down the same track. The opportunity came when Whitlam, to the surprise of his ministers and the consternation of the Chief Justice, the sturdily conservative Sir Garfield Barwick, appointed Lionel Murphy as a judge of the High Court. Murphy had more or less concluded his own program of legislative reform; it still stands as one of the most comprehensive on record. He was ready to move on to a more ruminative pasture. His departure left a vacancy in the Senate, to be filled by a selection of the New South Wales Parliament. In the past this had invariably involved a nomination by the party of the outgoing senator which was rubber-stamped by the state parliament; but for the conservatives of 1975 conventions were made to be broken. Lewis ignored the ALP altogether and appointed someone named Cleaver Bunton. As it happened Bunton behaved correctly and refused to vote against supply. But yet another precedent had been set.

Whitlam, outraged, brought the matter on in parliament; in the middle of his speech Snedden interjected, for no apparent reason: 'Woof woof.' His remaining supporters shuddered. The ambitious young Liberal Tony Staley, who had appointed himself Fraser's coup manager, broke into a broad grin. Watching from the press gallery I knew with a sinking certainty that the challenge was on again and that this time there would be no stopping the man with the Easter Island image, the stony visage that concealed a heart of solid lead, the iron fist in the barbed wire glove, the Squire of Nareen. And so it proved. After yet another dismal parliamentary performance during which Whitlam hammered Snedden into the ground like a tent-peg the plotters met in earnest; Snedden's deputy Phil

Lynch announced he was prepared to switch sides and a group of senators on whom Snedden had been relying did likewise. All that was needed was a trigger; this was provided by Andrew Peacock, whose on-again, off-again leadership ambitions were to bedevil the party for the best part of a generation. This time around he expected to be rewarded with the deputy's job, but alas, the hangman seldom receives an invitation to the victory feast. Fraser won reasonably easily and Lynch remained deputy.

Whitlam had effectively replaced King Log with King Stork, but really he had no choice; even if he had wished to prop Snedden up the man was long past help. Fraser had achieved the first part of his task; he was undisputed leader of the party. Within its ranks there would be resentment and recrimination, but there would be no more challenges. The die was cast and the Rubicon was crossed; no prisoners would be taken or conventions respected until the final triumph. By the election of Fraser and by the events that preceded it the Liberals had effectively torn up the rules of war. From now on unbridled terrorism was to prevail.

And of course the times were made for it. By 1975 the economy was deteriorating rapidly; this was in line with international trends, but that was no comfort to the beleaguered voters of the western suburbs. The public service was openly disaffected; a Treasury official calling himself Mr Williams, later to be identified in the Senate as Des Moore, was spilling his guts to Lynch on a regular basis. The media had turned; the main groups, Fairfax, Herald and Weekly Times and Murdoch were now baying for the fall of the government with Murdoch, a suitor spurned, leading the charge. Inside the government things were falling apart; the wave of sackings and resignations that was to bedevil the last tumultuous year was already under way and strange clouds with names like Junie Morosi and Tirath Khemlani were appearing on the horizon. The toboggan had left the hilltop and was gathering speed on its downhill run.

I wasn't feeling too flash myself; my own household, such as it was, had disintegrated and I was left to face the pity and terror of it all by myself. And like many others in the months that followed I went a little bit mad.

Chapter Twenty-three

I KNOW YOU CAN'T HAVE EVERYTHING BUT JUST THREE YEARS IN A LIFETIME SEEMS A BIT MEAN

The first signs of serious dementia appeared at the ALP's national conference. Two years earlier at Surfers Paradise the event had been pretty successful; at least no one had gone troppo. The organisers unwisely interpreted this as an omen that a seaside resort was the right kind of venue for a relaxed and comfortable conference which would generate a minimum of bad publicity. For the 1975 model they decided on Terrigal, a small beachside town in the middle of a marginal NSW Labor electorate. The delegates again packed their towels and sun cream and set off for what one described (with what was to prove depressing accuracy) our horror days at Terrible.

From the start it created the wrong impression; with the

economic crisis looming over the rest of the country readers (especially of the Murdoch press) were treated to the spectacle of their government frolicking around the swimming pool of the Florida Hotel and its environs. Michael Leunig, who had rather reluctantly accompanied me to the event, left after the first day claiming that there was just too much sex and violence for him to manage: the only cartoon he felt capable of drawing showed an overturned beach umbrella on a deserted patio. The was probably a little oversensitive of him, but there is no doubt that at least some of the participants seemed determined to turn it into a pilot for the Australian version of the last days of Pompeii; even today there are hardened reporters who dismiss eyewitness accounts of the week (was it really only a week?) as too extravagant for belief. The defensive took refuge in such activities as bird watching: Ian Moffitt claimed to have spotted a migratory Mongolian swift in the underbrush near the swimming pool. The non-political, which included a large group of Sydney reporters more accustomed to chasing ambulances and covering gangland warfare, ran around demanding to know who was up whom for how much and who was paying the rent. Most of the Canberra contingent felt somewhat overshadowed, and took refuge in drink; breakfast was a couple of bloody marys and it was all downhill from there. We felt, rightly as it turned out, that this was not really a political story.

Highlights included a picture of two of Don Dunstan's bikini clad male staff members locked in a tight embrace as they dived into the pool, which appeared under the headline 'Hi jinks at Terrigal'; the cognoscenti described it more bluntly as the flying fuck photo. Another shot of Your Government at Work showed Bob Hawke being flogged by a guard at Old

Sydney Town avidly watched by his girlfriend of the week (mistress would be the wrong term, implying as it does a quasi-stable relationship). But most interest centred around the unit occupied by the Treasurer, Jim Cairns. It overlooked a patch of scrub in which an enterprising News Limited photographer recently returned from Vietnam was detected one day building a hide. While his colleagues asked each other whether the war had finally got to him he merely smiled enigmatically; the point of his subterfuge appeared a couple of days later with a picture of Cairns breakfasting on the balcony with his office chief of staff, Junie Morosi. Accompanying it was an interview in which the Treasurer confessed that he had 'a kind of love' for his companion. The most insidious scandal to rack the government hit one of its frequent climaxes.

Defenders of the couple, and especially of Morosi, have always tried to portray the coverage of the affair as beset by sexism and racism: according to these critics the only reason for all the fuss was that Morosi was a woman in a position of power and a foreigner as well, which made it worse. She was also extremely attractive; indeed, for a 42-year-old grand-mother she was sensational. It was therefore easy to suggest that her detractors were motivated purely by bigotry and envy. If only it had been so simple; the affair would never have had legs if it had. Politicians and journalists around Parliament House have always been tolerant of such affairs, if only in self protection. The staid old building on the hillside was probably one of the most sexually promiscuous structures in the country. When people referred to it as a rabbit warren they were not just talking about the architecture. Politicians and their staff, journalists both resident and sessional, permanent staff members and just about anyone who happened to be passing through mingled happily in a voluptuous smorgasbord. There were, of course, those who for one reason or another remained aloof, but they were a decided minority.

In recent years a senior politician, National Party leader John Anderson, has suggested that sexual promiscuity is a symptom of wider misconduct, and that unchaste politicians should review their situation. If this standard had been applied in my days, the building would have looked like the aftermath of a neutron bombing with few visible signs of human life. Of the eight prime ministers from Chifley to Fraser I would have backed only one to pass the Anderson test; to one more I would have extended the benefit of the doubt. The other six were not in the race. The same ratio extended through the building. Scenes of illicit passion were the standard fare of the non-members bar. One of my favourites involved the young wife of a Labor man who was accosted by an equally young Liberal with a somewhat hangdog expression. 'You're not going to believe this,' he slurred pathetically, 'you're just not going to believe it. But it's true. I'm a 35-year-old male virgin. Can you believe that?' The woman in question looked him up and down. 'Yes, easily' she replied. Even before the incident the would-be seducer had been nicknamed 'Parliament's pet galah'; he now became part of the folklore. In this context the idea of a minister having an affair with his secretary was very much par for the course; in the normal course of events it would not have raised an eyebrow.

But there was more to the Cairns–Morosi relationship than just a casual affair. First there was the sheer intensity; Cairns in the past had always been something of an ascetic. Morosi turned him into a febrile adolescent. She could be seen hand-feeding him strawberries in the restaurants around town before the pair retired for the afternoon to a flat owned by Cairns's close friend Tom Uren. This was not a good look. Then there was the manner of her appointment; she had first appeared in the office of the excitable Immigration Minister, Al Grassby, whose partiality to colourful characters was already a minor worry among the government's more pressing concerns. Grassby had introduced her to Lionel Murphy, with whom she had formed an attachment. Then she had gone to Cairns. It was not exactly a spotless pedigree. Then there was the influence she exerted over the Treasurer's office; she took firm control of his appointment book and decided just who was to be admitted to the inner sanctum and, equally importantly, who was not. Many public servants, backbenchers and even ministers found themselves in the latter category and complained bitterly. All this was tiresome but tolerable; much the same grumbling had gone on over John Gorton's appointment of Ainsley Gotto. But the Cairns case seemed to go deeper into the processes of government.

In 1974 I had been part of the entourage that accompanied Cairns on a trip to China. It had been an exciting experience; I ended up writing a somewhat wide-eyed piece which reflected my preoccupation with the chaos of India. By comparison China, even in the wake of the dreadful cultural revolution and with the populace being adjured to cover the walls with mindless slogans pouring shit indiscriminately on Confucius and Lin Piao, looked pretty comfortable. Others in the party disagreed; a Foreign Affairs officer sent to keep an eye on us spent most of his time making ignorant and disparaging comments along the lines of 'even Chairman Mao can't stop the smell of pigs'. But there was one passenger whose role was more mysterious; a Hong Kong businessman who was rumoured to have 'contacts' on the mainland. His role was apparently to introduce Cairns, who at the stage was still Minister for Trade, to the right sort of people. This may have had benefits for Cairns, but obviously being in the company of a senior Australian minister didn't do the businessman's prospects any harm either. It made me a little uneasy.

After Cairns became treasurer there were a lot of similar stories of rather unlikely visitors to his office, many of whom looked suspiciously like carpetbaggers. A number of them had been sent by Morosi's husband, a fringe figure from the travel industry named David Ditchburn. As time went on, Cairns's other staffers and Treasury officials became concerned that Cairns was not talking to the right people and that Morosi, at Ditchburn's behest, was letting far too many of the wrong ones in.

The affair between Cairns and Morosi caused deep disquiet within the party. By and large Cairns's mates on the left stuck with him, although more than one tried to warn him that he was getting out of his depth; Cairns, hopelessly in love (or at the very least in lust; he was, as the new agers might put it, finally getting in touch with his sensual side) ignored them. His detractors saw proof of what they had always believed, that Cairns was far too naive and self-indulgent to be a real politician, and said so loudly. Whitlam himself refused to get involved. He regarded Cairns's private life as his own business and refused to listen to the scuttlebutt about Ditchburn and Morosi; to be fair he had enough scuttlebutt to deal with already, including one particularly silly rumour that he had impregnated his superwoman Liz Reid and that she had gone to Coonabarabran, of all places, for an abortion. But it was also in keeping with Whitlam's sense of justice; he invariably assumed innocence unless guilt could be proved beyond reasonable doubt, which predisposed him to think the best of people. In normal society this is an admirable quality, but in politics it can be disastrous, as was to be demonstrated in the course of the year as the dominoes began to fall.

The first had already gone: Lionel Murphy had successfully bailed out before any serious shit hit the fan. There were murmurings of jobs for the boys and a protest from Chief Justice Barwick, who complained rather preciously to the new Attorney-General, Kep Enderby, that the appointment had ruined the High Court; when Enderby passed this on to Whitlam, the Prime Minister snapped back: 'But did you tell him how much it has improved cabinet meetings?' Even after all they had been through together there was still no love lost between the government's two great reformers.

The next to go was the Speaker, Jim Cope, an amiable character whose main claim to fame had been that he was the best snooker player in Parliament House. Alas, his talents did not extend to controlling a bloodthirsty Opposition; the bully boys of the National Party in particular baited him mercilessly. He became known as Jim Can't Cope. The end came after a parliamentary brawl involving Clyde Cameron. When Cameron refused to withdraw something he said Cope named him; the Opposition's Ian Sinclair immediately moved for Cameron's suspension and in the vote that followed Whitlam and the Labor Party backed Cameron. It was reported that during the division Whitlam told Cope: 'If this goes against you you'll have to resign.' From where I was sitting it sounded more like 'Now you've stuffed it and you'll have to resign.' In any case Cope did so, to the wild applause of the Opposition. It was Snedden's failure to capitalise that led directly to the ascension of Malcolm Fraser. This signalled a major change in the balance of the chamber. Whitlam, hitherto the undisputed master of parliamentary debate, found it very hard to take Fraser's measure. In fact he never really got on top until the last desperate weeks following the blocking of supply and by then it was too late.

The loss of Murphy, and even of Cope, could have been excused as an aberration, but what followed could only be put down to carelessness or something worse. What became known as the loans affair now reared up to engulf the ship of state, sweeping too many of the key sailors overboard in the process. Ultimately it was to prove fatal; all that observers could do was to shake their heads and comment on what a very silly way it was to go. The genesis was in the oil price crisis; this left countries like Australia strapped for cash, while enriching the OPEC nations beyond their dreams. As a result there was a belief that the Arabs in particular had more of the stuff than they knew what to do with and might well be persuaded to steer a bit of it Australia's way in the form of a loan.

The plight of the government was well known; Whitlam, and in particular his formidable Minister for Resources and Energy, Rex Connor, were highly frustrated at not being able to afford even a start to the major projects they had in mind. At one cabinet meeting Whitlam expressed a yearning for something on a really grand scale, like the Suez Canal. Connor's dream of a national pipeline grid was second best, but it wasn't a bad second. The problem was that it would cost about $4 billion. Raising this sort of money in the normal way was out of the question; it would require the approval of the hostile premiers, which would not be forthcoming in a climate of mounting inflation and rising interest rates. But if it could be called a 'temporary' loan from unorthodox sources … well, that was a different tin full of worms altogether. Thus when people who claimed to know people who claimed to know where the Arabs kept their spare cash started slithering into ministers' offices they were not immediately shown the door.

As the Gair affair had already shown, the Whitlam government wasn't really very good at playing devious games. Even so, it is hard to understand why otherwise sane ministers were willing to believe that a series of sleazy characters wearing green sunglasses and white shoes with no track record of financial success and in some cases with the arse out of their strides held the keys to Aladdin's cave. More often than not they were the kind of people who would come up to you in a pub with an offer of a hot car radio, and if you showed any interest follow it up with some shares in Lasseter's lost reef and the deeds to the Sydney Harbour Bridge. At various times even such supposed hard heads as Cameron and Connor showed an interest. Connor was especially attracted. Known to journalists as the Strangler, he had once fixed a hangman's noose above his office door to remind visitors of his reputation. He would have been expected to be the last person to fall for what was, in essence, a simple confidence trick. But the lure of unlimited funds with which to realise his ambitions became too much; in the end he was reduced to a pathetic figure, spending his nights beside a teleprinter waiting for a message that never came – another victim of the carpetbaggers who insisted that all they needed was a letter of authority from the government and in a matter of moments the cheque would be in the mail.

Perhaps fortunately the Treasury could not be left out of the negotiations altogether; its conservative higher echelons, and especially the crusty secretary, Sir Frederick Wheeler, were appalled. It was at this stage that Mr Williams began feeding Lynch almost daily progress reports. The bureaucrats were not able to stop the process completely; Connor and Cairns now had the scent of petrodollars in their nostrils, and Whitlam apparently felt – wrongly – that the government had nothing to lose by making the attempt. In practice all the Treasury intervention achieved was to drive the process further underground. This not only left Cairns and Connor effectively out of control; it meant that when the stories started to emerge they were far more sinister and damaging than they need have been.

Lynch, with the aid of his Treasury drip, let the information trickle through; Fraser enthusiastically used it to construct a huge and horrendous conspiracy against the reputation and well being of the Commonwealth. The media fell on it with shrieks of delight; there is nothing the media like better than a good conspiracy. The *Age* in particular flung open the editorial chequebook in a quest for documentary evidence; naturally plenty was forthcoming and while much of it was fanciful and some clearly forgery there was enough solid stuff to reinforce what Lynch was getting from his own sources. Well before mid year the government was enveloped by accusations of incompetence, evasion, duplicity and at least the suspicion of criminal intent.

It was, of course, just what Fraser wanted. On becoming Leader of the Opposition he had paid pious lip service to the idea that governments should be allowed to serve out their full term without having to cope with the blocking of supply, but had added a few lines of fine print about the need for flexibility should unforeseen events take place. Things were falling nicely into line for what he was later to describe as an extraordinary and reprehensible circumstance. On the government side there was huge resentment and confusion; only a few senior ministers had been aware of the loans deal and the back-bench and most of the advisers had been kept completely in the dark. Now, without any knowledge or input, they suddenly found themselves in a series of mounting crises that even Whitlam seemed powerless to stop. It became a matter of every man for himself, with ministers openly blaming each other and their staff members coming close to blows in the non-members bar.

The press gallery was equally at a loss; attempts by Canberra staff to get a grip on the story and put it into some kind of perspective were invariably frustrated by out-of-towners who arrived from head office with a licence to kill. The mainstream press had already made its judgment. The Murdoch press had been baying for months. The *Sydney Morning Herald* had declared open war in April, ostensibly as a result of the government's acceptance of the communist victory in Vietnam. The *Age* had to justify its excess of chequebook journalism, and the Melbourne-based Herald and Weekly Times group, traditionally anti-Labor, now felt it had to outdo the *Age*. An alarming feature of this period was that the media all but abandoned the quest for real news and fell back on interviewing each other. Television specials consisted largely of talking heads recycling the morning's press comment, grave interviews with the hacks who wrote it and an occasional cross to an overseas journalist who claimed insights denied to Australians but seldom knew where the place was on the map. The anti-climax came with a one-day sitting of parliament in July, when a comedian (Gary McDonald) masquerading as a reporter (Norman Gunston) started interviewing real journalists about their views of other journalists' views of politicians. Seldom have the media been further removed from reality. But then, the same applied to the government. Ministers who had not been privy to the loans affair blamed those who had and the inner group said the outsiders were being selfish and disloyal. Everybody blamed everybody else for failing to keep the media, if not on side, at least marginally under control. Ministerial press secretaries, at the bottom of the heap, were particularly tough on each other. Parliament House echoed to free and frank exchanges: 'Piss off, you mug, you're nothing but an old has-been.' 'Well, sonny, better a has-been than a never will be.' 'Don't talk to me like that, you stupid drunk.' 'No, laddie, I'm not a drunk, I'm an alcoholic and when you grow up you can be one too.' To dementia had been added paranoia; we were rapidly drifting from the merely neurotic towards full-blown psychosis.

Cairns was the next domino to fall; his signature was found to be on some letters he did not recall signing. He was demoted from the Treasury, choosing, to the surprise of most, the junior portfolio of Environment as his fall-back position. Before he could make a mark on it he was found to have misled parliament and sacked from the ministry altogether. It was yet another might-have-been; a minister of Cairns's standing and charisma could well have elevated environmental concerns to real prominence some twenty years earlier than was actually to be the case.

Then Lance Barnard jumped ship; he had been unhappy since being replaced as deputy leader by Cairns after the 1974 election and his health was starting to suffer, but it was the worst possible time to cut and run, especially as he was given an ambassadorial job. From both sides of the House came claims that treachery was being rewarded, not unmixed with jibes about rats and sinking ships. Whitlam used the occasion to reshuffle his ministry, a process that was probably more trouble than it was worth; Cameron refused to surrender his Labour portfolio for some hours and in the end had almost literally to be dragged from his office. The only plus was that Bill Hayden, who had replaced Cairns as treasurer, produced a budget which finally accorded with the economic cycle. Inflation finally began to fall, but people were too preoccupied to take much notice.

The electorate, like the media, was in the grip of a feeding frenzy. Barnard's previously safe seat of Bass was devoured in the by-election that his departure had made necessary; the fact that Labor had selected possibly the worst candidate ever to stand at a by-election didn't help. Whitlam's attempts to play the straight man during a campaign of stunning ineptitude only made things worse. It was obvious that the government was now beyond salvation; all Fraser had to do was to wait around until the next election. But he was too eager for power to accept the delay. When Connor too was found to have misled parliament and was sacked by the punctilious Whitlam as a result, Fraser decided that the circumstance was sufficiently extraordinary and reprehensible to announce that the Senate would block the budget in order to force an election. The media agreed enthusiastically; by this time all sense of fairness and proportion had been lost in the lust for battle.

On a personal level this total loss of perspective was maddening. It was not that I was against passion and partisanship in journalism – far from it. But surely there needed to be some basis in reality for the kind of polemic that was now bombarding us. This was the most objectionable, immoral, corrupt, anarchic government since federation, we were assured. Any breach of convention, any political brutality that could be used against it was therefore legitimate; in the circumstances the end surely justified the means. I found this attitude on the part of the stern upholders of traditional justice and equity both stupid and hypocritical; it engendered a smouldering resentment which was to eventually blaze into rage.

A quiet look at the facts would have revealed that far from being reprehensible, Whitlam had acted with a scrupulous regard for the proprieties that was far above the usual standard of Australian politics. Ministers who had misled parliament got no second chance; there was no attempt at cover-up or excuse. Compared to the conduct of conservative ministers on (among other things) the Vietnam adventure, this was an exhibition of the highest integrity. Moreover, it should be pointed out that while Cairns and Connor were undoubtedly naive and occasionally a bit tricky there was never any suggestion of corruption, much less of personal gain. If nothing else, Whitlam's government was almost boringly honest.

It was perhaps this characteristic which made Fraser and his allies both inside and outside parliament believe that a government which had taken the kind of punishment that had been meted out to Labor would simply roll over; after all, when supply was blocked in 1974 Whitlam went straight to a double dissolution. But this time Whitlam decided to tough it out and fight the ultimate battle. The scene was set for a political Armageddon; or to put it another way, the government had entered its Götterdämmerung phase.

Chapter Twenty-four

SO THEY TURNED ON THE
LIGHTS, SHONE THEM IN OUR EYES,
AND REACHED FOR THE RUBBER
HOSES.

The first skirmish was a fight for the high moral ground. Here Fraser was at a serious disadvantage; his Senate majority was due purely to a piece of bastardry from the man described by Whitlam as the Bible bashing bastard, Queensland Premier Joh Bjelke-Petersen. Earlier in the year a Labor senator, Bert Milliner, had died; the ALP, in accordance with convention, nominated an ALP functionary named Mal Colston to take his place. But Bjelke-Petersen, following the precedent set by Tom Lewis, knocked Colston back, claiming, among other things, that he was an arsonist.

Instead he sent to Canberra a man named Patrick Albert Field, a French-polisher who was supposed to be a member of the ALP. Field turned out to be a few rags short of the full chamois, but he was smart enough to understand his orders, which were to vote against the government at all times. He fulfilled them diligently. Palbert, as he became known, was to be seen occasionally wandering blankly around King's Hall, a bathetic figure treated with patronising disdain by the Opposition, total contempt by the government and open derision by everyone else; he could never seem to understand why nobody liked him.

But he played his role, which was to give Fraser an absolute majority in the Senate. This was vital in that the Opposition parties could now carry a vote to defer consideration of the budget rather than be forced into actually rejecting it, a course which may have been too extreme for some of his colleagues. While the bills were simply batted backwards and forwards between the two houses of parliament they could kid themselves that they hadn't done anything truly radical; the budget was still in play. Some were a bit wary even of deferral; it took Fraser and his Senate leader, Reg 'The Toecutter' Withers, a mighty effort to keep them committed as the day when supply would finally run out drew nearer. At least four were known to be very unhappy indeed. At the start of the second week of November they were almost certainly ready to crack. It has since been denied (to my mind unconvincingly) that they would have done so; but the point is that this was the received wisdom at the time. It becomes an important factor in considering the timing of the dismissal.

In those early days the idea of Kerr sacking the government was considered simply ridiculous; governors-general had never done such a thing, and Kerr in particular, a Labor appointee, never would. But in retrospect we should have put it on the list of possibilities, because if it had not happened

Fraser would have been on a hiding to nothing, and that was not the way Fraser operated. The only ways he could win were if Whitlam backed down, which was clearly not about to happen, or if Kerr intervened. Fraser was to say that he had always been confident that the latter would be the case; it would be interesting to know just why, because it was a view shared by very few others at the time.

In the meantime Whitlam blossomed; the only outward sign that he was feeling the tension was that he developed a disconcerting habit of grinding his teeth in moments of elation. He had always been the greatest parliamentarian of his generation but in the period between October 16 and November 11 he reached new heights. His performances on the floor of the House were electrifying; the Labor party united behind him as it never had before. It was wonderful theatre dominated by a superstar. If the contest had been a purely dramatic one, the government would have walked away with the laurel wreath. The Opposition under Fraser was reduced to providing comic relief. At great expense it imported the weirdest figure of all from the loans affair, the London-based Pakistani banker Tirath Hassaram Khemlani, and locked him up with forty-eight hours' supply of salted peanuts and a couple of shadow ministers and their staffs. Eventually the shadow Attorney-General, Bob Ellicott, QC, emerged blinking into the daylight to reveal that the mountains of documents Khemlani had brought with him did not seem to implicate Whitlam in any misdemeanours at all. After a few explosive moments alone with Fraser he changed his mind; perhaps they could be made to if you sort of read between the lines.

The whole episode was sent up in a brilliant speech by

Fred Daly. It was a clear win for Labor. Shortly after the blocking of supply the ALP had issued a badge reading 'Shame
Fraser Shame'. It lent itself to adaptation; mine had gone
through Sham Fraser Sham and Ham Fraser Ham. After the
Khemlani interlude I altered it again: Ha Fraser Ha. But of
course Fraser was to have the last laugh; parliament, for all its
exhilaration, was only a sideshow. Still, it seemed that things
were going well for Labor; the opinion polls showed that the
electorate was coming back to the government. In spite of
the overwhelming support of the Establishment media Fraser
was losing voters. The press gallery itself was deeply divided,
but almost all the heavies and certainly the clear majority were
pro-Whitlam – or at least anti-Fraser. The aloof squattocrat
had never had many admirers; unlike Whitlam he had never
made any attempt to acquire the social graces, let alone the
common touch.

And unlike Snedden he was easy to dislike. Snedden had
his limitations, one of which was that he wouldn't have known
if you were up him with an open beach umbrella. Fraser, by
contrast, looked and acted as if an umbrella was permanently
up him and he actually found it rather comfortable. He was
generally thought of as a bit odd and a right bastard. I wrote a
song about it all to the tune of 'Carolina in the Morning':

Nothing could be crazier than Malcolm Fraser, grazier
    this morning;
Billy may be sillier but Mally wants to kill ya without
    warning;
When the fawning Tories
Slime around his door
He'll tell the same old stories

And have them rolling on the floor.
If you want a clincher look at Lynch the letter pincher
  in the evening;
Measure all the pleasure he is getting from the treasury
  and thieving.
If I had to cast a vote next Saturday
I'd write a note and here's what I'd say:
Nothing could be crazier than Malcolm Fraser grazier
  this morning.

It became, briefly, a hit around Parliament House; a number of tapes were made and played loudly, especially in the presence of Opposition members. Indeed, I was playing one myself over a leisurely lunch at the Lobby restaurant across the road from Parliament House when a member of Bill Hayden's staff came over to the table and informed me that Kerr had sacked Whitlam.

Of course I didn't believe her. But then I looked out of the window and saw something equally unprecedented: Laurie Oakes running. Something apocalyptic had clearly happened. A phone call confirmed it: the elected government, at a time when it was clearly regathering public support and still had the wherewithal to continue for at least another fortnight before it faced a serious supply crisis, had been sacked by a drunken megalomaniac representing the ageing matriarch of a dysfunctional family on the other side of the globe. It was not to be borne. With my lunching companions I too ran back to Parliament House and into the growing rage.

The story of that day has been well documented: how Whitlam went to Government House to request an election for half the Senate and was ambushed by Kerr telling him his commission was withdrawn, with Fraser waiting in the next room; how Whitlam, in a state of shock, returned to the Lodge and failed to inform his senators of what had happened, so supply was passed by early afternoon and Kerr was in a position to dissolve parliament almost immediately; and how the House of Representatives passed no confidence in Fraser and confidence in Whitlam, but Kerr refused to even admit the Speaker of the House with that message. To my mind too little has been made of this last point; parliament was still sitting at the time and Kerr's clear duty was to listen to it, even if the news was that his own appointed prime minister had been rejected. To lock the Speaker out was an act of autocracy quite unacceptable under the Westminster system; the monarchy and its viceroys had lost that power with the execution of Charles I. But not, it appears, in democratic Australia.

This brings up the wider issue of whether Kerr was entitled to act at all. There is still considerable dispute over whether the governor-general's reserve powers give him the right to sack a government; some very prominent legal experts believe that they don't. But for the sake of argument let's assume they do – under certain circumstances. Obviously it's not a blanket power; the GG can't just wake up one morning and think, well, I did the boy scouts yesterday and the baby health centre the day before; I reckon today I might sack the government. He has to have a reason. It would be nice to know if the blocking of supply by an Opposition and its allies fortuitously in control of the Senate (which, since the appointments of Bunton and Field, could not claim any kind of popular mandate) is deemed sufficient. It is true that the government was putting in place emergency arrangements so that it could carry on after supply ran out; but these were still a fortnight away and the prospect of one or more Opposition senators cracking was growing stronger by the day. At the very least it could be said that Kerr ejected prematurely.

He himself justified his actions in a curious document released next day, which appears to confuse the written Constitution with parliamentary convention, makes questionable political assumptions about the result of both a half senate election and a double dissolution and contains at least one thundering lie – that he would be surprised if the Law Officers (Attorney-General Kep Enderby and Solicitor-General Maurice Byers) would take the view that his actions had exceeded the reserve powers. In fact they had both given him that opinion in writing. Overall Kerr's reasoning lacks any semblance of credibility; it is hard to avoid the conclusion that it was dreamt up after the event rather than reasoned out beforehand. It is true that there were some eminent figures who supported Kerr, former Liberal Prime Minister Robert Menzies and former Liberal Attorney-General, now High Court Justice Garfield Barwick, among them. Interestingly Fraser also produced an opinion from one William Deane, QC, which said the government could not continue without supply – which of course it hadn't. But there were also plenty of opinions from equally eminent figures which went the other way. In the end it seems that Kerr made a personal and political choice and attempted unsuccessfully to rationalise it afterwards.

In the process he shook Australia's system of democracy to its foundations. There was talk of a CIA conspiracy, as a result of some mildly embarrassing disclosures in parliament about the agency's operations in Australia; certainly Washington would have been grateful to see the back of the Whitlam government. But I don't believe the CIA actively intervened (and nor does Whitlam). There was no need to take the risk; the government was clearly on the skids and would be gone in a few more months anyway. The simplest explanation is usually the right one: Kerr, addled by drink, allowed others to play on his vanity and saw a chance to secure at least a footnote in the history books. His supporters will say he paid a high price; his opponents will say that the price was not nearly high enough and would like to see him secured in the innermost circle of hell – the one Dante reserved for traitors.

The rage on that first afternoon had not reached quite that level of sophistication, but it was awesome enough. Whitlam made his appearance on the front steps and was cheered by the crowds, the Labor members left singing 'Solidarity Forever' and cheering each other on. Some clearly believed that they could still win the election which was to follow in a month's time. Euphoria and adrenalin carried them forward, as did the mass rallies which led up to the campaign proper. But the hard heads knew, even then, that it was all over. If Kerr's decision had done nothing else, it had ended the confusion. While still largely disapproving of Fraser's opportunism, middle Australia now turned against Whitlam. If the Queen's own representative, the Governor-General whom Whitlam himself had appointed, had found it necessary to sack the government, then the government must have done something terribly, horribly wrong. Even if no one could tell you what it was, an awful crime must have been committed. Therefore the government had to go.

In the meantime Parliament House became still more chaotic. Ministers of what became known as the elected government and their staffs, aided by large numbers of public servants who had taken leave or who had simply flexed off and by other supporters packed up their offices and handed them over to their appointed successors. In the intervals they – we – took over the non-members bar where one musically inclined staffer made noises like a police siren whenever a Liberal attempted to enter. One large Murdoch pressman offered to fight the bar when greeted in such a fashion; he explained he was joining the strike his Sydney colleagues had pulled on to protest against the coverage of the campaign. He joined in the singing of songs of oppression: 'Moreton Bay' and 'The Ballad of 1891' were particular favourites. They were, of course, also the songs of the losers. Subconsciously at least we knew where we stood.

The coalition, meanwhile, slid back into government. All but the inner circle seemed too dazed by their good fortune to do anything but luxuriate, which, given their invented 'care-taker' (Kerrtaker?) role, was probably just as well. Fraser gave a press conference to an unremittingly hostile gallery at which he accused Whitlam of having breached the Constitution. When asked which section Whitlam had breached, he simply repeated in Sneddenesque fashion: 'Mr Whitlam breached the Constitution.' It turned out he meant the conventions under-lying the Constitution; given his and Kerr's actions during the preceding weeks it was a surprise to hear that there were any left. He then went to Melbourne to open the campaign proper; instead he came down with flu and took to his bed for four days. Copies of his speech had already been distributed; I wasted a lunch hour helping to fax one to Whitlam in Perth, but it didn't help. This was not an election about policies or even personalities; it had become a matter of personal absolu-tion. Egged on by the press, the voters who had swung to

Labor in 1972 and 1974 were now preparing to cleanse themselves of their sins by returning to the rightful rulers of the nation. And if it proved to be a mean and punitive regime led by vengeful and tyrannical master, then that was just part of their penance and they thoroughly deserved it. As their campaign slogan the Libs pinched an old one from Margaret Thatcher: 'Turn on the Lights'. It had originally been intended for an England crippled by power shortages in the middle of winter; it seemed singularly inappropriate for the Australian summer. But again, it didn't matter. If the motto had been 'Let's Eat a Shit Sandwich' the electorate would have embraced it. In a last gesture of defiance *Nation Review* ran a front page 'Okay, let's turn on the lights – you can't trust the bastards in the dark' and retired to brood.

In a similar mood of masochism I hosted a small gathering at my home in Narrabundah on the night of December 13. We were, of course, all Labor supporters. We had no illusions about what was going to happen and we couldn't face the national tally room, with the triumphalism which was certain to follow the result. Instead, we relied on the ABC; even from the earliest figures it was clear that it was going to be a very bad night. The only optimist was the writer Xavier Herbert; the shock of the reality sent him tottering to bed, with the exit line: 'When it comes to the point, Australians can be relied on to behave like lice.' The papers carried a front page picture of Fraser playing dice with his family as he watched the results come in. His majority in the Reps was estimated at fifty-three and it was also clear he would have control of the Senate. I decided not to go to work for a couple of days. There didn't seem to be much point.

★ ★ ★

When I finally made the effort it was as though nothing had changed – not from the week before, but from 1969, when I had first arrived in Canberra. Labor was nothing if not resilient; the remaining members were already making plans for their next term in government, which they seemed to imagine was just around the corner. It seemed absurd that I felt more wounded than they did. I spent a lot of time hanging around Whitlam's office and did more than my share of Fraser-baiting, but it was more of a game than a vocation; it was fairly obvious that the powers that be in Australia would not let the left have another chance as long as the memory of Whitlam endured. They had opened the door in 1972, and the left had won; by fair means and foul – but mostly foul – that victory had been annulled. It would not be allowed to happen again. You couldn't always rely on a John Kerr to be in the crucial position at the right time. In future the left was to be kept in its rightful place – the Opposition benches – and allowed to let off steam in the streets, as long as it didn't frighten the horses. Until it abandoned any pretence of attempting to change the system, all the resources of the Establishment – big money, big media and not least a thoroughly cowed and cooperative public service – would be used to grind the bastards down. This was confirmed when Labor under Whitlam failed to improve its position in 1977; the years that followed were even bleaker. I started moving away from day to day politics and paid more attention to long-term causes, particularly in the field of aboriginal rights. It appeared to be one of the few issues in Australia where the left could play a worthwhile role.

Labor regained power in 1983, but it was a cautious, plodding Labor; Whitlam veterans such as Jim McClelland maintained that it wasn't a real Labor government at all. Bob Hawke and Paul Keating embraced much of the economic agenda of the right; socialism, even in its mildest form, was not on the menu. The government was obviously no threat to the Establishment; it can't have been because it kept getting re-elected. It was what might be called dynamically conservative: if you kicked it hard enough it would stumble forward, but only after making sure that it wouldn't intrude on anyone else's space. It was efficient enough, but it lacked vision and it lacked passion.

Above all it lacked pizzazz. I found that all that was left of the excitement of the Whitlam years – when no vision had seemed out of reach and no reform unattainable, when every day was another walk along the high wire to either glory or disaster – was the nostalgia. It wasn't enough, so I semi-retired to the beach. I still think of myself as on the left, and I still yearn for what might have been. But these days I recognise my limitations. The world is not ready for the left; nor is Australia. But Byron Shire just might be.

I once was an over-achiever
A true journalistic believer
But now I relax
With a phone and a fax
And a large curly coated retriever.